PLEASURE BOATING ON THE THAMES

A HISTORY OF

SALTER BROS

1858–PRESENT DAY

SIMON WENHAM

The History Press

Photographs are from the Salters' archive, unless otherwise stated.

First published 2014

The History Press
The Mill, Brimscombe Port
Stroud, Gloucestershire, GL5 2QG
www.thehistorypress.co.uk

British Library Cataloguing in Publication Data.
A catalogue record for this book is available from the British Library.

ISBN 978 0 7509 5833 2

Typesetting and origination by The History Press
Printed in Great Britain

PLEASURE
BOATING
ON THE
THAMES

Contents

Acknowledgements

Firstly, I would like to thank Amy Rigg, Rebecca Newton and the team at The History Press for all their hard work in publishing the book, and the directors of Salters', John Salter and Neil Kinch, for permission to access the company archive, without which the study could not have gone ahead. Secondly, I am especially grateful to Mark Smith and Christopher Day of Kellogg College, Oxford, for supervising my doctoral research and for all their invaluable advice, and to Clare Wenham for her tireless proofreading. I would also like to thank Michael Ramsden, Ian Smith, Amy Orr-Ewing and John Lennox for allowing me the flexibility at work to be able to conduct the research.

There are a large number of people who have provided guidance or information for the work. I am particularly grateful to Bill Dunckley, for filling in many gaps in my understanding, and Sidney Aster, for sending a number of interesting pieces from his related study. Others who have been very helpful include Robert Sackett, Margaret Clutterbuck, Bryan Dunckley, John Greenford, Graham Andrews, Peter Bowley, Steve Gaisford, Len Andrews, Ray Underwood, Steve Long, Albert Andrews, Merlyn Coates, David Nutt, Peter Robinson, Bob Dowthwaite, Gordon Smith, Paul Richmond and George Wyatt. I am also grateful to the Hobbs (Tony and Jonathan) and Turk (Mike and Richard) families for providing comparative information about their own family businesses on the Thames.

I would like to thank the many experts who have provided information or advice, including Iain MacLeod, Jeremy Burchardt, Liz Woolley, Tony Langford, Brian Hillsdon, John Foreman, Hugh McKnight, Roy Brinton, Rosemary Stewart-Beardsley, Janet Hurst, Frank Tallet, Laura Wortley, Dominic Erdozain, Mike Hurst, Martin Wellings, Peter Forsaith, Mark Davies, David Wenham, Emma Webster and Detlef Hempel. Those from the rowing community who have helped include Ian Smith, John Blackford, Eugene Crotty, Bryan Humphries, Theo Brun and Henry Myatt. Furthermore, Alan Birch provided information about sailing in the Midlands.

I would like to express my gratitude to those working in the many archives I have used, especially those at the Bodleian Library and the Berkshire Record Office. Those who have helped in the many other locations include Yvonne Taylor, Eloise Morton, Hettie Ward, Rosemary Joy, Chris Jeens, Amanda Ingram, Judith Curthoys, Emma Walsh, Julian Lock, Oliver Mahony, Robert Petre, Emma Goodrum, Emily Burgoyne, Cliff Davies, Alma Jenner, Rory Cook, Penny Hatfield, Clare Sargent and Claire Franklin. I am also grateful to Jim Cowan for permission to view his archive on the firm.

I would like to thank David Bowman for helping decipher the financial records, and Ian Farrell, Peter Southwell and Richard Carwardine for encouraging my work. I am also grateful for the contributions from those I have met at my speaking engagements, as well as those who have contacted the firm with historical information.

Finally, and most importantly, I must thank my wife, Angela (and son, Benjamin), for providing love, support and encouragement – and for putting up with me (and notes) cluttering up the house.

Author's Note

This book examines the history of Salter Bros Ltd and the firms connected with it, in order to show: firstly, how they fitted within the socio-economic context of Oxford and the Thames; secondly, the contribution they made to different forms of water-based leisure; and thirdly, how they evolved and ultimately managed to survive, bearing in mind the challenges such businesses faced. It takes a thematic approach, which involves examining the five main areas of the firm's commercial activities, which were: providing services for the sport of rowing (chapter 1), boat-building (chapter 2), boat-letting (chapter 3), passenger boat operating (chapter 4) and property development (chapter 5). The mainly quantitative data from the archive have been supplemented and put into context by drawing on wider qualitative sources, although there is not always much comparative information available. Finally, we examine the way in which the workforce evolved, which shows how Salters' managed to survive the impact of the industrialisation of Oxford (chapter 6), and the effects of being run by a single family over generations (chapter 7).

Sources

The main source used for researching this book is the extensive company archive, which contains the largest collection of documents relating to the firm. This resource survived partly because of the extent of property that Salters' came to own around Folly Bridge (see chapter 5), which ensured there was plenty of space in which records could be stored long term. Yet the majority of the documents date from the end of the nineteenth century onwards, which means there is little information about the firm's first three decades. Furthermore, the only comprehensive end of year accounts to survive date from 1915 (when Salters' became a limited company) to 1949. There are no records that show the firm's overall financial performance between 1950 and 1964, and the abbreviated accounts that were filed thereafter only show a summary, rather than how each individual department was faring.

The largely quantitative sources from the company archive have been supplemented by interviews conducted with past and present staff members, whose collective memories stretch back to the 1930s.[1] The Salter family also produced some written accounts, and a number of them were featured on local radio shows.[2] There is also a considerable collection of documents relating to the firm's history in private ownership.[3] Furthermore, the author has also been able to draw from his own knowledge of the firm and the river, having been a seasonal employee at Salters' from 1998 to 2000 and a full-time manager thereafter until 2005.

In terms of the wider primary source material, one of the most useful is what became known as *The Salter's Guide to the Thames*, of which there were fifty-seven editions published between 1881 and 1968. Other helpful resources include the annual *Rowing Almanack* (published from 1861), the *Lock to Lock Times* (from 1888) and *The Motor Boat* (from 1904). The archives of the Thames Conservancy (at the Berkshire Record Office) and the Oxford University colleges also provide invaluable information. Local newspapers help to shed light on many of the activities of Salters', and the British Library's electronic collection of these (and periodicals) from the nineteenth century is a particularly rich resource. The latter is one of a new generation of online facilities that have greatly aided historical research.

Finally, in writing this history of Salters', we have of course had to be sensitive to the fact that the firm continues to operate today. It has not been possible, therefore, to go into great detail about all the family dynamics at the business, for example, even though such relationships inevitably shaped how Salters' was run.

Notes

1   Those interviewed include Len Andrews (who began working at the firm in 1930), Albert Andrews (1936), Bill Dunckley (1944), Bryan Dunckley (1947), John Greenford (1955), Peter Bowley (1956) and Steve Gaisford (1970).

2   A. Salter, *Memoirs of a Public Servant* (London, 1961) and memoirs in the possession of the Sackett family. Centre for Oxfordshire Studies (COS) Radio interviews with Edward Arnold Salter (1931), reference: OXOHA: MT 1411, and Arthur Salter (1971), reference: OXOHA: MT 536.

3   Archive compiled by an unnamed employee in 1976, now in the possession of Jim Cowan.

Introduction

I have seen the Mississippi. That is muddy water. I have seen the St Lawrence. That is crystal water. But the Thames is liquid history.

John Burns MP, 1943[1]

Oxford owes not only its name but also its very existence to its waterways. It is by the banks of the river Thames at Folly Bridge, where the original ford may have been, that one of the city's oldest family firms continues to operate.

Founded in 1858 by the brothers John and Stephen Salter, the business – later known as Salter Bros Ltd (or Salters' for short)[2] – became one of the most important firms connected with the recent history of the Upper Thames,[3] substantially responsible for popularising pleasure boating on the waterway between Oxford and London. As well as becoming one of the largest boat-letters in the country, it became *the* major passenger boat operator on the non-tidal river, carrying hundreds of thousands of customers per year. Moreover, it developed into one of the foremost inland boat-builders in England, with its craft used widely around the country and its racing boats briefly enjoying worldwide fame. The firm also made a significant impact on the lives of many in Oxford, not only by providing leisure facilities, but as one of the larger non-university employers. Furthermore, the family would boast two mayors of the city, a Member of Parliament (and life peer) and a Waterman to the queen.

The business managed to survive in an era of immense change in the city. When the firm began, Oxford was still largely pre-industrial in character with the major source of both direct and indirect employment being the university, whose demands fluctuated with the academic terms. The city was said to be in 'great need' of major industry,[4] with levels of pay that were 'about the lowest in England' in 1908, owing to a surplus of labour and low agricultural wages in the surrounding countryside.[5] The city's 'air of almost studied backwardness'[6] lasted until the early part of the twentieth century when William Morris, who had previously had a cycle repair shop, started manufacturing cars. After Morris relocated his works to Cowley on the eastern outskirts of the city in 1912, his firm became the country's largest producer of automobiles between 1925 and 1939.[7] It was the expansion of the motor industry that made Oxford one of the fastest-growing cities in the inter-war period (Table 1). Its population doubled between 1911 and 1941 and the east side of Oxford was transformed into what John Betjeman described as 'Motopolis'.[8]

Table 1 Oxford's population[9]

Year	County borough population	Change
1901	49,336	+3,594 (7.9%)
1911	53,048	+3,712 (7.5%)
1921	57,036	+3,988 (7.5%)
1931	80,539 *(boundary extended in 1929)*	+23,503 (41.2%)
1941	107,000 *(estimated from the 1951 census)*	+26,461 (32.9%)
1951	98,684 *(taken when university on vacation)*	−8,316 (8.4%)
1961	106,291 *(boundary extended in 1957)*	+7,607 (7.7%)
1971	108,805	+2,514 (2.4%)

As one study has pointed out, 'it is difficult to exaggerate the impact that the interwar growth of the car industry had on the city of Oxford and its surrounding areas'.[10] The job market was transformed: by 1936 over 10,000 people were employed in the city's motor industry, which was approximately 30 per cent of the insured workers in the area.[11] There was not enough local labour to meet the demand and staff had to be recruited from the West Midlands, South Wales and London. Whilst some local firms benefited from the changes that occurred, many employers suffered because they were unable to compete with the levels of pay offered in the car industry. Furthermore, the old-established hierarchy of jobs was overturned, as semi-skilled factory workers could earn significantly more than those in professions previously considered to be of higher status, such as college servants.[12] The problem was particularly acute for the skilled trades, many of which relied upon lengthy periods of low-paid apprenticeship. Nevertheless, behind the long shadow cast by the motor works, a number of smaller firms survived and some, like Salters', even outlived the Morris brand.

Oxford and the Thames

Despite Salters' age, the firm's history is still relatively unknown; a short work by this author in 2005 was the first to examine the business in any depth.[13] A number of studies have been conducted on Oxford's recent history, but many of these focus on the impact of industrialisation and make little or no mention of the boat business.[14] Even the company's 150th anniversary in 2008 went largely unnoticed, as the milestone was only marked by *Limited Edition* (an *Oxford Times* supplement), which ran a feature on the firm's long-standing chief engineer, Bill Dunckley.[15]

A number of academic studies have examined the way in which waterway communities developed over the past two centuries. Mary Prior's work focused on those living and working at Fisher Row in Oxford, for example, but it also showed how the arrival of the railway in the city, in 1844, provided the *coup de grâce* to the ailing barge trade based at Folly Bridge. By the beginning of the twentieth century, the canal system had declined to such an extent that many of those whose livelihoods had depended on the waterway had either left the area or diversified into other trades.[16] Wendy Freer's work showed, however, that although the proportion of the nation's freight carried by the canals dropped drastically in the nineteenth century, and the industry 'never really recovered' from the Great Depression and the rise of motorised road transport in the inter-war period, some parts of the trade were still fulfilling a need beyond the Second World War. Her study also dispelled some of the stereotypes circulating about those working on the waterway, whilst also reaffirming that they were a marginalised, insular and distinctive occupational group.[17]

The transformation of the Thames from a working waterway into one primarily used for leisure is an area that has received relatively little attention from scholars – especially when compared to the amount of literature generated about the rise of seaside resorts – but there have been a number of studies showing how river communities adapted to these changes in the nineteenth century. David Blomfield's work on the watermen and lightermen of the Upper Tidal Thames (Teddington to Chiswick) from 1750 to 1901, for example, shows that by the middle of the nineteenth century many of those working on the waterway had started to cater for the leisure market, often as small side-lines from their main occupation. Indeed, he argues that a family's ability to remain on the river was strongly influenced by both their location and whether or not they were able to adapt their skills in response to the changing public demand.[18] Rosemary Stewart-Beardsley's study showed how five parishes located in the Goring Gap developed after the arrival of the railway in the 1830s, and included an examination of how the area changed as it became a popular tourist destination in the second half of the nineteenth century. New facilities emerged to cater for the growing leisure market, for example, and these included providing craft for pleasure boating, which she argues became a highly fashionable activity on the river in the 1880s.[19]

Whilst the academic literature on the recent history of the river is relatively sparse, a vast amount has been written at the popular level. The sheer range of topics is summed up in *The Thames 1580–1980: A General Bibliography*, which lists nineteen different categories, including engineered structures, natural history and craft on the waterway.[20] There are many popular works referring to Salters', from the more general, like Patricia Burstall's *The Golden Age of the Thames*,[21] to those with a narrower focus, like Frank Dix's *Royal River Highway: A History of the Passenger Boats and Services on the River Thames*.[22] Furthermore, there have been a number of short informal accounts written about the firm in specialist waterway magazines, although these do little to explain the company's development in terms of the wider changes that were occurring at the time.[23]

This book fills an important gap in the history of the river, by showing how the development of Salters' over the past two centuries fitted within, and contributed to, the socio-economic context of both the Thames and Oxford. In a sense it follows on from Mary Prior's work, as it represents the next chapter in the river's history, after the railway had destroyed the barge trade operating from Folly Bridge. This book, based on a doctoral thesis, is the first comprehensive work on any of the major historic firms operating on the Upper Thames.[24] Some of the other well-known river businesses, like Turks of Kingston (which traces its existence back to 1710), and Hobbs of Henley (founded in 1870), do not have the same level of archival material, meaning that only short informal histories have been produced.[25] The closest firms to Salters' that have had popular works written about them are the shipbuilders of John I. Thornycroft of Chiswick (founded in 1864)[26] and Sam Saunders of Streatley (1870).[27]

Drawing comparisons from these may seem inappropriate, but the larger businesses grew from smaller enterprises, and they not only faced the same kind of operational challenges as boat-builders, but could also be in direct competition with each other when it came to the sale of smaller vessels.

In this book we also show how an Oxford business managed to survive in a city that was transformed by industrialisation in the inter-war period. This is a topic that few of the popular histories of other local businesses cover.[28] Furthermore, it also sheds light on a distinctive waterway community, which, unlike those on the canal, has received little attention from scholars.

Leisure

An important topic which we will throw new light on is that of leisure, as this was the market on which Salters' was primarily focused. Sport and leisure are subjects in which 'an undeniably vigorous and extensive historiography' has emerged over the past three decades from a range of disciplines.[29] These have tended to be either 'social history with the sport left out, or sports history with the politics, society and economy left out'.[30] The approach favoured by many leisure historians has been to show how particular pastimes were created or moulded by political, economic, demographic, intellectual and other forces, which provides a useful 'window' through which the developments of other areas of society can viewed. Yet sociological studies have also helped to emphasise the social, psychological and cultural value of sport and leisure. They not only have a major influence on people's health and quality of life; they can also be one of the ways in which the participants derive meaning and purpose in life.[31]

This book is not intended to contribute directly to discussion of the conceptualisation of leisure by historians or sociologists, but to the study of the processes known as the 'commercialisation of leisure'.[32] This topic, which Pamela Horn describes as 'the most striking feature of the final years of the [nineteenth] century',[33] is one of two major themes that scholars examining popular pastimes have considered (the other being class conflict).[34] Peter Bailey suggests that it was a 'quickening of commercialisation', combined with the 'broadening impact of technology', that drove the transformation of leisure and popular culture from the 1880s onwards.[35] This led to the emergence of 'new leisure industries', which were 'both functions of material conditions and creators of employment'.[36] Competition between these could, at times, be fierce, although Stephen Jones suggests that it was not until the inter-war period that 'entertainment and leisure became big business'.[37]

Peter Borsay points out that one of the problems with this area of study is that historians often buy into the 'profoundly influential myth of progress'.[38] Irrespective of which of the last three centuries is being studied, 'the middle class are always said to be rising … [and] leisure is always said to be commercializing'.[39] He argues, therefore, that a more helpful approach to understanding the topic is to identify the variations that occurred in both supply and demand.

The 'demand-led view of economic change' continues to hold sway with leisure historians. This involves contextualising activities within specific chronological periods, 'each characterized by the absorption of a class or social group into the market place for leisure'.[40] The majority of scholars argue that the period between the mid-nineteenth century and the First World War, for example, marked a new era in the development of leisure activities, although it is the last quarter of the nineteenth century that is often seen as 'the most crucial stage in the general transformation'.[41] During the latter there was not only a 'scramble for sport' amongst the middle classes,[42] but it was also when the huge potential of the working classes as consumers of leisure was 'first properly realised' on a national scale, as a result of increasing spending power and greater amounts of free time.[43]

Salters' was involved with the supply of leisure activities, which was an area in which technology, capital, entrepreneurship, professionalisation and the development of cartels all played a part. Technological developments helped to deliver certain forms of leisure – although some activities offered little scope for innovation – whilst improvements to the transport network and the communication of news also helped to popularise certain pastimes. Entrepreneurship also played a significant role. Yet although historians have tended to focus on the most influential individuals, like the pioneer of the tourist industry, Thomas Cook, it was the mass of small-scale entrepreneurs who were 'far more important in promoting the commercialization of leisure'.[44] As the leisure industry grew, this led to the professionalisation of some activities, although it is important to note that 'certain aspects of leisure were at odds with or resistant to commercialization'.[45] Borsay argues that in order to understand how pastimes developed over time, it is necessary to acknowledge that they could be affected by a large range of factors, including the health of the economy, the role of the state, class politics, self and collective identities, geographical location, distinctions between urban and rural communities, and the availability of free time. Indeed, he stresses that each particular type of recreation can experience its own internal life-cycle, 'the rise and fall of which does not, of itself, reflect the fortunes of leisure as a whole'.[46]

In this book we will focus on three types of leisure activity on the Thames, the first of which is the sport of rowing. In *The Social History of English Rowing*, Neil Wigglesworth identifies Salters' as one of the two dominant racing boat-builders of the mid-nineteenth century; so this work provides the opportunity to examine in more depth why this was the case.[47] Indeed, it shows that the firm arguably had a greater impact on the sport than has been previously acknowledged.

A second area we will look at is the rise of pleasure boating on the Upper Thames. This remains a favourite topic for popular histories of the river, but it is one that has received little academic attention. Rosemary Stewart-Beardsley is one of the few scholars to examine the statistics behind the phenomenon,[48] whilst Lisa Tickner's article 'Messing About in Boats: E.J. Gregory's *Boulter's Lock: Sunday Afternoon* (R.A. 1897)' provides one of the best descriptions of how the Upper Thames changed in the late Victorian period.[49] Alison Byerly's work focuses on the literature that helped to shape perceptions of the waterway,[50] whereas Wigglesworth describes many of the different types of recreational boating that took off around the country at this time, including some on the river.[51] By examining one of main companies responsible for popularising pleasure boating on the Upper Thames, we will shed light on how different activities on the waterway developed, including the rise of camping as a recreational pastime.

A third type of leisure to be discussed is travelling by passenger boat. John Armstrong and David Williams argue that the steamboat, rather than the train, played a pioneering role in promoting recreational travel,[52] as is shown by the millions of passengers who were transported from London to seaside resorts like Gravesend and Margate between 1815 and 1840.[53] Yet the only detailed study of the non-tidal river is Frank Dix's popular work on the history of passenger boat services on the waterway as a whole. By examining the largest and most successful operator on the Upper Thames, this book not only gives more precise information about one of the major firms mentioned by Dix, but it also highlights the significant differences between running on the higher and the lower reaches of the river.

Another significant aspect of this work is the way it traces the evolution of a major provider of services on the waterway over one of the most significant periods in the development of sport and leisure – the end of the nineteenth century. Moreover, it shows how a firm was able to survive in an industry that is 'at the more volatile and risky end of the business spectrum',[54] because the leisure market is influenced so much by the 'flights of fashion'.[55]

Business History

In examining the history of Salters' we are contributing to the historical study of family firms. There has been a lot of discussion about such firms, and there is an on-going debate about whether they should be viewed as 'a source of economic growth or as a harbinger of conservatism and stagnation'.[56]

In his influential *English Culture and the Decline of the Industrial Spirit*, Martin Wiener argued that business owners were ultimately responsible for the decline of the British economy from the end of the nineteenth century onwards, because their desire to become landed gentry caused them (and their descendants) to become distracted from the primary focus of production and profit.[57] As David Landes explains, many industrialists 'sold out' to a role prescribed by the upper reaches of society, as 'rather than wear the short sleeves of their forefathers, they finish in silks and velvets, and focus on politics, culture, or the unabashed pursuit of the good life'.[58]

Linked to this notion is the so-called 'Buddenbrooks effect' (named after Thomas Mann's novel), which postulates that the important ingredients of entrepreneurial instinct plus a strident work ethic usually remain strong in those with a direct link to the founder, but that by the third generation this is often lost, as a result of family members being sent to select schools in order to enhance their social standing. This education provided neither the training nor the motivation to run a business and, instead, could nurture a desire to emulate the aristocratic lifestyle. Although some were able to sustain this transition, it could herald a family's economic ruin, especially if the 'effective direction of their businesses' was left to managers who were practical, but not entrepreneurial.[59] The Lancashire proverb 'From clogs to clogs in three generations' was not, therefore, without foundation, as Alfred Marshall explained:

When a man has got together a great business his descendants often fail in spite of their great advantages to develop the high abilities and special turn of mind and temperament required for carrying it on with equal success ... When a full generation has passed, when the old traditions are no longer a safe guide and when the bonds that held together the old staff have been dissolved, then the business almost invariably falls to pieces.[60]

This dilution of ability is supported by T. Nicholas' study of a number of successful British entrepreneurs since 1850. Although he concludes that further research is still needed in this area, he argues that the region of activity, type of occupation and religious affiliation were not determinants of entrepreneurial success, but that a 'high-status education was associated with inferior performance'. Indeed, 'firm inheritors performed less well than firm founders and managers', with the third generation failing, in particular, when compared to their *arriviste* counterparts'.[61] One possible reason for this, according to Matthias Doepke and Fabrizio Zilibotti, is that:

Parents shape their children's preferences in response to economic incentives. Middle-class families in occupations requiring effort, skill, and experience develop patience and a work ethic, whereas upper-class families relying on rental income cultivate a refined taste for leisure. These class-specific attitudes, which are rooted in the nature of preindustrial professions, become key determinants of success once industrialization transforms the economic landscape.[62]

Other classic weaknesses said to blight family firms are a lack of professional management skills, a failure to train successors adequately, a potential for in-fighting amongst relatives and an institutional conservatism that can cause both declining efficiency and a reluctance to embrace technological change.[63]

Yet, in spite of the potential vulnerabilities of such businesses, it would be wrong to view them as anachronistic oddities. Although few enjoy long-term success – in 1996, the Institute of Directors estimated that only around 24 per cent survive to the second generation and 14 per cent to the third[64] – family firms still account for between 60 and 90 per cent of all businesses in the European Union (the figure varying from country to country), as well as providing approximately two-thirds of jobs and overall gross national product.[65] Furthermore, the suggestion that the gentrification of business owners caused the country's economic decline at the end of the nineteenth century has been discredited. F.M.L. Thompson points out that between 1870 and 1990 the overall picture was generally one of growth in the economy, in terms of both gross national product and income per capita. It was not until the 1960s, when the British economy began to be overtaken by Germany, France and Japan, that commentators started to look for the long-term causes of the inefficiencies that were apparent in certain industries. This led, paradoxically, to the finger of blame being pointed at both the 'educated amateurs' (businessmen from public schools and universities), who were supposedly distracted by the trappings of wealth, *and* the 'practical men' (those who did not have elite schooling or a university education), who were left to run businesses and supposedly lacked the necessary entrepreneurial talent.[66] Yet Thompson points out that the former did not enter the business world in large numbers until after the Second World War. Moreover, it was entirely normal for those who had accumulated wealth to pursue different elements of a gentrified existence, like acquiring property in the country, sending children to elite schools and focusing more on leisure and the arts. Some purchased estates and withdrew from business, resulting in their families and descendants being assimilated into the landed aristocracy and gentry. Yet there were others, the so-called 'aristocratic bourgeoisie' (particularly those in banking, finance or brewing), for whom acquiring property 'may well have reinvigorated the industrial spirit', for it led to the founding of long-standing business dynasties. Thompson stresses that 'at no point would it appear to have had any pronounced effects on the performance of the national economy or on the overall economic performance of the gentrified new men', but that on balance it should be seen as 'a derivative of individual achievement and aspiration more than a determinant of economic advance or decline'.[67]

Mary Rose suggests that the success or failure of a business often hinged on whether it was able to overcome certain organisational challenges, such as a company's capability of moving with the times through investment in new technology, and the 'critical test' of succession, which she describes as one of the most crucial determinants 'not only of a family firm's future prosperity, but its very survival'.[68] Although she acknowledges some of the inherent vulnerabilities of such businesses, she argues that the prevailing socio-economic conditions of the early part of the Industrial Revolution were particularly suited to them: 'Small localised and often specialised markets, combined with the need for personal contact and trust in an age of unlimited liability, rendered the family firm a perfect organisational form.'[69]

As a result, 'a high level of regional specialisation' developed amongst nineteenth-century British businesses, although this started to erode as the expansion of the railway ushered in more of a national economy. Businesses sought to insulate themselves from the fragility of the economy by developing and operating 'networks of trust' within their geographical setting that reflected 'far more than flows of finance'. These ensured that the stratification and structure of the company was 'closely bound up with the culture and institution of the surrounding community'. Furthermore, shared religious convictions could help to influence business ethics and attitudes towards paternalism, as well as providing 'a common set of values and endogenous behaviour, which tied together extended families ... [and] could also provide the respectability crucial to business success'.[70]

Therefore, if potential hazards were managed well, family firms could benefit from a number of strengths. They tend to take a long-term view of business, they are often less bureaucratic, and the issue of succession can sometimes be less divisive, if the heir is already predetermined and if they bring with them a high level of specialist experience. Furthermore, those in charge can shape 'the prevailing attitudes, norms and values in the company', and this can produce greater productivity, if the workers feel part of the family and share in a common commitment, identity and purpose.[71]

Andrea Colli reminds us that research on this topic has broadened greatly over recent years and is now 'multi-disciplinary, drawing upon sociology, politics, and management, just as much as on economics and history'. He notes that 'There has been a growing tendency to analyse the role of the family firms at the different stages of growth of a dcfined national economy system' and that the minority of businesses that survived often did so by changing into either managerial or public companies.[72] Yet he also argues that 'Significant study evidence in Western economies now shows that family firms may have a positive influence in some sectors, especially in services, as compared with publicly owned and managerial companies in other spheres'.[73]

This is an interesting observation, as when it comes to focusing on boat businesses on the Upper Thames, it was family firms that enjoyed the greatest success. Indeed, this book shows how Salters' evolved over more than 150 years and how those in charge helped it overcome some of the difficulties that such businesses encountered. It also demonstrates how a company was affected by the changing social status and personal interests of those running it.

Notes

1   *Daily Mail*, 25 January 1943.
2   The firm was originally known as 'J. and S. Salter', but became 'Salter Bros' in 1890 (and a limited company of the same name in 1915).
3   In the late Victorian period the river above London was often described as the 'Upper Thames'. In this study it is defined as the waterway above Staines, which was where the majority of the firm's activities occurred. Staines was also the jurisdictional boundary of the river authorities.
4   *Oxford Times*, 4 January 1890, in C.J. Day, 'Modern Oxford', in A. Crossley (ed.), *The Victoria History of the County of Oxford*, vol. 4 (Oxford, 1979), p. 216.
5   Report of the Oxford Diocesan Social Services Committee (1908), p. 33, in Day, 'Modern Oxford', p. 217.
6   S. Ward, O. Stewart and E. Swyngedouw, 'Cowley and the Oxford Economy', in T. Hayter and D. Harvey (eds), *The Factory and the City* (London, 1993), p. 67.
7   Ibid., p. 70.
8   J. Betjeman, *John Betjeman's Oxford* (Oxford, 1938), p. i.
9   Day, 'Modern Oxford', p. 182.
10 Ward, Stewart and Swyngedouw, 'Cowley and the Oxford Economy', p. 71.
11 Ibid., p. 117.
12 J.M. Mogey, *Family and Neighbourhood* (Oxford, 1956), pp. 6–7.
13 Published as S. Wenham, 'Salters' of Oxford: A History of a Thames Boating Firm over a Century of Evolution (1858–c. 1960)', *Oxoniensia*, vol. 71 (2006), pp. 111–43.
14 See Hayter and Harvey, *Factory and the City*, T. Sharp, *Oxford Re-Planned* (London, 1948), R.C. Whiting, *The View from Cowley* (London, 1993), and R.C. Whiting (ed.), *Oxford: Studies in the History of a University Town since 1800* (Manchester 1993).
15 *Limited Edition*, 12 December 2008.
16 M. Prior, *Fisher Row: Fishermen, Bargemen and Canal Boatmen in Oxford, 1500–1900* (Oxford, 1982), pp. 298–325.
17 W.J. Freer, 'Canal Boat People 1840–1970' (Nottingham University PhD thesis, 1991), pp. 132–330.
18 D. Blomfield, 'Tradesmen of the Thames: Success and Failure among the Watermen and Lightermen Families of the Upper Tidal Thames 1750–1901' (Kingston University PhD thesis, 2006), pp. 90–2, 259–61.
19 R. Stewart-Beardsley, 'After the Railway: A Study of Socio-economic Change in Five Rural Parishes in the Upper Thames Valley, 1830–1901' (Reading University PhD thesis, 2009), p. 193.

20 B. Cohen, *The Thames 1580–1980: A General Bibliography* (London, 1985).

21 P. Burstall, *The Golden Age of the Thames* (Newton Abbot, 1981).

22 F. Dix, *Royal River Highway: A History of the Passenger Boats and Services on the River Thames* (Newton Abbot, 1985).

23 *Waterways World*, January 1974, pp. 32–33 and March 1998, pp. 54–55, *Canal and Riverboat*, November 1981, pp. 39–41, *Old Glory*, March 1996, pp. 28–33, and *Canal Boat and Inland Waterways*, April 2005, pp. 78–83 and February 2011, pp. 60–63.

24 S.M. Wenham, 'Oxford, the Thames and Leisure: A History of Salter Bros, 1858–2010' (Oxford University DPhil thesis, Michaelmas 2012).

25 Turks' history is recorded in *Classic Boat*, August 2010, pp. 62–65, whilst Hobbs' is in *Thames Guardian*, spring 1998, pp. 16–17.

26 K.C. Barnaby, *100 Years of Specialized Shipbuilding and Engineering* (London, 1964).

27 A.E. Tagg and R.L. Wheeler, *From Sea to Air: The Heritage of Sam Saunders* (Newport, 1989) and R.L. Wheeler, *From River to Sea: The Marine Heritage of Sam Saunders* (Newport, 1993).

28 Popular books have been written about Blackwell's (bookshop), Cooper's (marmalade), Lucy's Ironworks, Morrell's (brewery), Morris (car manufacturer), Oxford University Press, Symm's (builder) and Taunt (photographer).

29 J. Hill, *Sport, Leisure and Culture in Twentieth Century Britain* (Basingstoke, 2002), p. 1.

30 Ibid., p. 2.

31 K. Roberts, *The Leisure Industries* (Basingstoke, 2004), p. 3.

32 J. Walton and J. Walvin (eds), *Leisure in Britain 1780–1939* (Manchester, 1983), p. 3.

33 P. Horn, *Pleasure and Pastimes in Victorian Britain* (Stroud, 1999), p. 19.

34 Walton and Walvin, *Leisure in Britain*, p. 3.

35 P. Bailey, *Leisure and Class in Victorian Britain* (London, 1978), p. 182.

36 J. Walvin, *Leisure and Society 1830–1950* (London, 1978), p. 62.

37 S. Jones, *Workers at Play: A Social and Economic History of Leisure* (London, 1986), pp. 3–15.

38 P. Borsay, *A History of Leisure* (Basingstoke, 2006), p. 218.

39 Ibid., p. 21.

40 Ibid., p. 25.

41 P. Bailey, 'The Politics and the Poetics of Modern British Leisure: A Late Twentieth-Century Review', *Rethinking History*, vol. 3, issue 2 (1999), p. 137, in Borsay, *History of Leisure*, p. 15.

42 J. Lowerson, *Sport and the English Middle-Classes 1870–1914* (Manchester, 1993), p. 7.

43 Borsay, *History of Leisure*, p. 24.

44 Ibid., p. 30.

45 Ibid., p. 40.

46 Ibid., p. 13.

47 N. Wigglesworth, *The Social History of English Rowing* (London, 1992), p. 50.

48 Stewart-Beardsley, 'After the Railway', p. 112.

49 L. Tickner, 'Messing About in Boats: E.J. Gregory's *Boulter's Lock: Sunday Afternoon* (R.A. 1897)', *Oxford Art Journal*, 25 February 2002, pp. 1–28.

50 A. Byerly, *Are We There Yet? Virtual Travel and Victorian Realism* (University of Michigan, 2013), pp. 1–134.

51 Wigglesworth, *History of Rowing*, pp. 92–116.

52 J. Armstrong and D.M. Williams, 'The Steamboat and Popular Tourism', *Journal of Transport History*, vol. 26, issue 1 (March 2005), pp. 66–77.

53 D.M. Williams and J. Armstrong, 'The Thames and Recreation, 1815–1840', *The London Journal*, vol. 30, no. 2 (November 2005), pp. 25–36.

54 Borsay, *History of Leisure*, p. 38.

55 Roberts, *Leisure Industries*, p. 3.

56   M.B. Rose, 'The Family Firm in British Business 1780–1914', in M.W. Kirby and
      M.B. Rose (eds), *Business Enterprise in Modern Britain: From the Eighteenth to the Twentieth
      Century* (London, 1994), p. 61.

57   M.J. Wiener, *English Culture and the Decline of the Industrial Spirit* (Cambridge, 1982).

58   D. Landes, *Dynasties* (London, 2006), p. xiv.

59   F. Crouzet, *The Victorian Economy* (London, 1982), p. 407.

60   A. Marshall, *The Principles of Economics* (London, 1890), pp. 299–300, in T. Nicholas,
      'Clogs to Clogs in Three Generations? Explaining Entrepreneurial Performance in
      Britain since 1850', *Journal of Economic History*, vol. 59, no. 3 (September 1999), p. 688.

61   Ibid., p. 711.

62   M. Doepke and F. Zilibotti, 'Occupational Choice and the Spirit of Capitalism',
      Quarterly Journal of Economics, vol. 123, issue 2 (2008), p. 747.

63   M.B. Rose, 'Beyond Buddenbrooks: The Family Firm and the Management of
      Succession in Nineteenth Century Britain', in J. Brown and M.B. Rose (eds),
      Entrepreneurship Networks and Modern Business (Manchester, 1993), pp. 7–11, and
      M.F.R. Kets de Vries, *Family Businesses: Human Dilemmas in the Family Firm* (London,
      1996), pp. 18–22.

64   Institute of Directors, *Family Businesses* (London, 1996), p. 5.

65   Landes, *Dynasties*, p. xi.

66   F.M.L. Thompson, *Gentrification and the Enterprise Culture* (Oxford, 2003), p. 140.

67   Ibid., pp. 160–61.

68   Rose, 'Beyond Buddenbrooks', pp. 3–14.

69   Ibid., p. 5.

70   Rose, 'The Family Firm', p. 76.

71   Kets de Vries, *Family Businesses*, p. 17.

72   A. Colli, *The History of Family Business, 1850–2000* (Cambridge, 2003), p. 13.

73   Ibid., p. 26.

I

The Sport of Rowing

Were its colleges to disappear one by one, were Ruskin to be forgotten, so long as Salter's boat-house stands by Folly bridge, it will be a trysting-place for the oarsmen of England.

Elizabeth Robins Pennell, 1889[1]

John and Stephen were the fourth and seventh of eight children born to James and Elizabeth Salter, in 1826 and 1835 respectively (see family tree, p. 187). At the time, the family were living in 'The Duke's Head' pub in Parsons Green (near Fulham),[2] where James was the publican. He was also a carpenter, which may have influenced his sons subsequent move into boat-building. By March 1836 they had crossed the Thames to take over 'The Feathers' pub, in Wandsworth by the mouth of the river Wandle.[3]

'The Feathers Boat House, c. 1890.

The distance of the relocation was less than a mile, but it was significant because it brought the family into direct contact with the world of aquatic leisure. Not only was the pub situated on a section of the Thames that was becoming one of the major centres for rowing in the country, but the move coincided with a 'vital stage' in the development of the sport (1830–80). This was when a 'new breed' of professional oarsmen was emerging, whose contests helped greatly to increase the popularity of rowing. In this 'era of professional champion and personality', the oarsmen benefited from 'good training waters, expert coaching and excellent equipment', before prohibitive legislation was introduced towards the end of the century, which would begin to marginalise non-amateurs in the sport.[4]

Waterside taverns, like that owned by the Salters, played an important part in the development of rowing:

> Small groups of enthusiasts got together and bought or hired boats and rented changing-rooms from boatyards or pubs, and these associations or groups of oarsmen often took their names from those of the boats in which they rowed.[5]

Many clubs 'owed their very existence to boat hirers' because they were reliant on members being able to use craft at a reduced rate.[6]

Rowing histories seldom mention 'The Feathers', but in the Victorian period it was a well-known training establishment with on-land exercise facilities, including a 100-yard cinder track.[7] As well as renting out pleasure boats, the pub, whose licence had transferred from James to Elizabeth in 1840,[8] hosted a large number of clubs, including some that regularly competed in the early years of the Henley Regatta, like Wandle and Wandsworth. The crews probably used craft constructed on the premises and it is likely that this is where the Salters first learnt to build boats. By 1855, 'The Feathers' had also established a reputation for being where 'the North countrymen train' and 'the champions are cared for'.[9] The former was a reference to the number of famous Tyneside oarsmen who used the premises, whilst the latter was a reference to the work of Harry Salter.

Sporting activities were often arranged or promoted at pubs, and it was Harry who was the key individual responsible for elevating the reputation of 'The Feathers'. By the mid-1850s he was considered to be 'highest among trainers', owing to 'the great number of winners' he had trained.[10] In particular, it was by coaching a string of competitors for the Championship of the Thames, the most prestigious professional race at the time, that he made a name for himself. The event, which at that time involved the two leading oarsmen of the day (the title-holder and a challenger) competing over the university course for a typical prize of £400, was hugely popular and drew large crowds to the river.

Harry was associated (as coach, agent and occasionally umpire) with at least one of the two competing oarsmen in every Championship race from Thomas Cole's victory in 1852 to Henry Kelley's defeat in 1868. Furthermore, in his testimonial from the late Wandle Rowing Club, he was described as 'frequently neglecting his own interests' in order to play 'a most active part in nearly every rowing match of his day'.[11] Another indication of his reputation was that his 'Hints on Rowing' (both for 'the gentleman amateur' and 'watermen and tradespeople') was included in the first two editions of the annual *Rowing Almanack* (1861 and 1862). This was ahead of its time in taking a scientific approach to the condition of the oarsmen,[12] and it combined rowing on the water with land-based training, like the 'novel' exercise of skipping and the use of dumbbells.[13]

Given that they were brought up in such a centre of rowing, it is unsurprising that the Salter family became competitive oarsmen themselves. One of the earliest records of their competing was in the Thames Regatta of 1841 when Harry's Isis crew (from Wandsworth) lost to Lambeth Aquatics Club in the four-oared Tradesmen's Challenge Cup.[14] He was around 18 at the time and it was at a similar age that his younger brothers (John, George, Stephen and Alfred) all began rowing in the major regattas, sometimes with other family members and presumably in boats that the family had built. The Salters were not amongst the famous professional oarsmen of the day, like 'Coombes, Cole, the Mackinneys, Newell, Messenger, Kelley and Chambers',[15] but they would have been well known in rowing circles as they regularly competed at the top non-amateur contests, including the waterman's race at the Henley Regatta of 1851. It was Stephen, who coxed in the Thames Regatta of 1841 at the age of 6, who became the most accomplished individual oarsman. In 1856, he was Henry Kelley's (the Champion of the Thames) 'principal companion in practice'[16] and he enjoyed success on both the home front, including winning the Apprentice sculls at Thames National Regatta in 1857 (for which he received the freedom of the Thames), and several of the rivers of Europe, including winning the International Regatta at Antwerp in 1858.[17] He considered his greatest personal triumph to be his victory against the Chelsea Landsman George Drewitt over the university course for a wager of £40 each.[18]

In terms of the future business, the most important result of their early involvement with the sport may have been the relationship the Salters forged with the Clasper family from Newcastle. Harry Clasper (1812–70) was one of the most important figures associated with rowing. As well as becoming a famous and successful oarsman, he helped to popularise a number of significant design changes to the racing craft, including, most notably, the use of outriggers in the 1840s. These enabled boats to travel much faster because of their narrower, lighter, construction.[19]

It is not clear exactly when the two families first met, but the Claspers had trained at 'The Feathers' regularly enough for it to be called their 'old quarters' by 1849.[20] This was also the year when some kind of arrangement between the two families was struck. By September, John had travelled up to Newcastle to spend an extended period of time with Harry Clasper.[21] The following year he competed with them in a number of northern regattas, resulting in a second place at the Talkin Tarn regatta, and victories in both the Manchester and Salford Regatta (the Chadwick Cup and the Ellesmere Plate) and the Tees Regatta (the Tradesmen's Plate).[22] The main purpose of the trip was probably to gain practical boat-building experience. This was presumably the implication of the later statement in *Bell's Life*, which described him as 'John Salter of Wandsworth who was formerly with Clasper of Newcastle'.[23]

Immediately following this, the family was building racing-craft to a high standard. Their boats had considerable success in the 1850s, including victories in both the professional and amateur Championships of the Thames (in 1852 and 1853 respectively), and in a number of the contests in Cambridge, including the Colquhoun Sculls in 1854 and both the college four-oared and sculling races in 1856.[24] The arrival of the Salters at the pinnacle of their field was confirmed in 1857 when they built their first eight used by Cambridge University in the Boat Race against Oxford.[25] This particular craft was not victorious, but the following year John and Stephen Salter, now leading racing boat-builders, decided to set up a partnership (known as 'J. and S. Salter Boat Builders') in Oxford, a city with one of the most vibrant and active rowing scenes in the country. They bought Isaac King's business for £1,300 (paid in instalments), which included the boats and 'stock in trade'.[26] It is likely that they heard about the sale of the yard through their connections in the sport of rowing and it is also possible that the 'great stink of London', caused by pollution in the Thames and an unusually hot summer, may have encouraged their decision. *Jackson's Oxford Journal* suggested that the brothers came with quite a reputation: 'From the high position occupied by Messrs Salter, in the aquatic world, there can be no doubt that Mr King has found worthy successors in that well known firm.'[27]

Salters' and the University Boat Race

The first rowing contest between the universities of Oxford and Cambridge was held in 1829, and it was on the barge of a Folly Bridge boat-builder, Stephen Davis, that the initial challenge (from Cambridge) was posted.[28] The event, which was held annually from 1856, was significant for the boat-builders who supplied the craft, because of the publicity it received, not only in Britain, but also internationally. It has been argued that the race helped to launch modern sports journalism,[29] and the subsequent reporting helped its popularity further. This was part of a wider transformation in the communication of sporting news through specialist publications, like *Bell's Life in London and Sporting Chronicle* (first published in 1822), which had a circulation in excess of 30,000 by the 1860s.[30]

Table 1.1 The leading racing boat-builders associated with the Boat Race during the era of wooden construction (based on the winners only)[31]

Date	Leading firm	Number two
1829–1836	No market leader	
1839–1856	Searle	King / Hall
1857–1860	Taylor	Searle
1861–1869	**Salter**	
1870–1875	Clasper	**Salter**
1876–1881	Swaddle and Winship	
1882–1891	Clasper	
1892–1898	Rough	Clasper
1899–1908	Sims and Sons	
1909–1914	Rough	Sims and Sons

1920–1936	Sims and Sons	Bowers and Phelps
1937–1954	Sims	
1955–1964	Banham	Sims
1965–1972	Sims	
1973–1976	No market leader	

By tracing the history of the boat-builders involved with the Oxford and Cambridge Boat Race (Table 1.1), one can gain an insight into how the racing boat industry worked and which were the leading firms at any given time. Many factors dictated whether a firm was used by one of the crews to build a craft. Firstly, it needed to have a history of success at a lower level, which is what Salters' enjoyed at Oxford and Cambridge before it was commissioned to build its earliest craft for each of the universities. It was important for the constructor to have a close relationship with those competing in their boats,[32] and it is unsurprising, therefore, that many of the leading boat-builders were also professional oarsmen themselves. Indeed, the design of the racing craft was slowly refined through an on-going 'arms race' between the respective boat-builders, by which they (or a client) tested both their muscle and the merits of their vessel in competition. If a loss was blamed on the craft, they could copy a competitor's design and/or refine their own boat in order to make it faster. This process led to the eights slowly changing in appearance. The first winning boat of 1829, for example, was 45ft in length, weighed 972lb and resembled a pilot gig from Cornwall,[33] whilst those used a century later were typically 62ft 6in in length and weighed approximately 350lb.[34] There were also certain 'schools' of boat-building that influenced one another. Initially firms based on the Thames dominated the event, but by the middle of the nineteenth century the balance of power had shifted to Tyneside. Between 1857 and 1898 all but one of the victorious craft were built by firms from the Newcastle 'stable', such as Taylor, Clasper and the partnership of Swaddle and Winship. The only two seeming exceptions (Salter and Rough) were both trained by the Claspers; the former, as mentioned, had been with Harry Clasper in 1850, whilst the latter was John Clasper's son-in-law and ex-employee. The Thames yards then regained the ascendency and much of the twentieth century was dominated by George Sims and Sons of Putney (founded in 1891) and a rival firm set up in Hammersmith by his grandson of the same name. The Cambridge firm of H.C. Banham enjoyed a brief period of success in the mid-1950s, but by the mid-1970s there was no overall market leader.

Secondly, the location of the boat-builder was important. The Oxford firms of Salters' and Rough produced many more boats for the dark blues than they did for the light blues, whilst the opposite was the case for Searle and Banham, who both had bases at Cambridge.[35] It was common for boat-builders to try and increase their market share by relocating to new areas or by operating from more than one yard. Salters' was not only based at Oxford, but it also had a second site at Eton from 1870 to 1875. The latter was a strategic location, because Eton College provided nearly a third of the individuals who competed in the race up to 1954 (over five times as many as the next most prolific school).[36] In 1870, for example, the Oxford crew (including five Etonians) requested that their boat from Salters' was a facsimile of their college craft that had been built by

Mat Taylor.[37] As this suggests, the same firm did not always build eights in an identical manner and requests like this could help with the refinement of their design. According to *Lock to Lock Times*, Salters' did 'much towards perfecting the racing boat',[38] and the two fastest times its craft set in the nineteenth century came after a number of years of building for the race (in 1868 and 1869).[39] The latter, a 56ft 4in craft that had taken around a month to build, was said to have benefited from an unusual design feature:

> … she seemed to us to trim somewhat more towards the stern than is usual … but we were informed by her builder that this was an intentional peculiarity … with the object of exposing as little as possible of her stern to the action of the wind.[40]

Thirdly, the result of the race had a significant bearing on which supplier would subsequently be used. Between 1839 and 1873 the losing crew changed their boat-builder on sixteen occasions, whilst the victor only changed theirs on five occasions. Although this was not the case with the first craft that Salters' built for Cambridge, the two times that Oxford switched to using the firm (1861 and 1976) was following a loss in the previous year. By the same token, a prolonged series of victories for one crew could mean a corresponding period of dominance for their boat-builder. This was the case for both Oxford's unbroken run of nine successive victories from 1861 to 1869 and Cambridge's run of thirteen successive victories from 1924 to 1936, when the crews kept faith with their constructor (Salters' and Sims respectively). These periods included races when both crews used the same supplier of craft, which was said to be 'the summit of every boat-builder's ambition'.[41] During the 1860s, for example, Salters' was 'at the head of the trade'[42] (see p. 35) and the firm was described as the 'usual' provider of the craft, because it built for both Oxford and Cambridge for five successive years between 1865 and 1869 (as well as in 1862).[43] Yet this was one of the reasons why commentators looked elsewhere to explain Oxford's dominance at this time. The dark blues were said to have been helped by the retirement of Cambridge's coach, Tom Egan, in 1861, for example. Furthermore, the resurgence of the light blues in the 1870s was believed to have been heavily influenced by both Oxford's head coach, George Morrison (1863–68), switching allegiances in 1869, and the arrival of John Goldie, one of the most famous Cambridge rowers, who competed between 1869 and 1872.[44]

By the end of the nineteenth century the crews were switching their suppliers less often, which suggests that the differences between the respective makes of craft may have been less apparent than they once had been. In the forty races between 1873 and 1914, the losers changed their boat-builder on ten occasions, whilst the winners changed theirs on six (although the ratio becomes ten to three, if you treat Clasper and Rough as one, as they were part of the same family).[45] Although there is not enough data to compare trends beyond this,[46] the design of racing craft continued to evolve. By the mid-1970s there were still notable differences between craft, as *Rowing* reported that the leading British companies were basing their designs on the superior and more expensive foreign boats (Donoratico of Italy and Stämpfli of Switzerland).[47]

Yet the impact that the craft had in affecting the outcome of the race was often overlooked as commentators tended to focus on the composition and merits of the respective crews. An exception to this was if a particular design innovation was first introduced, like the outrigger (1846), the carvel-built keel-less hull (1857) and the sliding seat (1873). As most of the significant changes were adopted by both crews in the same year – having been tested first at a lower level – this gives the false impression that neither crew had a particular advantage in any given contest. Yet in the era leading up to the First World War, the majority of races (54 per cent) were contested by crews rowing in craft constructed by different boat-builders (Table 1.2).

Table 1.2 Number of races when the respective crews rowed in boats made by different boat-builders[48]

1820s: 1 out of 1 (100%)	1830s: 2 out of 2 (100%)	1840s: 6 out of 7 (86%)	1850s: 3 out of 6 (50%)
1860s: 4 out of 10 (40%)	1870s: 5 out of 10 (50%)	1880s: 3 out of 10 (30%)	1890s: 6 out of 10 (60%)
1900s: 4 out of 10 (40%)	1910s: 4 out of 5 (80%)	**Overall total: 38 out of 71 (54%)**	

This was significant because there could be considerable differences between the boats, as was observed in the very first contest: 'The Cambridge boat, though London built and launched new for the occasion and much gayer in appearance than the old Oxford boat, was far inferior in the water, dipping to the oar whilst the other rose to every stroke in fine style.'[49]

Specialist publications often provided information about why a certain craft was superior to the other. In the Clasper boat used by Cambridge in 1871, for example, the rowers sat approximately half a foot lower in the vessel than they did in the Salters' craft used by Oxford, which made it more stable. Furthermore, it was also both stiffer and lighter than its counterpart, because it had permanently fixed stretchers and wooden support bars across the boat (rather than ones made from iron).[50]

Yet the issue is more complicated than one make of craft being better than another, because in the early years of the contest the respective crews did not always adopt the same rowing technique. In the early 1860s, for example, there was a distinct 'Oxford style' which involved a stroke that was said to be loftier, more powerful, but slower than that of Cambridge.[51] This meant that, although there was generally a leading racing boat-builder, one make of craft could potentially be more suited to one side than the other. In 1870, for example, Oxford rejected the boat built by Taylor, because it had 'no way on the feather, like a Salter', although it was known for being steady in the water, 'lively off hand' and requiring a fast stroke.[52] Some of the changes in the rowing style were dictated by design innovations, such as the introduction of sliding seats, but ultimately it was the coach who often determined the type of boat and stroke that the crews used. Although professionals were officially excluded from coaching in the 1850s, *Baily's Magazine of Sports and Pastimes* speculated in 1869 that one of the Salters may have played a role in this respect too:

We have heard divers mighty names noted as the founders of the present Oxford form, but fancy that Stephen Salter, the boat-builder, had as much to do with it as any one, and Oxford's great improvement certainly bears a date about contemporary with his commencing business on the Isis when he used to give many a useful hint to the oarsmen of the day, though now his attention is fully taken up with the boats instead of their occupiers.[53]

Yet even when the crews used the same rowing style and make of boat, there could still be significant differences between the craft, because no two vessels were the same. This is because those used by the late 1850s were bespoke vessels tailored to the specific weight of each of the rowers. In 1953, for example, George Sims built his craft with an extra ⅛ of an inch freeboard for every additional 7lb over 11½ stone that the average rower weighed.[54] This could be crucial if the race was contested in bad weather; there were five races in which a craft sank from taking on too much water, although this only affected the outcome of three races (1859, 1925 and 1978), as two were subsequently re-run (1912 and 1951). In 1859, Oxford made the right decision to use a larger boat built by Taylor, because the one they had commissioned from Salters' (their first order to the firm) was rejected for being too small – the crew had turned out to be 5lb a man heavier than expected.[55] As this suggests, the performance of the craft in testing was also critical in determining whether a boat would be used in the race.

Furthermore, certain boats just turned out to be exceptionally fast. The *Rowing Almanack* of 1914 described Cambridge's boat of 1913, built by Bowers and Phelps, as having 'the undeniable advantage in naval architecture' and being 'the best model since Oxford's boat of 1908 and probably superior to that, in which case one might be harked back to the celebrated "Swaddell" [sic] used by Oxford ('77–'82)'.[56] W.B. Woodgate agreed with this, although he also added Cambridge's Clasper-built boat of 1883 to the list.[57] As this suggests, a particularly fast craft could be used in more than one contest, which is what occurred with the first boat that Salters' built for Oxford in 1861. The crew won by the considerable margin of fourteen to sixteen lengths (or three-quarters of a minute) and it was subsequently retained the following year.

Although the firm was not credited with producing one of the fastest craft, W.B. Woodgate suggested that an enforced design change ensured that the eight used by Oxford in 1865 was 'certainly never surpassed by any other boat which Salter built'. The firm was usually 'tenacious' in sticking to its 'own creed' of having the widest part of the boat at number five (towards the middle of the craft), but on this occasion it was 'scared' into altering this because of the large size of the bow rower.[58] As a result the boat was designed with the widest part at number three (towards the bow), which was the way that Taylor built his craft, to mimic the shape of a fish. The eight was used again by Oxford in 1866 and after it was sold (to the Oxford Etonians) it went on to win the Grand Challenge cup of 1866 and 1867, as well as the eight-oared race at the International Regatta in Paris.[59]

In 1978, Arthur Salter summed up the business as being 'more like breeding race-horses. Your reputation has to make itself, on the way your boats perform.'[60] It was a results-based industry and this meant that a boat-builder's livelihood was bound up with a host of other factors that could dictate whether or not their craft won. In 2011, the former Oxford oarsman Dan Snow reminded television viewers that the contest is 'all about tiny twists of fate that can turn the entire race'.[61] The power and the skill of the crews – including the role played by the coach and the tactics employed on the day by the coxswain – were obviously the most important factors in determining the outcome, but others included the weather,[62] the toss of the coin, the physical and mental condition of the rowers on the day, as well as more unusual occurrences, such as last-minute changes to the crew or equipment failures. Yet as *The Saturday Review* acknowledged in 1874, it is clear that the boat design and set-up did play a larger role in determining the outcome than has often been acknowledged:

> We shall content ourselves with drawing the conclusion that in rowing, as in more serious matters, the conditions which it is convenient for historians to overlook are frequently the most important. Armies have been defeated, it is said, from the fault of the shoemaker as well as from the mistakes of the general; and, if justice were fairly distributed, Messrs. Searle, Clasper, Salter, and other builders would frequently deserve a large share of the glory or the blame which is too frequently bestowed upon the oarsmen and their trainers.[63]

Amongst all of the boat firms associated with the race, Salters' was unique, because it was the only one to achieve success in the competition that was not confined to a relatively short time frame. Following reinvestment in the racing boat department in the 1970s (see pp. 40–1), the firm gained the contract to build Oxford's 1976 boat (the first the company had built for the race since 1872 and probably only the second built in the city since 1914). Neither university nor boat-builder was dominating the contest at this time and the respective crews were experimenting with both foreign and British craft. The eights built by Salters' were not the lightest on the market, but they were very rigid, which was necessary for speed. Indeed, the boat used by Oxford in 1976 won the race in a then record time of sixteen minutes and fifty-eight seconds, which was described by Arthur Salter as 'the proudest day for Salter Bros this century'.[64] Fittingly, this was also the last-ever contest using a wooden-hulled craft, before corporate sponsorship transformed the event and new composite materials were introduced that led to the dominance of a new generation of boat-builders. The contract ensured that Salters' was the firm with the longest association with the contest (1857 to 1976), and it still holds the most record-breaking times (three, in 1868, 1869 and 1976). Furthermore, if one takes the era of wood construction alone, the ten victories ranks the company as the fifth most successful boat-builder in the history of the race.

Rowing at Oxford

Identifying those associated with the Oxford and Cambridge Boat Race is a convenient way of finding which firms were at the very pinnacle of racing eight construction, but it was still only a single contract in a year – albeit a highly prestigious one. On a day-to-day basis, it was the local market that largely determined the fortunes of a boat-builder, as can be illustrated by the Cambridge firm of H.C. Banham, which was proud to advertise that over 100 of its craft were being used on the Cam in 1948, before it was even deemed good enough to build for the university crew.[65]

In *The Social History of Rowing*, Neil Wigglesworth examines the commercial exploitation of the sport by a number of outside agencies, including local councils that sponsored races, and railway companies that carried spectators to the events. He does not accord the boat-builders any great significance in this respect, however, other than acknowledging that they sold and rented out craft to clubs, and that some were amongst the well-known oarsmen of their day, who helped popularise the sport during the heyday of professional rowing between 1830 and 1880.[66] By examining the early history of Salters' in Oxford, however, one can see that in a thriving centre of rowing, a proactive business could exploit the sport financially to a much greater degree than first might be realised.

Competitive rowing at Oxford is thought to have evolved from informal contests between those using boats for leisure and the first intercollegiate competition was a light-hearted affair between eights from Brasenose and Jesus in 1815.[67] A number of entrepreneurial boat-builders played an important role in encouraging rowing during these early years by competing in races for payment (including in the main university races up to 1823), organising contests (with bets staked on the outcome) and building (or modifying) the craft that were used. The sport was given 'tremendous impetus' by the famous victory of seven Oxford rowers over eight from Cambridge at Henley in 1843,[68] and by the middle of the nineteenth century it had assumed an unrivalled significance amongst university sports. This stemmed from its accessibility for participants,[69] the culture of athleticism propagated by the private school system,[70] and the popularity of the annual procession of boats (held until 1893), which rivalled Encaenia as an attraction.[71] This pre-eminence was reflected in literature about the city, with rowing figuring prominently in novels like Thomas Hughes' *Tom Brown at Oxford* (1860) and Max Beerbohm's *Zuleika Dobson* (1911).

Chris Nilson defines an entrepreneur as someone possessing 'a sense of market opportunity combined with the capacity needed to exploit it',[72] and it was this instinct that John and Stephen Salter displayed when they chose to move to Oxford in 1858. The firm's craft were already successful in Cambridge and it was a strategic move for an 'up-and-coming' boat-builder to relocate in order to tap into another of the most thriving rowing centres in the country. As the *Oxford Flying Post* recorded in the same year:

> Among the amusements which have been introduced during the present century in England, amateur rowing takes a very high place, and nowhere has it been carved to greater excellence than at Oxford and Cambridge … the numbers of those who practise it at these two universities far exceed the total of the amateur oarsmen who are elsewhere engaged in this healthy amusement.[73]

The proximity of the market was extremely important, in much the same way as the output of shipbuilding firms during the era of wooden construction was 'proportionate to the trade of the ports'.[74] It was advantageous for coastal businesses to be located near major shipping lanes and, by the same token, it was clearly lucrative for Salters' to be situated in a city that became such a hub for boating (of all types). The business John and Stephen took over was strategic, as Isaac King's firm was already the leading racing boat-builder in the city, responsible for producing nine of the fifteen boats used in the 1856 university eights.[75] It was also situated close to the city centre on one of the busiest sections of the river for rowing, whilst backing onto a weir stream was advantageous, as it meant that large numbers of craft could be moored outside, as the reach was not used by through-traffic. The character of the local area inevitably shaped the way in which the business developed, as was also the case for Hobbs of Henley, for example, which became closely associated with the annual regatta,[76] and Turks of Kingston, which did a lot of work for the nearby film studios in the second half of the twentieth century.[77]

The success of Salters' is shown by the areas of the sport from which it managed to derive income, which included, firstly, providing craft for the respective crews. The firm was clearly pursuing customers energetically from the outset, because within days of arriving in Oxford it agreed to rent a boat that had won 100 guineas at the Thames Regatta to Balliol College for the four-oared races[78] and Jesus College had accepted a proposal to provide a practice boat for the Torpid and another for the race in part exchange for the college's boat *Prince of Wales* and £5 in money.[79] The firm's rise to leading constructor in the city is shown by its craft winning the four-oared race of 1861 and accounting for the top six boats in the eights in 1862 – a year in which it also produced craft for the Cambridge colleges of Sidney Sussex, St John's and Trinity Hall.[80] Another sign of its pre-eminence is that Salters' was given the honour of building a special craft used to row the Prince of Wales to the university barge for the annual procession in 1863.[81]

The firm's early success is shown by the number of racing craft it had in its fleet. Between 1861 and 1865 the number of its fastest craft (the eights, fours, pairs and singles) increased from 64 to 118. Although there was then a slight reduction of these to 102 by 1875, Salters' was more than compensated for this by a significant increase in the other types of boat used in the sport. The number of gigs and whiffs the firm had in its fleet increased from 60 in 1861 to 205 by 1875.[82] These were used for lesser races, like the Torpids, as well as for training oarsmen in half-outrigged boats called 'tubs'.

The Prince and Princess of Wales at the university barge. (*Illustrated London News*, 27 June 1863, p. 441)

This meant that the firm had over 300 racing craft in the mid-1870s, and by the end of the decade this had risen further to around 400.[83] This number was far in excess of the 100 boats that Banham proudly advertised that it had on the Cam in the 1940s. Indeed, it was probably the largest commercially owned collection of racing craft in the country and it is likely to have peaked in size around 1887, as this is when the number of vessels in the firm's overall fleet, including pleasure boats, was at its greatest (see chapter 2). This is close to the period described by W.E. Sherwood as the 'high-water mark of boating enthusiasm' in the city, which was 'five or six years' before he wrote *Oxford Rowing* (1900).[84]

The reason the firm owned so many craft is that, like many clubs around the country, the college crews largely relied upon rented boats. Len Andrews, who started working for the firm in 1930, recalled that Salters' had long-standing agreements where a boat would be leased for three years, after which a new craft was built and the old model would be passed down to a lesser crew at a reduced rate.[85] Although some colleges bought boats, the majority entered into some kind of rental agreement. Many hired craft for a whole year, such as Christ Church which in 1877 agreed to pay £25 for one year's rental of an eight-oared gig and a torpid eight for the races (with the latter 'to be new each alternate year'),[86] although they could also be leased for one-off events. In several instances the firm provided a college with a whole 'suite' of rowing equipment.[87]

As well as building and renting craft, a third service the firm provided was boat-repair and on-going maintenance. Accidents were not uncommon on such a congested section of river, which is why the university imposed fines on those whose craft collided with rowers out practising (£1 for hitting a college eight and £2 for a varsity eight at the beginning of the twentieth century).[88] Furthermore, the university contests involved a series of bumping races where craft had to make contact with one another and this inevitably ensured that regular running repairs were needed.

A fourth service provided by the firm was boat storage, which involved taking advantage of the many waterside yards at Folly Bridge that it came to occupy, including the University Boat House until 1881 (see chapter 5).[89] Space came at a premium and Salters' was charging £5 a year for housing a single eight in the 1870s.[90] The expense of accommodating many craft was one of the reasons that college clubs often broke up their old boats, once they were no longer needed. Finding space was a constant challenge and after the Second World War the firm even considered a plan to try and store racing craft vertically on a rotating rack, although this was deemed impractical.[91]

As custodians of the boats, another service offered by the firm was the transportation of craft. Moving large and fragile boats required specialist equipment and Salters' developed a comprehensive delivery and retrieval service (see pp. 35–6).

The firm also offered a variety of facilities for the rowers themselves, which included providing changing rooms (in the University Boat House) for Wadham, Lincoln, Keble and Corpus Christi, as well as another for public use, in 1875.[92] By that point, however, many of the college crews were using barges moored at Christ Church Meadow for this purpose, which was an unusual feature of rowing life in Oxford. Many of these craft were provided by Salters' (see chapter 2), which had acquired at least two (*Nelson* and 'the green barge') from King.[93] The latter was particularly significant because it was '*par excellence*, the barge of the river' and was 'the great centre of the Oxford navy'.[94]

The green barge (*c.* 1870).

It was not only the main place where many rowers changed in the mid-nineteenth century – as it was considered both inappropriate and an offence to be in the Meadows in boating costume – but it was also the site of the finish line for most races, with its flagpole used to display the order of the colleges.[95]

Salters' built up the number of barges, by both purchase and construction, until they numbered fourteen by 1875. Furthermore, it sought to maximise the revenue produced by the craft by using some of them for other purposes, like storage or as holiday houseboats for rent. Up until around the Second World War, the firm would tow a number of them down to Henley each year for those who wanted to use them during the regatta,[96] although this practice was not popular with the colleges. In 1896, Wadham started to raise money for a new barge, as it deemed it 'humiliating … to see its colours hired out to the use of strangers'.[97]

Another source of income relating to the barges arose from the assignment of watermen to them; they were employed to perform a variety of tasks, like ferrying the crews across the river. For safety reasons, each club was required to have its own waterman from 1889, although Salters' had employees living on its barges from at least the mid-1860s.[98] These staff ensured that the firm had regular contact with the crews, which would have been important for the development of further commercial opportunities. Salters' also played a significant part in the growth of women's rowing in the city. It not only provided craft for Falcon Rowing Club, one of the earliest to feature female participants in a race (1869),[99] and Lady Margaret Hall, the first women's college to start a boating club (1885), but in 1893 it also supplied St Hilda's with its first boat and a waterman (William Best) to coach them.[100] At the beginning of the twentieth century, St Hilda's started regularly practising on the Isis in a four, and in 1911 rowers were allowed in an eight, 'a hitherto unheard of thing for a women's college'. Coaching took place at 9 a.m., in order to be less conspicuous.[101] Fittingly, it was the firm's barge that was used as the headquarters for the first-ever women's contest between Oxford and Cambridge in 1927.

Finally, the founders were also personally involved in actively promoting the sport. Stephen, who was in the twilight of his rowing career when he moved to Oxford, was involved in a number of notable races, like the Championship of the Isis in 1859, which he was forced to pull out of owing to illness, and a town-versus-gown eight-oared challenge match the following year.[102] After retiring from racing, he established himself as a successful coach, training, amongst others, W.B. Woodgate, as well as becoming a 'renowned umpire'[103] officiating at regattas across the UK during the 1860s. Stephen and John were both also involved in an organisational capacity with a number of events involving the city crews, including, most notably, the Oxford Royal Regatta,[104] of which John became Honorary Secretary (and steward).[105]

Given the variety of areas that the business was able to exploit commercially, it is unsurprising that the sport was very lucrative. There are a number of sources that provide an indication of how well the firm was faring at this time. One is an inventory taken in 1874, which valued the business at approximately £10,000.[106] This was more than eight times the price paid for King's firm sixteen years earlier and the increase was partly owing to the additional buildings Salters' had accumulated (see chapter 5). Another is the college boat club records, which show that by the 1870s a number of crews had amassed significant debts to Salters'. The annual running cost for Jesus College Boat Club was around £105 per annum, but as it was only managing to pay off around half of this each year, its debt to John Salter had risen to £160 5s in the three years up to October 1877, forcing it to arrange a special collection in order to pay it off.[107] By contrast, Worcester College Boat Club was more frugal, operating at just under £70 per annum between 1874 and 1881, but as it was only paying around a third of this off each year, the overall bill had reached £312 9s by the end of this period.[108] In this instance John Salter agreed to accept a 10 per cent discount for 'prompt settlement of the whole year', although he claimed 'for the seven years I have had this business on my own hands I have been paying 5 per cent interest on a large amount' (suggesting that he had significant debts).[109] By the end of the Victorian period, approximately a quarter of the firm's overall turnover was accrued on credit, and concessions such as this may explain why Salters' slowly reduced the amount of work it did on account during the twentieth century.[110]

The Wider Influence of Salters' on the Sport

The majority of racing boat-builders focused on providing craft for their immediate locality, but Salters' was one of two firms identified by Wigglesworth (the other being

Searle) that were into business in a 'big way', because it supplied craft to clubs 'all over the country'.[111] It was particularly significant, as it not only built the fastest craft in the 1860s, but also combined a prolific output of boats with a far-reaching distribution network.

The available evidence does not allow us to give a precise figure for the number of craft that were produced during its heyday, but there is no reason to doubt Stephen Salter's claim that between 1858 and 1874 the firm built more racing boats than any other business in the same time frame.[112] Indeed, when John Salter died in 1890 a number of newspapers reported that his business had seemed to have almost a monopoly of the trade.[113]

It was, after all, the market leader in the 1860s and the performance of its craft established the firm's reputation, which also helped to attract more business. This was the period 'when Salter was king of the river'[114] and customers had to pay a premium for its craft, with prices (in 1866) ranging from £15, for a sculling boat, to £60, for a racing eight.[115] One can gain an idea of the company's prestige by the range of prominent races the firm's craft were winning. By 1864, this included the Oxford and Cambridge Boat Race for four years running (1861–64), the Grand Challenge Cup at Henley in 1861, 1863 and 1864, the Wingfield Sculls from 1862 to 1864, the eights at both universities, and an unspecified number of 'Winning boats at most of the principal Amateur Regattas'.[116] A Salters' craft also won the Doggett's Coat and Badge in at least 1863 and 1864, whilst its victorious boat of 1866 was said to be 'the best specimen of her class'.[117] Furthermore, the firm also provided the umpire eights for the Henley Regatta,[118] because the official had to be rowed in the fastest possible boat.[119] Indeed, the business was linked with so many successful crews and oarsmen that in 1874 *Punch* included in its humorous 'Things not Generally Known' that 'Julius Caesar crossed the Thames in a boat built specially for him by Salter, of Oxford'.[120]

Yet, despite the variety of success its craft had, Salters' was not universally considered to be the best builder of every type of boat. During the build-up to the Oxford–Harvard race of 1869 (an event that attracted an estimated half a million spectators – one of the largest crowds ever seen for a rowing contest),[121] London Rowing Club told the American crew that the fours built by the Oxford firm were too strong and heavy, making them slower than those of Jewitt or Clasper. Nevertheless, the visitors favoured it in training and although they eventually opted for one built by their normal constructor, Elliott of Green Point (who had travelled over with them), they narrowly lost the race to the Oxford crew, rowing in a college four built by Salters'.[122]

Although the American crew chose not to use the firm's boat, Salters' managed to develop a delivery network that was on an unprecedented geographical scale, helped by both the company's reputation and its output of craft. Wigglesworth suggests that Searle, the other major distributor of racing boats, used a horse and cart to deliver its products, which was also a mode of transportation used by the Oxford firm. In the 1860s, the customers supplied by Salters' in this manner came from within a 100-mile radius of the city and they included Cambridge colleges, as well as numerous Thames rowing clubs, such as Albion, Kingston, Leander and London.[123] The horse and cart had its limitations, however, as it was a slow form of transportation (the trip to Wandsworth took two days, for example), and journeys were largely confined to the warmer months, when the roads were in a better condition. Furthermore, accidents did occasionally happen, as in 1886 when a horse managed to back a racing craft through a glass merchant's window on St Aldate's.[124]

In order to distribute its craft further, and at a faster speed, Salters' regularly used the railway, which was a significant development because Searle (its major competitor before Clasper) chose not to, as he deemed it unsafe for transporting long boats.[125] Although there were occasional accidents,[126] the railway enabled Salters' to reach a wide geographical area, as can be seen by the number of clubs around the country that bought ex-rental craft from the firm between 1877 and 1879 (Table 1.3) and those that purchased boats or accessories in 1893 (Table 1.4). Some of these orders would have gone by sea, however, because the firm also regularly sent craft to the docks, as in 1863 when boats were shipped to the rowing clubs of Cork Harbour and Dublin University respectively.[127]

Table 1.3 Clubs purchasing second-hand ex-rental craft from Salters' between 1877 and 1879[128]

Ancholme RC	Birmingham and Edgbaston RC	Boston RC	Bradford ARC
Bradford-on-Avon RC	Clifton RC	Dundalk RC	Grosvenor RC (Chester)
Kensington RC	Lancaster RC	Liverpool RC	Mersey RC
North London RC	Reading RC	Thames RC	Winchester College BC

Table 1.4 Clubs purchasing boats or accessories from Salters' in 1893[129]

Ancholme RC	Bath Amateur BC	Belfast RC	Bewdley RC
Boston RC	Bradford on Avon RC	Clarence RC	Clifton RC
Derby Town RC	Downton College BC	Edinburgh University BC	Gainsborough RC
Hereford RC	Hereford School BC	Hill Lands BC	Kensington RC
Mumbles RC	Naiad RC (Ipswich)	Newark RC	Northwich RC
Ross RC	Royal Engineers BC	St Augustine's College BC	Stourport BC
Stratford on Avon BC	Union RC (Nottingham)	Wareham RC	Warwick BC
Weymouth RC	Winchester College BC	Worcester RC	

An even better indication of the firm's success and reputation is the extent to which its craft were distributed internationally. The Oxford and Cambridge Boat Race received a lot of coverage from around the world and it is likely that this was the most important event for stimulating demand on a global scale. Nevertheless, the family was exporting some craft whilst in Wandsworth, including Thomas Cole's Championship of the Thames-winning craft, which was bought by a Melbournian boat-letter in 1855.[130] There continued to be a market for the firm's craft in Australia. In 1863 *Bell's Life in*

Sydney recorded that 'Few branches of colonial industry have been more extensively patronised than that of boat building' and that, because the country's firms could not cope with the demand, orders had gone to Salter, Clasper and Searle.[131] Those built by the former included gigs named *Oxford* and *Cambridge* that were rented out on the river Yarra in 1861, a craft exhibited at the 1866 Ballarat Exhibition, fours used at the Melbourne and Geelong regattas of 1877, and an eight used by the Victoria crew against New South Wales in the inter-colonial races of 1878 and 1879.[132]

The firm's impact appears to have been even greater still in New Zealand, although this may have been a reflection of the more detailed reports from the country's newspapers on items being imported. Indeed, the reports show that there were many more crews using Salters' equipment than would be apparent from the fragmentary records in the company archive. The Inventory Book of 1877–79 only lists three New Zealand clubs (Table 1.5), for example, but the local newspapers show that at least another ten were using Salters' craft during the 1870s.[133] The firm was clearly well known in rowing circles and in 1874 four of the six boats used in the four-oared race at the Interprovincial Regatta were built by the firm.[134]

Table 1.5 Ex-rental craft bought by international crews, 1877–79[135]

Auckland RC (New Zealand)	Beuel Bonn RC (Germany)	Budapest RC (Hungary)
Colombo RC (Ceylon)	Gothenburgian RC Uppsala University (Sweden)	Madras BC (India)
Stockholmian RC Uppsala University (Sweden)	Timaru BC (New Zealand)	Union BC (New Zealand)

By the 1880s, Salters' was trying to build up its international reputation as it advertised that 'especial attention' was given to foreign orders.[136] The firm's global ambitions are shown by the variety of boat shows it attended, which included major London events, like the Sportsman's Exhibition in the Agricultural Hall (1880s), the Yachting Exhibition at the Royal Aquarium (1890s), and the first Boating Exhibition in Earl's Court (1902), which was organised by the Thames Boat-Builders Protection Association (formed in 1887), whose president was John Henry Salter.[137] Furthermore, its craft were displayed at shows targeting the worldwide market, including the 1886 International Exhibition of Navigation Travelling Commerce and Manufactures held in Liverpool (in which it won a silver award) and the St Petersburg Yachting Exhibition of 1897.[138]

C.V. Butler's survey of Oxford mentions only books and marmalade being exported from the city in 1912,[139] even though around 10 per cent of the craft Salters' built were destined for overseas by that point, with the majority of orders going to the British Empire. Jan Morris described the firm as an 'infinitesimal cog in the imperial machinery', because the firm was used by the many ex-Oxbridge students who were dispersed around the world.[140] T.E. Lawrence is an example of one of these, as he had a Salters' canoe sent to him in Beirut in 1913.[141] Writing in 1907, R.W. Jeffery suggested that certain markets had already been lost by that point, as he recorded that the firm:

... have an order for fifteen boats for the Orange River Colony, and in the past they have sent many boats to India, Ceylon, and China; but in the last two cases there is no longer so great a demand for English-built boats, as the natives have learnt to construct them on the same lines.[142]

Despite this mention of an order from Africa, the continent was not a major market for the firm, although on a trip there in 1912, an employee was conducting market research and sending out brochures to local clubs.[143] The order books confirm Jeffery's suggestion that India was the most important country for exports. In 1924, six of the nine international locations to which Salters' sent craft were located in that country (Bombay, Calcutta, Karachi, Kodaikanal, Lucknow and Madras – the others being Durban, Montevideo and Rangoon).[144] The majority of the clients were boat clubs, although one prestigious customer was the Maharaja Gaekwad of Baroda, who was sent two gigs in 1895.[145]

Given the extent of their global reach, one can see why P.H. Ditchfield claimed in 1912 that the 'names of Salter and Clasper are famous all the world over for their splendid racing craft'.[146] The documents in the archive list over sixty international clubs using the firm's craft between 1877 and 1960, but it is clear from the example of New Zealand that the actual number would have been much higher still, especially as there is little information from the firm's 1860s heyday. Although this global trade would have gone largely unnoticed by those outside rowing circles, a number of its craft received more attention. These included the 6-year-old *Oxford Torpid*, which became the first university racing boat to cross the Channel in 1885, in four hours twenty-five minutes (thereby inspiring a number of copycat attempts),[147] and the ex-Brasenose four, re-christened *Emil*, that was used in the 1890s by members of the Heidelberger Ruder Klub to explore 40 miles of the Neckar river.[148] The international demand for the firm's craft declined sharply after the Second World War, however, and 1946 was the last year in which significant numbers of any type of boat were exported (eleven in total). After that point Salters' sent very few boats overseas and the last orders went to the Rhodesian boat clubs of Hunyani (1953), Zambesi (1956) and Rhokana (1960).[149]

Decline from the 1870s

The decline of the racing boat department was set in motion by two principal events in the 1870s. Firstly, the departure of Stephen Salter in 1874 not only deprived the firm of its most passionate rowing enthusiast (as he directly supervised this side of the business), but seems to have precipitated the closing of the firm's second yard at Eton. The younger brother had exerted himself to such an extent that his doctor recommended that he stop working altogether. Believing he only had a few years to live, he left the firm at the age of 40 to 'enjoy his remaining years', which turned out to be sixty-two years of retirement.[150] He sold his side of the business to his brother in 1875 and eventually settled on the Isle of Wight to enjoy a gentrified existence. By the time he died, in 1937, he was best remembered as a 'great breeder of fancy pigeons' rather than as one of the co-founders of the Oxford firm.[151]

Secondly, the firm was affected by the arrival of local competitors which were building superior boats. John Clasper was the first of these, in 1870, and although he had left Oxford by the middle of the decade (in order to take over 'The Feathers', following the suicide of Harry Salter in 1874),[152] his yard was then taken over by his son-in-law, Frederick Rough, who became the market leader at the end of the century. Losing the university contract to a local competitor must have been especially hard for the firm, as it relied on the Oxford rowing scene for so much of its business. In 1873, the president of Christ Church Boat Club was one of those to record the difference in the performance of the craft, as he noted in his log that their new torpid from Clasper was 'easier to sit, and faster through the water than an ordinary Salter'.[153] The wider impact on the business would have been gradual, but by the end of the century the firm's best boats were considered antiquated. In 1895, for example, the Birmingham Rowing Club ordered a new craft from Rough (the leading builder at the time), because a senior crew concluded that they were 'heavily handicapped, owing to the old-fashioned build of the boat supplied to the club by Messrs. Salter Brothers'.[154]

The firm also became slowly marginalised from the sport in Oxford during the twentieth century, as its 'core' customer base, the colleges and local clubs, moved towards providing many of the services they required 'in house', which was partly an attempt to reduce the costs associated with relying on external businesses like Salters'. After the First World War many boat-builders around the country severed ties with local clubs, because they could make more money from renting craft for pleasure boating.[155] Salters' did not do this, probably because it had a large enough fleet to be able to serve both markets, but there was a steady reduction in the number of craft being rented, partly because many colleges started to buy their craft, as the crews began to train more regularly.[156]

The number of privately owned craft that the firm stored for university crews also fell from twenty-one for twelve colleges in 1919 to six for six colleges in 1948, plus a further six belonging to the Oxford University Women's Boat Club.[157] Purpose-built boathouses with better facilities were being constructed by the colleges themselves from 1936 onwards – a process that was accelerated after the war. Similarly the city clubs, like Falcon and Neptune, which had once revolved around the firm, moved to their own premises from the 1950s.[158] The construction of the new boathouses also meant that the college barges were dispensed with, which cost Salters' not only the rental income, but also the income associated with their regular upkeep. The latter could be considerable, as many of them were in a bad state of repair by the middle of the twentieth century. This also meant that Salters' lost the personal contact it had with many rowers, as the colleges hired independent watermen, rather than relying on employees from the firm. Furthermore, the family's active involvement with the local rowing scene ceased once Frank, who had been on the committee of the Oxford Waterman's Regatta, died in 1956.[159] The firm continued to transport craft for local crews, until the proliferation of sectional craft (designed to make moving them easier) in the 1970s, removed another source of income.[160]

The picture was not one of total decline, however, because the firm continued to provide a range of training craft, like the 'tubs' used by the clubs in Oxford. In 1928, Salters' constructed an innovative boat for Rangoon University Boat Club that could be steered from any point along the central gangway,[161] which it believed was a precursor to Oxford University Boat Club's training craft *Leviathan*, built by George Harris in 1952.[162]

The firm also rented out a number of coaching launches to OUBC. These included *Swan*, a fast steamer built by Clark that was used to start the Boat Race of 1891,[163] and *Niceia*, a motor boat constructed by Salters', which was a gift to the club from William Morris in 1936.[164] Furthermore, it also built early land-based and floating rowing machines, as well as the rafts upon which craft were launched.

Salters' also managed to re-specialise by building different types of racing boat. By the late 1930s the company was able to claim that its inrigged six-oared gigs were being used by many clubs 'on the great lakes at Killarney', whilst its four-oared galleys had 'proved successful in nearly all the races at South Coast Regattas in which they have competed'.[165] Furthermore, in the 1970s the racing boat department experienced a renaissance, which ensured that Salters', once again, became a market leader.

The 1970s Renaissance and Subsequent Decline

Arthur Salter may not have had a rowing background, himself, but he had served his apprenticeship in the building where the racing boats were constructed, and in 1970, possibly because of nostalgia or wanting to boost the firm's reputation, he decided

Salters' twelve in 1928 and OUBC's *Leviathan* (c. 1950s).

to invest more heavily in this side of the business.[166] The most important part of this process was the employment in 1970 of Ted Wilde, an expert from George Sims (the leading British firm at the time), who had been building 'Oxford and Cambridge boats for some years'.[167] He was responsible for revitalising the racing boat department by introducing the latest building methods.[168] This ensured that the number of orders the firm received leaped from four in 1970 to fourteen the following year.[169]

A testament to the standard of craft he produced was the return to the firm of many of its old customers (although not those from overseas), some of which had not ordered boats from Salters' for over a century. These included leading rowing schools, such as Eton and Westminster, Oxford colleges (as well as Caius, Christ's and Girton in Cambridge), and a number of UK clubs, such as Henley Rowing Club, Reading University and the Furnivall Sculling Club.[170]

Rowing's survey of boat-builders in 1972 showed that the racing craft built by Salters' were amongst the most expensive of the British firms, although they were still significantly cheaper than the foreign constructors (Karlisch, Donoratico and Stämpfli). Furthermore, the Oxford firm offered the shortest build time of any of the suppliers (one to three months, as opposed to eight months for Karlisch, for example), although this was partly because it was an Olympic year, which meant that some of the other companies were busier than normal.[171]

The firm's renaissance was short-lived, however, as its output declined after peaking at twenty-two boats in 1973. The short-term cause of the decline was the loss of three of its six racing boat-builders in 1974,[172] but the long-term cause was the introduction of new composite materials (using carbon fibre), which Salters' did not have the expertise to embrace.[173] There was a slow decline in demand for wooden craft and in 1987 the firm only sold a single racing boat (to Wadham College's Women's Boat Club) – the last it ever built.[174] This was also the final year in which the firm was listed amongst the suppliers in the *British Rowing Almanack*, a publication in which it had featured since the first edition of its forerunner (1861).

The demise of the racing boat department had a further implication for the business, which was the loss of an important source of low-season income. The university rowing scene was busiest during term time, which included the autumn months, when the boat-building industry as a whole usually experienced a 'period of great slackness' (see chapter 2).[175]

• • •

When Salters' finally bowed out of the market, it was one of the oldest racing boat-builders still in existence,[176] with a tradition probably stretching back to the late 1830s. It had been one of the most important firms associated with the sport of rowing, as its supremacy in the 1860s and its far-reaching distribution network ensured that its craft played a part in the history of a large number of clubs, including the formative years of competitive racing in countries as far afield as Sweden and New Zealand. Indeed, as one commentator put it, Salters' appeared to be the 'embodiment of muscle'.[177] Yet over the course of a century it went from being a global market leader, positioned at the heart of Oxford's rowing scene, to one whose main interests lay elsewhere. This fact was not lost on the employees themselves. Even though he worked during the 1970s revival, Steve Gaisford was one staff member whose enthusiasm for rowing led him to join the rival Oxford business of G. Harris, which revolved more heavily around the sport.[178] Yet the firm's priorities had already begun to shift a century earlier, as it started to focus more heavily on producing craft for the pleasure boat market.

Notes

1   E.R. Pennell, 'The Stream of Pleasure', in *The Century Magazine*, vol. 38, no. 4 (August 1889), p. 483.

2   *The Pigot and Co's London and Provincial New Commercial Directory for 1826–7*. The pub is now called 'The Duke on the Green'.

3   Wandsworth Heritage Service Battersea Library (WBL) General Annual Licensing Meeting of the Justices of the Peace, March 1836.

4   Wigglesworth, *History of Rowing*, pp. 40–66.

5   G. Page, *Hear the Boat Sing: The History of Thames Rowing Club* (London, 1991), p. xiii.

6   Wigglesworth, *History of Rowing*, pp. 50–52.

7   L.G. Applebee, *Vesta Rowing Club 1870–1920* (London, 1920), p. 6.

8   WBL General Annual Licensing Meeting of the Justices of the Peace, 5 March 1840.

9   *The Era*, 17 June 1855.

10   Ibid., 17 May 1857.

11   *Bell's Life*, 28 February 1858.

12   This predated the publication of Harry Clasper's regime, which was identified by Roberta Park as being advanced for its time in R.J. Park, 'Athletes and their Training in Britain and American, 1800–1914', in J.W. Berryman and R.J. Park (eds), *Sport and Exercise Science: Essays in the History of Sports Medicine* (University of Illinois, 1992), p. 69.

13   *The Rowing Almanack and Oarsman's Companion 1862* (London, 1862), pp. 119–23.

14   *The Aquatic Oracle or Record of Rowing from 1835 to 1851* (London, 1852), p. 122.

15   E.D. Brickwood, *Boat Racing* (London, 1876), p. 6.

16   *Jackson's Oxford Journal*, 20 November 1856.

17   *Oxford Times*, 8 June 1907, p. 4.

18   *The Times*, 14 December 1934.

19   Argonaut, *The Arts of Rowing and Training* (London, 1866), pp. 4–8. See also T. Harris, *250 Men, Women and Animals Who Created Modern Sport* (London, 2009). The inventor of many of the innovations is disputed.

20   *Bell's Life*, 8 July 1849.

21   *Bell's Life*, 9 September 1849 and *Lock to Lock Times*, 5 August 1893, p. 1. Stephen also spent some time with him.

22   *The Newcastle Courant*, 27 September 1850.

23   *Bell's Life*, 20 July 1851.

24   Ibid., 7 December 1856.

25   *The Era*, 5 April 1857 and *Daily News*, 6 April 1857.

26   Receipt for £50 from I. King, 30 December 1859 (from archive compiled by an unnamed employee in 1976, now in the possession of Jim Cowan).

27   *Jackson's Oxford Journal*, 25 September 1858.

28   Davis and Isaac King built the first eight used by Oxford in the Boat Race.

29   F. Brittain, *Oars, Sculls and Rudder* (Oxford, 1930), p. x.

30   T. Mason, *Sport in Britain* (London, 1988), p. 46.

31   Data from *Rowing Almanacks*, newspapers, periodicals and specialist magazines. 'Leading

firm' is defined as one whose craft won at least 60 per cent of the races and a run of at least three victories in a row in that time-scale.

32　W.B. Woodgate, *Boating* (London, 1888), p. 67.

33　M. Edwards, 'An Oxford Boat with a Cornish Accent', in C. Dodd and J. Marks, *Battle of the Blues* (London, 2004), p. 19.

34　G. Ross, *The Boat Race* (London, 1954), p. 153.

35　Searle's headquarters was in Stangate, but it had a yard in Cambridge.

36　Ross, *The Boat Race*, p. 243.

37　L.S.R. Byrne, *The Eton Boating Book* (Eton, 1933), p. 117.

38　*Lock to Lock Times*, 25 January 1890, p. 50.

39　The times were twenty minutes fifty-six seconds and twenty minutes four seconds respectively.

40　*The Observer*, 6 March 1869, p. 6. For dimensions of the firm's racing craft, see Argonaut, *Arts of Rowing*, pp. 13–14.

41　T. Cook, *Rowing at Henley* (Oxford, 1919), p. 89.

42　Stonehenge, *British Rural Sports* (London, 1868), p. 559.

43　*The Observer*, 6 March 1869.

44　R.P.P. Rowe et al., *Rowing. Punting* (London, 1898), p. 115.

45　These figures do not include 1878, because the 1877 race was declared a dead heat.

46　By the second half of the twentieth century, firms were less likely to advertise their involvement with the contest, partly because of the growing prestige of other rowing contests, like the Olympics and the World Rowing Championships (first held in 1962).

47　*Rowing*, March/April 1976, p. 6.

48　Data from *Rowing Almanacks*, newspapers, periodicals and specialist magazines.

49　W.F. MacMichael, *The Oxford and Cambridge Boat Races 1829–1869* (Cambridge, 1870), p. 38.

50　*Nautical Magazine for 1871*, vol. 40, May 1871, p. 323 and *Sporting Gazette*, 8 April 1871.

51　*The Morning Post*, 30 March 1863.

52　*Oxford University Herald*, 19 March 1870, p. 9.

53　A.H. Baily, *Baily's Magazine of Sports and Pastimes*, vol. 16 (London, 1869), p. 253.

54　Ross, *The Boat Race*, pp. 157–8.

55　*Bell's Life*, 17 April 1859.

56　*Rowing Almanack 1914*, p. 52.

57　Woodgate, *Boating*, p. 147.

58　W.B. Woodgate, *Reminiscences of an Old Sportsman* (London, 1909), p. 382.

59　Woodgate, *Boating*, p. 152.

60　*The Oxford Times*, 18 August 1978, p. 11.

61　Dan Snow, *The Boat Race 2011*, television programme for BBC1, 26 March 2011.

62　See B.J. Morris and I.D. Phillips, 'The Effect of Weather Conditions on the Oxford–Cambridge University Boat Race', *Meteorological Applications*, vol. 16, issue 2 (June 2009), pp. 157–68.

63　*The Saturday Review*, 4 April 1874, p. 429.

64　*The Times*, 23 March 1976, p. 10.

65　*Rowing Almanack 1948*, advertisement.

66　Wigglesworth, *History of Rowing*, pp. 34–55.

67　W.E. Sherwood, *Oxford Rowing* (Oxford, 1900), pp. 5–8.

68　Ibid., p. 25.

69　H.S. Jones, 'University and College Sport', in M.G. Brock and M.C. Curthoys (eds), *A History of the University of Oxford*, vol. 6 (Oxford, 1997), p. 518.

70　P.R. Deslandes, *Oxbridge Men: Masculinity and the Undergraduate Experience, 1850–1920* (Indiana University, 2005), pp. 168–82.

71　Jones, 'University and College Sport', p. 522.

72   C. Nilson, 'The Entrepreneur in the Industrial Revolution', in Brittain, *Oars, Sculls*, p. 74.

73   *Oxford Flying Post*, 22 May 1858.

74   S. Pollard and P. Robertson, *The British Shipbuilding Industry, 1870–1914* (London, 1979), p. 56.

75   *Jackson's Oxford Journal*, 26 April 1856. Three other firms built two each respectively.

76   *Thames Guardian*, spring 1998, pp. 16–17.

77   *Classic Boat*, August 2010, pp. 62–65. These were Shepperton, Pinewood and Teddington studios.

78   *Jackson's Oxford Journal*, 29 November 1858.

79   Jesus College Archive (JCA) College Boat Club Minute Book 1856–85, 7 December 1858.

80   *Oxford University Herald*, 7 June 1862, p. 8. Two of the eights were newly built.

81   Ibid., 20 June 1863, p. 12 and *Daily News*, 18 June 1863.

82   From the *Rowing Almanacks* (1861, 1863 and 1865) and Salters' Archive (SA) Agreement Dissolving the Partnership between John and Stephen Salter, 21 June 1875.

83   SA Inventory Book 1877–79.

84   Sherwood, *Oxford Rowing*, p. xii.

85   Interview with Len Andrews, 31 August 2004.

86   Christ Church Archive (CCA) Christ Church Boat Club Minute Book 1875–98, Memorandum of Agreement made in January 1877, 17 November 1879.

87   SA Agreement between St Edmund Hall Boat Club and Salter Brothers, 12 December 1911.

88   J. Corbin, *An American at Oxford* (Boston, 1903), p. 90.

89   A new University Boat House was completed in 1881 (after one built in 1880 had burned down).

90   Worcester College Archive (WCA) Statement of Boat Club's Account with John and Stephen Salter, October 1871–72. Some craft were also stored on the outside of the barges.

91   Interview with Bill Dunckley, 3 March 2010.

92   SA Agreement Dissolving the Partnership between John and Stephen Salter, 21 June 1875.

93   *Jackson's Oxford Journal*, 29 July 1843.

94   E. Cook, *Eliza Cook's Journal*, vol. 9 (May to October 1853), p. 262.

95   Sherwood, *Oxford Rowing*, p. 8.

96   *Thames*, April–June 1951, p. 69.

97   Worcester College Archive (WCA) Letter to Boat Club Members, 14 December 1896.

98   *Oxford University Herald*, 29 April 1865, p. 8.

99   Wigglesworth, *History of Rowing*, p. 159.

100 K.A. Morgan, 'The Lady Blue: Sport at the Oxbridge Women's Colleges from their Foundation to 1914' in J.A. Mangan, *A Sport-Loving Society* (Abingdon, 2006), pp. 162–66.

101 St Hilda's College Archive (SHC) C.M.E. Burrows, 'Working Notes on the College History' and extract from 'Reminiscence of Student, 1910–1913'.

102 *Jackson's Oxford Journal*, 21 April 1860.

103 *The Times*, 30 September 1859.

104 N. Selwyn, 'Social and Cultural Activities', in Crossley, *The Victoria History of the County of Oxford*, vol. 4, p. 428. The university also participated in the event until 1890.

105 *Jackson's Oxford Journal*, 23 June 1877. His son, John, who rowed for Neptune, also became a committee member (and sometimes the official starter).

106 SA Agreement Dissolving the Partnership between John and Stephen Salter, 21 June 1875. The inventory was conducted in 1874 and, after some property was given to Stephen, John paid £4,845 for his brother's half of the business.

107 JCA Papers Concerning College Barges 1878–1962, Boat Club Meeting, 16 March 1878.
108 WCA Statement of Boat Club's Account with John Salter, October 1874–October 1882.
109 WCA Letter from John Salter to Worcester College Boat Club, 16 November 1881.
110 SA Finance Book 1896–1900.
111 Wigglesworth, *History of Rowing*, p. 50.
112 *Oxford Times*, 8 June 1907, p. 4.
113 *Isle of Wight Observer*, 25 January 1890, p. 4 and *Yorkshire Herald*, 25 January 1890, p. 8.
114 *Time*, vol. 15, issue 21 (September 1886), p. 278.
115 Argonaut, *Arts of Rowing*, p. 11.
116 *Rowing Almanack 1865*, p. 158.
117 T.A. Cook and G. Nickalls, *Thomas Doggett Deceased: A Famous Comedian* (London, 1908), in Blomfield, 'Tradesmen of the Thames', p. 215.
118 SA Carmans Boat Work, 24 June 1863, 22 June 1864 and 27 June 1865.
119 For a history of the umpire's craft, see R. Goddard, 'The Umpire's Launch at Henley Royal Regatta: an Historical Review' (1997) from the Consuta Trust's website: www.consuta.org.uk (accessed 20 December 2011).
120 *Punch*, vols. 66–67 (London, 1874), p. 187.
121 Ross, *The Boat Race*, p. 61.
122 *The Times*, 27 August 1869 and *Jackson's Oxford Journal*, 4 September 1869.
123 SA Carmans Boat Works.
124 *Jackson's Oxford Journal*, 15 May 1886.
125 Wigglesworth, *History of Rowing*, p. 50.
126 *Jackson's Oxford Journal*, 8 July 1874.
127 SA Carmans Boat Works, 4 May 1863 and 12 August 1863.
128 SA Inventory Book 1877–79. This is the earliest inventory book.
129 SA Order Book 1893.
130 *Empire*, 1 September 1855, p. 4.
131 *Bell's Life in Sydney*, 31 January 1863, p. 4.
132 *The Argus*, 29 October 1861, 29 August 1866, 4 August 1877, 7 March 1878.
133 *Press*, 20 February 1872, p. 3, 22 October 1873, p. 2, 19 December 1873, p. 2 and 28 March 1874, p. 2; *Star*, 6 February 1863, p. 3, 20 November 1876, p. 2 and 15 September 1885, p. 3; *Evening Post*, 17 February 1873, p. 3; *Wellington Independent*, 18 November 1872, p. 2.
134 Ibid., 28 March 1874, p. 3.
135 SA Inventory Book 1877–79. Private orders to Paris and St Petersburg are also listed.
136 J.H. Salter, *The River Thames: From Its Source to Wandsworth* (London, 1881), advertisement.
137 *Thames*, December 1901, p. 7 and 15 March 1902, p. 10.
138 *Thames*, 8 March 1902, p. 6.
139 C.V. Butler, *Social Conditions in Oxford* (London, 1912), p. 38.
140 J. Morris, *Oxford* (London, 1965), p. 258.
141 T.E. Lawrence, *The Home Letters of T.E. Lawrence* (Oxford, 1954), p. 247. He was also a friend of the Salter family, having gone to school with them.
142 R.W. Jeffery, 'Industries', in W. Page (ed.), *The Victoria History of the County of Oxford*, vol. 2 (Oxford, 1907), p. 275.
143 SA Letter from W.H. Gillams to Mr Salter, 2 December 1912.
144 SA Order Book 1924.
145 SA Order Book 1895.
146 P.H. Ditchfield, *Oxfordshire* (Cambridge, 1912), p. 80.
147 *Bell's Life*, 21 July 1885.

148 D.D. Braham, 'Forty Miles on the Neckar in a Racing Four', in *Badminton Magazine of Sports and Pastimes* (September 1899), pp. 313–21.
149 SA Master List of Boats 1937–87.
150 Salter, *Memoirs of a Public Servant*, p. 15.
151 *Oxford Monthly*, October 1937, p. 2.
152 *Jackson's Oxford Journal*, 21 March 1874.
153 CCA Boat Club: Captain's Private Log 1880–1909, p. 30.
154 Extracts from the Secretary's Report of 1895: www.birminghamrowingclub.co.uk/?page_id=31 (accessed 7 April 2011).
155 Wigglesworth, *History of Rowing*, p. 53.
156 R. Hutchins, *Well Rowed Magdalen* (Oxford, 1993), p. 9.
157 SA Housing Book 1919–48.
158 Interview with Bryan Humphries and John Blackford (members of Falcon since the 1950s), 17 January 2011 and Wigglesworth, *History of Rowing*, p. 170.
159 *Oxford Times*, 20 May 1927, p. 14. His father James, who rowed for Falcon, had been president of the event.
160 Conversation with Ian Smith (coach at the Oxford City Rowing Club since the 1970s), 25 September 2010.
161 *Oxford Mail*, 1 July 1955, p. 8.
162 SA H.G. Salter, 'History of Salter Bros' (*c.* 1958).
163 *The Standard*, 23 March 1891.
164 Interview with Albert Andrews, 26 March 2005 and SA Master List of Boats 1911–36.
165 SA Salter Bros. Ltd Brochure (*c.* 1930s).
166 Interview with John Salter, 20 December 2011 and COS radio interview with Arthur Salter (1971), reference: OXOHA: MT 536.
167 *The Oxford Times*, 18 August 1978, p. 11.
168 Interview with Steve Gaisford (employee 1970–74), 4 October 2010.
169 SA Master List of Boats 1937–87.
170 Ibid.
171 SA J. Langfield, '*Rowing*'s Boatbuilding Survey 1972'.
172 SA Racing Boat-Building Schedule 1973–75. They worked in pairs and a trainee assisted them.
173 Interview with John Salter, 20 December 2011.
174 SA Master List of Boats 1937–87. An old racing four and eight from St Aldate's Yard are stored at the Slipway.
175 *The Motor Boat*, vol. 9, no. 222 (8 October 1908), p. 237.
176 Stämpfli (founded in 1896) claims to be the oldest today: www.stampfli.co.uk/about/ (accessed 27 June 2012).
177 *Bow Bells*, 8 June 1894, p. 569.
178 Interview with Steve Gaisford (employee 1970–74), 4 October 2010.

2

Boat-Building

> Mr Salter knows as much about the art of boat-building from steamers down to punts, dinghies, gigs, skiffs, scullers, randans, whiffs and Rob Roys and funnys, as any man alive.
>
> F.V. Morley, 1927[1]

Salters' established its early reputation through the construction of racing boats, but other types of craft became increasingly important to the firm. The number of craft constructed by the firm gives an indication of how significant Salters' was, although there is little information from other Thames businesses to compare it with. In 1863 Salters' was constructing approximately two craft per week[2] and this had risen to three per week by 1865 (approximately 150 boats per year).[3] The inventory books provide a useful indication of the firm's output of boats from the 1870s onwards, because each craft was assigned a reference number according to its year of construction (the first and last numerals) and its order number (the middle digits). Therefore, for example, the fifteenth and 150th boats built in 1874 would be numbered '7154' and '71504' respectively, and if these were listed in an inventory book, this would indicate that the firm had built *at least* 150 boats in this year. This method, which also shows the close links between the boat-building and rental departments, is fairly accurate, as the later data can be cross-referenced with the exact numbers that are recorded in the 'Master List' of boats built (from 1911), and this confirms that the majority of estimates are within five or six of the actual figure. Not all of the craft were constructed by the firm, however, as a number of canoes were outsourced to Canadian firms (see p. 48).

During the 1870s the company was producing between 150 and 200 boats per year, but afterwards the figures fluctuated more widely from a high of at least 200 in 1897 to a low of at least 103 in 1904. This shows that the firm was already a major Upper Thames boat-builder, as many other businesses operated on a smaller scale, like Hobbs of Henley, which was building between twenty and thirty small craft per year at the start of the twentieth century.[4] Indeed, the figures suggest that Salters' had orders for approximately 7,000 vessels between 1858 and 1910.

From 1911 the 'Master List' provides precise figures and, unlike shipbuilders, whose orders rose and fell in a regular cycle over a number of years (according to the demands of the freight industry),[5] the output at Salters' showed no discernible pattern. There were certain periods *within* each year when the output of craft was particularly high.

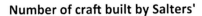

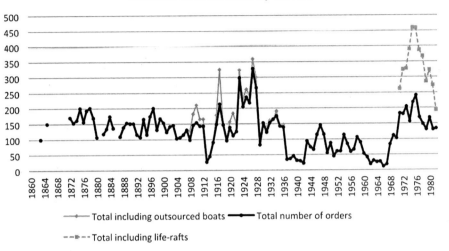

Like other boat-builders, the firm was busiest in the spring time, although it was unusual because the orders also picked up slightly in the autumn, which was partly the result of the craft it supplied for the university rowing scene (see chapter 1).

The most prolific years were 1920, 1926, 1930 and 1931 when the firm produced over 300 boats, but some of the canoes were built by three businesses in Canada, all located within 10 miles of each other (the Canadian Canoe Company, Lakefield Canoe Company and Peterborough Canoe Company). Craft from Canada were widely marketed in the UK from the 1880s onwards, but it was not until the 1890s that they began to be mass produced. The Peterborough Canoe Company, for example, exported approximately 600 to the UK between 1892 and 1898.[6] Writing in 1936, William Luscombe claimed that 'over fifty years ago' Salters' built its own, before realising that the cost of importing them was 'not much more than the price of English labour'.[7] Indeed, the reliance on imports, which continued until the Second World War, was a crucial part of the department's flexibility, as it helped to insulate the firm from the risk associated with market uncertainties. It meant that Salters' did not have to retain as many employees, because when demand was particularly high the output could be increased (through outsourcing) to well beyond what its workforce was capable of producing, whilst when it was low, as in the 1930s Depression, the work could be reassigned internally. In 1920, for example, the boat-building department reaped a 'golden harvest' owing to a large rise in the number of students matriculating at the university (more than double the pre-war total),[8] and a widespread strike that affected many other Thames boatyards from mid-June to the end of October.[9] During the industrial action Salters' built seventy-three craft, but this output was nearly doubled again by a further sixty-six from its Canadian suppliers, making a total of 139. This represented a considerable increase from its normal summer output, as in the same timeframe in 1919 the firm built fifty boats (and imported a further thirty-one), whilst in 1921 it constructed fifty-five (and none was imported). The greatest number of canoes Salters' imported was III in 1920, although the normal figure was between twenty and thirty per year.[10]

If one excludes the outsourced craft, the firm was still constructing between 100 and 200 boats per year. Output was at its highest between 1926 and 1931 when over 200 boats were built for six consecutive years, the zenith being in 1930 when 328 were constructed (or 359 including the imported canoes) – the equivalent of more than one a day, as the workforce did not work on Sunday. The firm stocked twenty-seven different types of wood at this time,[11] and its oar-making department was also very active. In 1925, for example, it produced 1,334 sculls, 239 poles (mainly punt poles), 217 oars, 174 paddles and six miscellaneous items, including piles, a flagstaff and a boathook.[12] There was a sharp fall in orders for boats in 1932 and after that point the output of craft returned to its pre-war level of between 100 and 200 per year. Far fewer craft were built after the Second World War and the most significant period of decline was in the mid-1960s, culminating in a nadir of just twelve craft being constructed in 1969.

This was followed by a notable resurgence in the 1970s when the output reached a post-war peak of 241 in 1979. If one includes the life-rafts that were introduced from 1973 (see p. 66), then the output of craft was briefly higher than at any time in the firm's history. Between 1977 and 1981 Salters' constructed over 350 craft each year, of which over 200 were life-rafts. The peak came in 1978 and 1979 when 460 and 459 vessels were built respectively. The record-keeping deteriorated after that point, but the data suggest that the combined orders for life-rafts and boats had reduced to around 200 by 1985.

The figures show that the firm built approximately 10,000 craft between 1911 and 1980, including outsourced canoes, pontoons and life-rafts. If one combines this total with the pre-1911 figure, Salters' produced approximately 17,000 vessels between 1858 and 1980.[13]

Type of Craft: Pre-1911

The firm's early boat-building revolved around the sport of rowing, but in the 1860s it was also supplying a range of small pleasure craft, including punts, canoes, dinghies, gigs and sailing boats, in addition to accessories.[14] As well as constructing standard Thames boats, Salters' became 'firmly established as barge builders to the colleges'.[15] Its clients included, at the very least, Exeter (1873), Brasenose (1882), Magdalen (1887), Oriel (1892), Keble (1898), Merton (1900), Pembroke (1903), Jesus (1911/12) and Corpus Christi (1930).[16] Each craft was built to bespoke specifications and the price paid by Exeter was £375, for example, which was a considerable reduction from the initial bill of £469, which had included an unexpected charge of £100 as 'compensation for site' (meaning the hire of the slipway space needed to build it).[17] The firm's pre-eminence in barge-building was confirmed by the order it received in 1909 to construct what was described as 'one of the most luxurious house boats not only on the Thames, but in the world'.[18] The craft was built for Alfred Vanderbilt of the famous American dynasty, who also bought a motor boat to accompany it from a different firm – which suggests that Salters' was not held in the same regard for all types of craft.[19] There were other ostentatious barges on the river, but at £1,200, *Venture* was one of the most expensive ever built and its size required the river to be lowered in places to transport it under some of the bridges on its way downstream to Shiplake. There was considerable prestige attached to building such vessels. In the 1920s, for example, in order to maintain his firm's reputation, Mr Salter refused to provide a quotation for Brasenose because he deemed the design for its new barge to be too ugly.[20]

The barges may have been the most impressive craft that Salters' built, but in terms of its standard range of products, it was the award-winning Oxford Collapsible Boat that became its 'showpiece' model by the end of the nineteenth century.[21] This appears to have been the firm's first – and probably only – product to carry the city's name, which became fashionable with other local companies, like Frank Cooper (Oxford marmalade) and Morris (Oxford cars).

Collapsible lifeboats were developed by Reverend E.L. Berthon, following the sinking of SS *Orion* (1849), and by the 1870s his models were being widely used by the Navy.[22] Salters' probably entered the market through its links with Oxford Lifeboat Day, a fundraising event for the Royal National Lifeboat Institution, first held in 1866, which involved launching a boat (not built by the firm) from St Aldate's Yard.[23] The Oxford Collapsible Boat ranged in size from 21ft (capable of carrying thirty-five people) to 28ft (capable of carrying sixty-two) and the firm claimed it had a number of advantages over others in the market. It had a double skin of oak to protect the canvas, four or more could be stacked in one place, it automatically distended when lifted by davits (or this could be done manually in thirty to forty seconds), it could be launched whilst flat (with passengers on board) and it was strongly built to ensure it was as 'sea-worthy as a normal craft'.[24] One explorer even recommended it for polar expeditions because it collapsed flat, making it easier to transport on snow.[25] The firm also built the Berthon-type lifeboats and in 1903, for example, it had twenty-two of these in stock, the majority of which were 10ft by 4ft in size.[26]

SALTER BROS. LIMITED. FOLLY BRIDGE. OXFORD.

HOUSEBOAT "Venture."   Built for the late Mr. A. G. Vanderbilt.

HOUSE BOATS of all sizes built to order.

Specifications and Quotations sent on receipt of Customers' requirements.

Venture, built in 1909.

The Oxford
Collapsible Boat.

Salters' managed to attract a number of orders from high-profile clients, including Cabinet minister Robert Hanbury, but despite a rumour that remains amongst the staff today, it did not build any for the *Titanic*. Nevertheless, the sinking of the ship did have a brief but significant impact on the business. In 1911 the firm built only one small folding boat (a Berthon model), but the following year, it received twenty-nine orders for the largest (28ft) Oxford model, all dated after 15 April 1912, just after *Titanic* sank.[27] It also prompted Salters' to revisit the original design and to submit a new patent for an improved distending system.[28] The demand for lifeboats quickly subsided and the firm did not build any more of the Oxford craft after 1912.[29]

Type of Craft: 1911–80

An analysis of the 'Master List' of the boats built by the firm (from 1911) provides a fairly accurate picture of the type of craft that were sold and how the boat-building department developed over time. It shows that it went through four distinct stages.

The first period was prior to 1925, when the firm was mainly building small manually powered craft. The majority of orders were for racing boats (28.7 per cent of the recorded sales in the 1910s, excluding 1910 and 1915–18),[30] punts (26 per cent) and canoes (24 per cent). The latter were virtually all the Canadian type, whilst there were a great range of punts and racing craft (see chapter 1). Almost two-thirds of the punts were of the pleasure variety, although the firm also produced a good number of skiff-head rowing punts (approximately a quarter), as well as smaller numbers of ferry, fishing, sailing and standard rowing punts. After this, in descending order of popularity, came the skiffs (11.6 per cent), collapsible craft (3.7 per cent), dinghies (3.5 per cent) and motorised boats (1.3 per cent). The miscellaneous craft (1.3 per cent) included a number of 10ft cockle boats.[31]

The second stage stretched from approximately 1925 to the start of the Second World War, which was when the greatest number of new models was introduced. In particular, it was the introduction of dinghies, paddle boats and motor boats that drove output to unprecedented levels (see pp. 59–63). The new models had a significant impact on the orders the firm received, with the proportions much more evenly balanced between the different types of craft. In the 1930s, the canoes (20.9 per cent of orders), dinghies (18 per cent) and racing craft (16 per cent) were the most popular, followed by paddle boats (12.7 per cent), motorised vessels (11.2 per cent), skiffs (10.3 per cent) and punts (9.7 per cent). The miscellaneous craft (1.3 per cent) included a weed scow (1937).[32] Although it was not classed as a new type of vessel, perhaps the most unusual modified product was a canoe sidecar that Rudge-Whitworth was offering its customers in the mid-1920s.[33]

The third stage ran from 1945 to 1969, which was when the boat-building department went into decline with little further innovation. Although the firm introduced short slipper-stern 'runabouts' (1952) and 'manor class' houseboats (1966) during this period, only a small number of each were built.[34] The cheapest models sold particularly well during this period, as the dinghies were the most popular craft (26.8 per cent of the orders in the 1950s), followed by the skiffs (20.8 per cent), owing to the success of the corporation model (see p. 65). These were followed by the canoes (15.2 per cent), paddle boats and racing craft (both 12.8 per cent), and punts (8.3 per cent). By contrast, the more expensive motorised craft were the least popular, accounting for only 3.1 per cent of the orders in the decade.

Rudge-Whitworth canoe sidecar (mid-1920s).

The fourth period began in 1970, which was when fibreglass versions of Salters' craft were introduced (see pp. 65–6). The boat-building department was revitalised by the introduction of new models, including, most importantly, the life-raft, which accounted for 41 per cent of the total orders during the 1970s. Skiffs were the most popular boat, accounting for 25.8 per cent of the orders, whilst Salters' continued to produce smaller numbers of the other types of vessel, such as dinghies (9.4 per cent), paddle craft (7.3 per cent), racing boats (6.2 per cent), punts (5.6 per cent) and motorised craft (4.4 per cent). The only exception was the canoe, which was the one type of craft that could not be replicated from fibreglass.[35]

Technological Development

The introduction of new craft appears to have been important for stimulating sales, but by examining four aspects of the department's activities (steel manufacturing, motorised boats, corporation craft and fibreglass construction) one can gain a better understanding of, firstly, how successful the firm was in keeping up with technological developments and, secondly, how its customer base shaped the direction of the business.

Steel Craft

Johnston Robb argues that a major challenge for shipbuilders was coping with the 'rapidly changing conditions of the nineteenth century, which was dominated by the great transitions from wood to iron and then steel, and from sail to steam'.[36] Sidney Pollard and Paul Robertson point out that when wood was the primary material used for shipbuilding, prior to the mid-1860s, the industry was dominated by small-scale family firms operating in almost every port. These required relatively little capital to run, as the yards needed only a few basic tools and the training of staff was done through a straightforward system of apprenticeship. The situation changed significantly when metal construction was introduced, because it required not only a greater outlay on machinery (to move and shape huge metal components), but also more specialist training. The mechanisation of the industry as a whole was slow, however, because the nature of the job was predominantly that of construction, requiring large numbers of skilled workers, as there was little scope for the mass production of ships.[37] As this suggests, therefore, the wage bill was the major cost for firms making this transition, although there were still other associated costs, like introducing machinery and, if new or larger premises were needed, buying land.

The development of Salters' steel building department did not follow the normal evolution described by Robb, however, as the firm by-passed the iron stage altogether,[38] because it was very late in moving into metal construction. When it finally made the transition, the decision was unusual because it was not directly prompted by demand from customers, but resulted from the company's need for more passenger boats. The firm started operating a service between Oxford and Kingston in 1888 (see chapter 4) and it initially enlarged its fleet by purchasing craft from Edwin Clark, a boat-builder based in Brimscombe, Gloucestershire. Clark was an engineer who started his own business in 1884, having spent a short period of time in Abingdon building steamboats for Gabriel Davis. As there was already a lot of competition on the river, he chose to move to Gloucestershire, where he could take advantage of cheap property and labour (owing to the demise of the woollen mills), as well as the 'direct link with the Thames via the Sapperton Tunnel' (part of the Thames and Severn canal).[39] Salters' had a say in the design of each craft and the orders were placed through W. Sissons and Co., the Gloucester firm that provided the steam engine. The price of *Nuneham*, built in 1898, was £1,620.[40] It was only after Clark's firm went out of business in 1900 (following his death in 1896, aged 35) that Salters' decided to start building its own steel craft.

The first step in this process was the enlargement of the firm's yard at Iffley, completed in 1900 (see chapter 5). This was a convenient location because not only was it (slightly) nearer to the raw materials than many of its competitors further downstream, but importantly, the surrounding area had some of the lowest wages in the country (see introduction). The second step was the employment of Thomas Arnold Baker, who was probably Clark's foreman, as he was building craft in Brimscombe in both 1881 and 1891. He was also a Methodist preacher, which may have endeared him further to the Salter family (see chapter 7).[41] It is likely that the firm used his existing business connections to set up its operation and he established quite a reputation as the term 'Baker-built' became associated with exceptional craftsmanship.[42] His early contracts show that he operated, at least initially, like a sub-contractor for Salters'. He was paid a flat rate for each of the craft, but he had to 'undertake, provide and superintend' all of the labour he required. Nevertheless, there were two other steel workers on the company payroll in 1901 and this had risen to five by 1906 (see chapter 4). The arrangement appears to have been far cheaper than purchasing boats from Clark, as in 1902 Baker was paid £245 to complete the hull of an 85ft steamer (a job that took around two months), after which it was passed on to the carpenters to finish.[43]

T.A. Baker (front left) in the workshop (*c.* 1905).

Between 1901 and 1931, at a time when London's last major Thames shipbuilding yards were closing,[44] Salters' built at least twenty-one large passenger boats in conjunction with W. Sissons,[45] which included some for external customers (see p. 56). These were produced at a rate of one – or occasionally two – per winter, although none was built between 1915 and 1922. The last two were *Mapledurham* (1927) and *Cliveden* (1931), which were much larger at 105ft in length and, therefore, more expensive to construct than the earlier steamers (the latter being £1,682, including wages, materials and machinery instalments).[46]

The firm's standing as steel boat-builders can be gauged by their dealings with the Baptist Missionary Society at the beginning of the twentieth century. The Society had begun to focus its attention on Africa in the late 1870s, following the death of David Livingstone in 1873, and this led to the pioneering missionary George Grenfell being sent to the Congo (Musuku) in 1880.[47] To aid his exploration he was provided with the steamboats *Peace* (operational from 1884 to 1904) and *Goodwill* (1893 to 1915), which were purchased from Thornycroft. By 1903, a third was needed and the Society contacted a number of the leading Thames and Clyde boat-builders for quotations. Their requirements were for a craft measuring 100ft by 18ft (and a draft of 2ft 4in) that was capable of doing 9 knots whilst carrying 25 tons. The initial quotations ranged widely (Table 2.1), but Salters' was able to undercut its nearest competitor by almost £1,000 and the previous boat-builders, Thornycroft, by over £2,000.

Table 2.1 Quotations to build *Endeavour* (1904)[48]

Boat-builder (location)	Quotation
Thornycroft (London)	£7,800 (for craft measuring 111ft by 19ft 3in)
	£7,000 (second quotation for craft of 100ft by 19ft)
Russel and Co. (Glasgow)	£6,000
Alley and MacLellan (Glasgow)	£6,000
Ritchie, Graham and Milne (Glasgow)	£5,710
Salter Bros (Oxford)	£4,750

It is possible that a favourable quotation may have been given because of the Salter family's religious convictions (see chapter 7). Yet if the price was representative of the cost at which the firm could construct steel craft – albeit, in this case, for a non-standard build – then this was significant, as a number of the shipbuilding firms on the Thames (in London) were closing at this time, since they were unable to compete with the lower production costs of the northern yards.[49] Nevertheless, a lack of experience in naval architecture showed: although Salters' was deemed competent to carry out the work, it did 'not quite realise the requirements of the case', after it emerged (through Thornycroft) that a boat of those dimensions would not be able to hold the prescribed load. A naval architect, George L. Watson, decreed that it needed to be widened by a foot and after much subsequent negotiation, mainly about the set-up of the boiler and engines, a price of £5,525 was agreed upon.[50]

The firm's close relationship with W. Sissons may have helped to keep the costs down, although it is likely that a small workforce was used, as the Society described the construction of the craft as being 'leisurely'.[51] This was in comparison to the speed with which its engineer, Charles Williams, reconstructed the boat in Africa, which 'astonished' the naval architects.[52]

The hull was launched from the slipway on 20 March 1905 and after its completion and trials, a dedication service was held by Folly Bridge on 20 July. The craft was named *Endeavour*, as it had been funded by over 500 Endeavour societies, although Salters' also helped. Visitors were charged 6*d* a head to see inside the boat, whilst a steamer was put at the Society's disposal for two days after the dedication, so that more money could be raised. *Endeavour* was then dismantled, crated and sent to Liverpool for shipment.[53]

This was followed by another order from the Society in 1910 for a smaller craft (68ft), *Grenfell*, capable of accessing the higher reaches of the Congo. This was built to replace *Peace* and was dedicated at a service on 29 March 1911.[54] Both *Endeavour* and *Grenfell* were unusual enough to be featured in *International Marine Engineering*.[55]

Despite these prominent orders, the firm never managed to develop this side of the business significantly. Prior to the First World War, Salters' provided such craft for a small range of customers, including the Thames Valley Launch Company of Weybridge (1903) and the International Engineering Company (1907), which ordered the 66ft *Kassid Kareem* for use on the Nile.[56] By contrast, after the conflict, the firm only built steamers for its own fleet and one external client, Joseph Mears. Mears, who operated passenger boats between Westminster and Hampton Court, ordered nine steamers from the firm between 1908 and 1926 (including the *Marchioness*), a number of which were later used in the evacuation of Dunkirk.[57] The last three boats were 110ft in length, which was close to the longest that could be transported on the Upper Thames, owing

Endeavour, built in 1905.

to the restriction imposed by the size of some of the locks. Salters' appears to have been happy with this limitation, however, because it did not relocate in order to build larger vessels, as Thornycroft had done in 1904 by opening another yard near Southampton.[58] This is perhaps not surprising, as the craft Salters' produced were almost exclusively for the Thames market.

The firm's failure to expand this part of the business significantly was partly self-inflicted, however, because it had a policy of not selling large steamers to any of its direct competitors between Oxford and Kingston, although Mears' operation did have a small amount of overlap. This shows that the firm was giving priority to the passenger services over its boat-building department.

Although the steel side of the business provided the firm with cheap passenger vessels, in 1920 John Salter was forced to concede that it was not performing well. In a letter to Baker that was intended to clear up an unspecified misunderstanding about the level of work the firm could offer, he said that if the launch business could not be developed substantially by taking on work from outside, it might be better for all concerned if the whole thing were abandoned.[59] A short-term formal agreement was subsequently reached, but the steel side of the business was eventually discontinued in the early 1930s, after both Mears and Salters' called a temporary halt to the expansion of their fleets. By this stage, launches were still much less popular than manually powered craft in Oxford (see chapter 3), whilst the decision may also have been linked to the rapid growth of the motor industry in the city, as steel workers were in great demand and they could earn much higher wages in the car factories (see chapter 6). Salters' subsequently relied upon second-hand craft for its passenger boat needs and it was not until 1980 that it purchased a new craft, *Lady Ethel*, this time from an external source (see chapter 4).

Motorised Boats

It is not clear when Salters' began building motorised craft. The firm was not a pioneer of steam or electric propulsion,[60] but the introduction of the internal combustion engine provides the opportunity to see how successful it was in exploiting an emerging technology. In 1904, *The Motor Boat* suggested that although the market was already dominated by newly established businesses, Salters' appeared to be taking advantage of it:

> Oxford may be said to be distinctly 'coming on' with regard to motor boats; and Messrs. Salter Bros. are quite alive to the great future of the motor ... One hears so much of new firms in the motor boat line that it is interesting to see an old-established firm prepared to energetically cater for the new sport.[61]

Salters' had actually been one of the earliest British firms to be involved – albeit indirectly – with the testing of the technology in 1894. The automobile engineer Frederick William Lanchester had decided that the best place to trial his engine (a single-cylinder, high-revving vertical engine that ran on Benzoline through a wick carburettor) was on water, because of the stifling legal regulations on land. The boat was collected by Salters' from Olton and tested at Folly Bridge before a modified version of the same engine was then used in one of the first British-built motor cars in 1896.[62] The vessel, which remained on the river for a number of years, was not the very first to be powered by a British-built combustion engine – *The Motor Boat* traces the history back to a rudimentary vessel trialled in London in 1827[63] – but it was certainly one of the earliest, as it was not until the mid-1880s that the technology became a practical proposition, with the German firm Daimler being an early pioneer.[64]

Salters' was exhibiting such craft at events from at least 1903,[65] but this did not translate into much business. Up until the mid-1920s it was typically building fewer than five motorised craft, including steamboats, per year. Nevertheless, it did attract some prestigious clients, like the Mir of Khairpur (1905) and Nawab Salar Jung Bahadur of Hyderabad (1921),[66] and it also occasionally produced more unusual craft, like one of the first cabin launches on the river (1923).[67] Unlike some of its competitors, however, Salters' did not change its overall focus to concentrate more heavily on this market. James Taylor of Chertsey (established 1850), for example, reinvented himself as a launch specialist and by the end of the Edwardian period his business was producing around thirty motor boats per year.[68]

There are a variety of reasons why Salters' initially had a relatively small output of motor boats. Firstly, there were difficulties associated with the development of such craft in the early years, as engine manufacturers would not lend their engines out to boat-builders.[69] This gave an advantage to those who built both boats and engines, like Sam Saunders (Streatley), or those who had a close relationship with a particular manufacturer, like the boat department of Simms Manufacturing Company (Putney), which had the rights for the Daimler engines.[70] Yet, conversely, the development of engines was expensive, and by retaining its independence Salters' was able to choose the most appropriate supplier for its needs. In 1903 it was relying mainly on American engines like those of Palmer, or Fay and Bowen,[71] but by 1906, it had switched to using predominantly English firms such as J.W. Brooke (Lowestoft), L. Gardner (Manchester) and Simms.[72] The firm also produced more unusual craft, including one running on coal-gas in 1917, and a number of launches using hydraulic propulsion from 1922 onwards (fitted by Hotchkiss, the manufacturers).[73]

Secondly, it took a number of years for motor boats to become popular, because there was initially a general prejudice against them, as they were viewed as being unreliable and dangerous. This was partly owing to the cheap imports that were 'particularly numerous' on the Thames, which meant that they were frequently seen at a standstill, owing to engines being incorrectly installed by inexperienced boat-builders.[74] A number of fires that affected craft in 1905 caused the Thames Conservancy to impose by-laws on them to try to ensure their safety standards. This not only added to the expense of running them, but it also helped to fuel a lingering feeling amongst those in the industry that the river authorities were hostile to them.[75] Yet the stigma surrounding them slowly receded as their safety and reliability improved. Furthermore, the engines were not only more fuel efficient and smaller than those powered by steam, but they did not require constant attention from someone in order to keep them going.

Thirdly, in spite of the technological developments, there was less of a market for motorised craft in Oxford. Certain riverside resorts nearer to London became particularly popular for motor boating in the first half of the twentieth century (see chapter 3), whereas the higher reaches were less suited to motor boats because the river was shallower and more overgrown, and there were fewer places with facilities for them. Furthermore, Oxford had one of the lowest bridges on the river, at Osney, which represented a barrier that larger craft were unable to pass (see chapter 3). Yet Salters' was able to specialise in boats with a small draft, which were suitable for shallower waters. One of these was *Bosphorus* (1936), a cabin cruiser built for Warren Lewis (and often used by his brother, C.S. Lewis),[76] who wrote a number of articles encouraging others to explore the inland waterways – 'ditch crawling', as he called it.[77] Yet such craft were not widely marketable, because the small draft not only rendered them less suitable for deeper water, but also restricted the internal space.[78]

Finally, the firm was not at the forefront of building motor boats because its owners did not have a personal obsession with them. A number of the market leaders were run by individuals with a particular interest in producing high-end racing craft, like Sam Saunders and John Thornycroft, for example, who were both included in *The Motor Boat*'s 'Prominent personalities associated with marine engineering'.[79] By contrast, Salters' built very few motorised boats in the first quarter of the twentieth century. Indeed, it was not until the sudden popularity of hydroplane racing in the late 1920s that the firm experienced a notable increase in orders.

Motor boat racing started to become popular in the early twentieth century through the regular contests organised by the British Motor Boat Club and the Motor Yacht Club, both formed in 1905. The Motor Yacht Club organised its first event for outboard-powered craft in 1923,[80] but it was not until around 1927 that the activity started to gain widespread appeal. In August 1928, the *Illustrated London News* ran a feature entitled 'Outboard motor-boating for all: a popular new pastime', in which it acknowledged the 'tremendous increase' in the activity, owing to price reductions that enabled 'people of ordinary means' to be able afford both the hulls (typically priced from £25 to £35) and the engines (£40 to £50).[81] The 'sudden vogue of the outboard'[82] was also helped by technological advances, as outboard craft were able to reach speeds within a few miles an hour of those achieved by inboard craft that cost approximately twenty times as much.[83] Furthermore, it was considerably cheaper than motor car racing, but being on water provided a greater thrill.[84]

There was not much profit to be made in building hydroplane hulls, but by 1928 the demand was so high that Salters', like many other businesses, entered the market. The firm's first model was a 14ft boat costing £45, and by the end of the year nineteen hydroplanes had been built.[85] By 1929, five standard types were being offered, which ranged from 10ft to 14ft in length, 85lb to 139lb in weight, and £31 to £44 in price, excluding the cost of the engine.[86] Bespoke craft were also offered and the firm constructed more than twenty different models in total, the best-seller being one designed for the motorcycle manufacturer Dunelt (Dunford and Elliott), which produced one of the most powerful outboard engines for its size (and whose managing director was a customer of the firm).[87] The hydroplanes were marketed as 'inexpensive and very speedy'[88] and a peak of fifty-five orders was achieved in 1929 – plus a further thirty-five for 'outboard motor boats', which may have included some that were used for racing.

The Thames was not suitable for testing such fast craft – which is one of the reasons why Sam Saunders relocated his business to the Isle of Wight[89] – and although Salters' tried to lobby for their acceptance (as a much-needed fillip for business), this was an imposition that the Conservancy was unwilling to accept.[90] Instead, it was the family's ownership of the reservoir at Edgbaston (see chapter 5) that enabled the firm to move into the construction of hydroplanes. This not only provided a suitable waterway for their development (one that was also used by engine manufacturers), but also had an all-important local market connected with it, in the form of the Midlands Outboard Racing Company, founded in 1929. The latter even included a race for Salter-class boats in one of its first contests. Frank Salter and an employee, F.E. Gillams, were on the committee, but by far the most important member was the commodore, R.D. Weatherell, who was one of the most successful competitors of the era, racing in his range of *Itsit* craft that he designed himself. Seventeen of these were built by Salters', including *Itsit VII*, which established a record speed of 31.79mph for a craft powered by a Class C engine (less than 500cc) off the Isle of Wight in 1929,[91] and *Itsit XVII*, which won the Thames International Championship Trophy in 1931.[92]

Weatherell's importance can be illustrated by Salters' advertising in September 1929 that its craft had notched up over eighty victories that season,[93] of which the majority were Weatherell's, as he won sixty-nine races that year. Another well-known competitor, and committee member, was Captain J. Palethorpe of Tipton, who was responsible for getting the firm an order from its most prestigious client, the Prince of Wales (the future Edward VIII). The prince had tried a hydroplane at a charity fête early in 1931 and this resulted in his ordering two, at least one of which was built by Salters' to Palethorpe's design.[94]

R.D. Weatherell's record-breaking *Itsit VII* (1929).

The outboard racing craze was short-lived, however: orders for hydroplanes dropped to fifteen in 1930 and only three in 1931 – the last that the firm built. The Depression appears to have ended the sport's widespread appeal, although its popularity was already on the wane.[95]

Salters' continued to build motor boats beyond this, but again, few were produced for the Thames market. The more unusual models included an airscrew launch (1936) and two hydro-gliders (1938). The last model to sell in large numbers, before the introduction of fibreglass, was the small 'lake boat' (6ft to 8ft) produced for local councils and amusement parks (see p. 62), which accounted for forty-six and thirty-five orders in 1933 and 1938 respectively. After the Second World War the output of motorised craft dropped to pre-1920 levels, which was part of a more general shift in the boat-building department towards the production of cheaper 'corporation craft'.

Corporation Craft

At the end of the nineteenth century the majority of orders that Salters' received were from rowing clubs (see chapter 1), private individuals (including some via Harrods department store) and other boatyards.[96] Although Salters' advertised that it produced craft for 'lakes and ornamental waters' in the early 1870s,[97] it was not until the twentieth century that it started to attract increasing business from councils around the country. This was another example of the firm expanding beyond its local market and this type of client became the boat-building department's central focus after the Second World War.

Local government bodies only accounted for two orders in 1893 (both from Southport Corporation for a total of six boats and four sets of oars), one order in 1894 (from Southport Corporation for four Belgian sliding seats) and two repairs in 1895 (to a scull and a canoe for the Metropolitan Board).[98] It was a growing market, however, because in 1913, the first year that the 'Master List' shows some of the customers (though not all of them), a combined total of twenty-one craft (gigs, skiffs and dinghies) were recorded as going to the corporations of Scarborough and Manchester.[99] The Yorkshire seaside resort became one of the firm's most important customers: it was responsible for ten of the fourteen orders placed by councils in 1925; the other four consisted of two orders from the borough of Warwick and one from the corporation of Hull and the borough of Henley.[100]

Although there are some early examples of council-run facilities, like Birkenhead's municipal lake that opened in 1844, it was not until after the First World War that many local authorities started including such initiatives in their plans.[101] The firm understood this market, as it ran its own reservoir at Edgbaston from the 1890s onwards (see chapter 5), and John and James Salter both served as councillors in Oxford from the end of the nineteenth century (see chapter 7). Yet it was not until 1925 that it experienced a large rise in orders from local authorities, owing to the introduction of a new range of small dinghies, including the paddle boat, designed for children. The firm had built boats for this market since 1917, the first model being a 9ft children's punt, but with the exception of the First World War, when a number of small collapsible craft were produced (see p. 219), vessels measuring less than 10ft in length tended to account for less than 5 per cent of the company's output. From the mid-1920s onwards, however, this was typically between 20 and 50 per cent, and in some years orders for these diminutive boats outnumbered those for all other types of craft put together.

The earliest children's dinghies were 6ft in length and square at both ends, but a 7ft 'skiff head' version was also offered from 1927. The short-term demand for paddle boats was particularly spectacular, despite the fact that other firms, such as Walter Johnson of London, were already building them at the start of the decade.[102] After they were introduced at the end of 1925, when the firm built nine, Salters' received orders for 220 the following year, which was approximately three-quarters of its overall output. This was the closest the firm came to the mass production of any of its wooden craft,

Lake boat in use at Southsea.

6ft paddle boat.

6ft pram dinghy.

requiring the workload to be shared between seven boat-builders and their assistants, and it is likely that customers took advantage of the discounts it provided for bulk orders. Salters' built a further sixty-one in 1927 and although this was followed by more modest amounts, by the end of the decade they still accounted for 15.1 per cent of the boats that had been built – the equivalent of almost a third of those produced in the second half of the decade.

The standard children's dinghies were not quite as popular, although they remained fairly consistent sellers. Orders peaked at seventy-two and ninety-two in 1928 and 1930 respectively, but their popularity dropped in the 1960s, only to grow once again in the 1970s with the introduction of fibreglass models.[103]

By the 1930s, the firm had taken the first step towards specialising in craft for local councils by dedicating a section of its brochure to 'Boats for Public Boating Stations'. The marketing emphasised both the money that could be made from them and the need to stock different boats for different age groups:

> The provision of Boats on Lakes in Public Parks and at Seaside Resorts creates a certain source of revenue. In order however to secure the best results and meet the requirements of everyone, boats of many classes should be available. For instance, for **CHILDREN Paddle Boats** are in first demand, but a child soon thinks he ought to row and then a **Pram Dinghy** is required; afterwards **Canoes, Cycle Pedal Boats**, and more especially **Motor Boats** will be demanded, so that every child instead of being the hirer of one boat only is a **potential customer for every class of boat provided**. [emphasis as shown in the advert]

It suggested that motorised craft were 'by far the most popular and profitable craft', because some operators 'had earned two or three times their cost in their first season'. Furthermore, it claimed that 'A Lake crowded with these boats all running at speed and colliding with one another is an amusing sight to spectators and a most exhilarating experience to the boat's occupants'. It stressed, however, that the craft were 'perfectly safe, being practically non-capsizable'.[104]

Another step was taken in 1938, when Salters' produced its first designated 'council type' (or 'council pattern') craft: a skiff that could be either 16ft or 18ft in length. By the late 1940s, its range of craft for public boating lakes (built for 'strength and safety') had enlarged further to eleven, which included some unusual models, like a pedal boat with an aluminium swan's head and wings on it, first built in 1939.[105]

After the Second World War the boat-building department shifted its focus to concentrate more heavily on this market. In 1946, for example, over half of the ninety-four boats built went to five locations: Colwyn Bay (twenty boats), Nottingham (thirteen), Scarborough (ten), Trentham Gardens (ten) and Walsall (two). Orders from this type of client continued to grow and in 1957 over two-thirds of the craft produced went to the local authorities of Colchester, Lowestoft, Malvern, Prestatyn, Redcar, Sheffield, Swindon and Weston-super-Mare. The firm's main clients (those buying five or more craft in a single year) were widely spread across the country (Table 2.2) and Salters' also offered advice on the construction of boating lakes.[106]

Table 2.2 Major clients (1946–70)[107]

Aberdare (1947, 1962)	Bexhill (1961)	Bexleyheath Borough (1955, 1956)
Burnham Beeches (1950)	Cheltenham (1956, 1957, 1961)	Colchester (1957)
Colwyn Bay (1946)	Coventry (1960)	Derby (1947, 1949, 1950)
Edmonton (1959)	Gillingham Borough (1955, 1956, 1968)	Gunnersbury Park (1947, 1948)
Leeds (1949, 1950, 1962)	Llandudno (1960)	Malvern UDC (1957)
Manchester (1960, 1961)	Newcastle (1950)	Nottingham (1946, 1947)
Nuneaton Borough (1956)	Prestatyn UDC (1957, 1963)	Redcar (1957)
Rhyl (1950)	Ruislip UDC (1955, 1962)	Scarborough (1946)
Sheffield (1957, 1958, 1961)	Sutton-in-Ashfield (1947)	Sutton Coldfield (1960, 1963, 1968)
Swindon Borough (1957, 1958)	Southern Miniature Railways (1958)	Tottenham Borough (1955)
Trentham Gardens (1946, 1961)	Walsall (1947)	Weston-super-Mare (1957)

Yet, ultimately, the price of focusing on this market was that instead of developing new craft incorporating the latest technology, the firm arguably went in the opposite direction by concentrating on producing boats that were cheap, functional and sturdy (or 'rough' boats, as they were nicknamed). This can be seen in the design of a number of craft, which were much more austere and plain than their aesthetic predecessors. The longitudinal strip canoe, for example, was replaced by both a cheap angular frame canoe and a more elaborate, but functional, steel child's safety canoe.

This shift in emphasis was partly a reflection of changing market forces, as there was fierce competition in the post-war period of austerity, with the boat-building industry heavily dependent upon the production of small craft at a price that was 'reasonable to all pockets'.[108] In this respect, there are some parallels with what occurred to the canoe-builders of Canada six decades earlier. Ted Moores describes the period leading up to the 1880s as being a 'self-indulgent time' for boat-builders when they were able to construct craft with 'great finesse', as part of their 'private search for excellence'. (One is reminded of Salters' refusing to provide a quotation for Brasenose College's new barge in the 1920s, on the grounds of its appearance.) Yet eventually:

> … the demand for a cheap serviceable canoe was growing and could not be
> ignored … When the change did come it was from outside the area from builders
> who didn't possess the same obsession with craftsmanship. In order for builders

to consider compromises in construction methods, the business had to be driven by the tough atmosphere of love for commerce rather than love of the board dugout [canoe].[109]

This, as well as financial difficulties for the business as a whole (see chapter 4), explains why Salters' adopted a variety of cost-cutting measures after the war, including streamlining its range of products and trying to source cheap supplies of wood. Indeed, in 1953 the firm even collected unwanted telegraph poles from near Woodstock, which were used in the construction of a cabin cruiser (*Meanderer*). Furthermore, Salters' also suffered from dwindling numbers of skilled boat-builders after the war, because of the problems in the local employment market (see chapter 6).

Fibreglass Craft

In October 1956 the firm wrote to a number of chemical companies to enquire about building out of fibreglass,[110] but it was not until 1970 that the firm sold its first craft made from the material. The new material helped to revive sales, but it marked a further reduction in the level of craftsmanship at Salters'.

The quality of fibreglass took a number of years to be refined, but the firm was still very late in making the transition to the material, as in 1964 already 30 per cent of craft on display at the International (London) Boat Show were made from it, compared to 4.4 per cent a decade earlier.[111] It is likely that the reticence of Salters' to embrace fibreglass was the main cause for the declining output of its boat-building department during the 1960s, because the new material was not only cheaper, easier and quicker to use than wood, but the finished product also required little on-going maintenance. Furthermore, finding good-quality timber was becoming more of a challenge for the firm at that time.

By introducing fibreglass craft, Salters' was able to drop the price of its craft by approximately a third. The impact this had on orders can be seen by the number of orders more than quadrupling in a single year from nineteen boats in 1970 to eighty-four in 1971, of which seventy were fibreglass. Indeed, in the 1970s the output of craft increased more than five-fold (2,541 in total) from the previous decade (475).[112]

Many of the craft resembled their wooden predecessors, because the moulds were made from the previous models, which was one way of keeping down the costs associated with developing the new range of boats. This was also an important element of their popularity, because unlike some of the craft produced by competitors, the boats had a more 'traditional' look. Furthermore, they could be produced in different colours of fibreglass, which was appealing to rental operators wanting to be able to distinguish their craft from others.

The best-selling boat was the skiff, which had a clinker appearance that was further enhanced by wooden trimmings. This was popular with other boat firms (including many on the Thames), local councils (including some new clients), and companies that either sold craft or specialised in providing water-based leisure services. Salters' also introduced a range of petrol 'runabouts', which resulted in the output of motorised craft reaching its highest level since the 1930s.

The most important innovation for over forty years was the introduction of the life-raft (1973),[113] a bright orange vessel filled with foam buoyancy that did not require any on-going maintenance. This came in two sizes, for fourteen or twenty people, and was designed to stack on board passenger-carrying craft and then to 'float free' in the event of the boat tipping or sinking. Salters' sold over a thousand of these in just six years to a range of customers, including shipbuilders, passenger boat operators and ferry companies. The domestic market included businesses on the Thames, like Catamaran Cruisers, and those further afield, like the Guernsey Boat Building Company. Furthermore, the firm's export trade, which continues today, was revived with orders during the 1970s from Belgium, Denmark, Finland, Germany, Ireland and Malta.[114]

Salters' subsequently introduced further fibreglass craft by purchasing moulds from other companies. These included a range of diesel and electric day-boats, which sold in small numbers, as well as some less successful boats that were only marketed for a brief period, like the Salter 775, a 26ft 'family motor-sailer' that was showcased at the 1980 London Boat Show.

The ultimate cost of using fibreglass, however, was that it ushered in the end of the skilled wooden boat-building that had been a hallmark of the firm for over a century – although the racing boat department continued to operate into the 1980s (see chapter 1). A single unskilled employee could produce a skiff in two to three days, for example, whilst the wooden equivalent could take a boat-builder (and apprentice) three to four weeks.[115] Furthermore, it caused a fundamental shift in the industry, as firms could no longer rely on craft needing to be replaced as regularly. The threat that this posed led to the formation of a number of organisations dedicated to keeping the skills associated with wooden boat-building alive, like the Thames Traditional Boat Society (formed in 1979), which still includes some ex-employees of Salters'.[116]

Innovation

The firm produced a large range of craft, but what is less apparent is *how* Salters' developed new products. Boat-building businesses regularly copied one another, so there are few that can be considered pioneering, in the sense of introducing new designs that could transform the market. Sam Saunders is a good example of a proactive and forward-thinking Thames business owner, as his engineering and entrepreneurial talent led him not only to patent over 100 innovations between 1886 and 1930,[117] but also to move into a number of new markets, including aeroplane construction. Salters' did not diversify to this degree and the European Patent Office only credits the firm with two patents submitted in 1912 and 1973, for the lifting mechanism on the Oxford Collapsible Boat and the design of the life-raft respectively. Yet it was able to make a significant impact in the market, by producing its own version of craft that were already produced by other businesses.

We know that there was some innovation from within the firm, because a number of key workers were responsible for developing certain craft. These included Stephen Salter and Ted Wilde, who were responsible for overseeing the construction of the successful racing boats in the 1860s and 1970s respectively, Thomas Arnold Baker, who built the steel craft, Bill Gillams, the firm's foreman during the inter-war period, and Ian Cullingworth, the naval architect who was responsible for designing the fibreglass life-rafts.[118] Furthermore, Salters' relied upon a highly skilled and versatile workforce that was able to build almost any type of small boat.

There was also innovation from outside of the firm, as Salters' gained the expertise of building more unusual craft from fulfilling bespoke orders. Many of these, such as the college barges and a number of the hydroplanes, were designed by external naval architects. Each new model was tested after completion and some were added to the standard range of products, because Salters' retained the blueprints in order to duplicate the boat, if required.

Yet, arguably, the firm's position within the industry was such that it did not require significant innovation. It did not produce engines, for example, and its main focus was on building fairly standard Thames craft, which did not change radically in appearance over time. It was also partly because some types of vessel, like punts, became particularly popular and were eventually viewed as being those that one 'traditionally' used for pleasure boating (see chapter 3). Nevertheless, leisure on the river could not have taken off without working craft being appropriated for recreational use, and the designs of boats were gradually refined for their new purpose.

Innovation could shape the demand for craft, as much as it could be shaped by it, which is why certain types of boat became fashionable at different times. R. T. Rivington argues that in the early Victorian period, for example, punts were usually wide-beamed craft made from pitch and tar mainly associated with fishing or ferrying. Yet from around 1860 they started to be built from mahogany to a much narrower (and therefore lighter) design more suited to pleasure use.[119] He suggests that the innovation reached Oxford later, between 1880 and 1900, which is broadly supported by data from Salters'. The firm's earliest surviving Inventory Book (1877–79) lists the type of wood used for a number of the pleasure boats and this shows that the majority were made from deal (pine) or oak, whilst mahogany was only occasionally used.[120] By 1903, however, mahogany was used for over 90 per cent of such craft – a shift that appears to have occurred sometime in the 1880s.[121] Rivington also suggests that a crucial part in the growing popularity of the punt for leisure was the introduction of a 'saloon' to the design of the craft in the late 1880s. This allowed passengers to sit in the middle of the boat opposite one another, where there had once been a well for storing bait or fish.[122] It is impossible to say whether Salters' was responsible for either of these innovations in Oxford, but it was obviously a major supplier of boats to the city.

Even if the business was not very pioneering, it still required a keen sense of timing to be able to exploit the emerging opportunities. Indeed, one of the key strengths of Salters' was that it managed to sell large numbers of its own version of craft that were already in existence, like the paddle boats and the hydroplanes. The firm was certainly well placed to be able to judge the market, because it had its own large rental fleet (with which to gauge what boats were popular), its steamers were regularly travelling between Oxford and Kingston (so it could see what other firms were doing), it had close ties – and some business arrangements – with other boat companies, and its personnel attended many different exhibitions (where competitors would showcase new products).

The Economic Impact of the Wars

By examining the economic performance of the boat-building department during and after the two world wars, one can see how adaptable the firm was, as well as the reason why this part of the business declined in the second half of the twentieth century. The firm's commercial activities were greatly affected by the two conflicts. In a letter dated 5 February 1918, George Salter wrote to Mallam's, the landlords of St Aldate's Yard, to explain the impact the war had had on the business. He claimed that it had 'completely destroyed' the university trade and for more than three years a large number of its best boats 'of all kinds' had been laid up. He concluded that 'In all probability it will be years before this trade recovers the position it previously held'.[123]

Although he neglected to mention the areas of the business that had been very lucrative during the conflict (see pp. 70, 97, 127) – perhaps unsurprisingly, as the letter was in response to notification from Mallam's that it intended to raise the rent – the war did pose a considerable challenge for boating companies. The nearby business of Frederick Rough, the leading racing boat-builder prior to the conflict, for example, was declared bankrupt in 1923 with the war being cited as the major contributing factor. The firm had temporarily closed between December 1914 and June 1915, after the death of Rough, but it was subsequently revived by his son, Jack Clasper Rough, who was initially forced to rely upon aircraft contracts in order to keep the business going. The comparison with Salters' is not perfect, however, because Rough was forced to buy a lot of new stock after the destruction of his yard in 1913 by the suffragettes (see chapter 5). This caused him to accrue significant debts (over £2,000 by 1923, including £71 19s 8d owed to Salters'), which he was unable to pay off.[124]

The income from boat sales at Salters' was very low during the First World War, although there were also significant drops in revenue during the Great Depression and the Second World War. Unlike Rough, it had other areas of its business to fall back upon during the war (see chapters 3–5), but it also struggled during the conflict, at least initially. Yet although the firm became heavily reliant on contract work, by the end of the war this area of the business was helping Salters' to make significant profits (see the conclusion), as it produced revenue of £17,167 10s 4d and £25,115 11s 4d in 1917 and 1918 respectively, which was over half of the total turnover at this time.[125]

Salters' started producing craft for the war effort in 1915 and initially the orders were mainly for pontoons, collapsible boats and cutters. During the latter stages of the conflict, the firm produced a much wider range of craft, as well as a number of accessories, like buoys, sails, life floats, oars, paddles and even some items used in the construction of airships.[126] A number of the manually powered craft were sent by rail to go on board larger ships being built elsewhere, like the 30ft carvel gig sent to Palmer's yard (Jarrow) in 1918 for the cruiser HMS *Dauntless*. The other shipbuilding firms supplied by Salters' were Armstrong Whitworth (Newcastle), Fairfield (Govan), Cammell Laird and Co. (Birkenhead) and Scott's (Greenock).

Salters' had the closest ties with Thornycroft, for which it built thirteen coastal motor boats (or CMBs),[127] as well as two seaplane tenders. The CMBs were 'one of the fastest pieces of naval weaponry in the world',[128] capable of over 30 knots, and 123 were ordered from Thornycroft between the summer of 1916 and the end of the war. This required the assistance of numerous subcontractors, including Salters'.[129]

The Oxford firm produced 280 military vessels (including 154 pontoons) in total during the First World War (see the appendix). Although some of the orders were lucrative, such as four steam pinnaces sold for over £10,000 in 1918, gaining the contracts was not straightforward. Around half of the quotations that the firm submitted for cutters and collapsible boats were turned down on the grounds of cost, whilst the proportion was more than three-quarters for whalers and dinghies.[130]

This provides an interesting backdrop for what occurred during the Second World War. By 1940 the firm had received two orders from the Admiralty (as well as one from Trinity House for 170 oars), but after the first (for eight 32ft cutters) had been completed, the second (for two 45ft fast motor boats) was put on hold because of the price. Despite numerous attempts to resolve the situation, Frank Salter was unable to make any headway. This led him to write an exasperated letter to his brother, Sir Arthur Salter, the parliamentary secretary to the minister of shipping, in which he claimed to be 'absolutely in despair at the dilatory way the admiralty works'. His major concern was that the firm was losing its workforce because of a lack of orders (see chapter 6):

We have a good staff of men very anxious to work hard but we have very little to work at. Why can't the Admiralty if it wants boats give us all we can do instead of quibbling about prices all the time? We will work for <u>nothing</u> if they will guarantee us against loss ... I am quoting the Ministry of Supply today for some boats, but if I get a reply in three months' time I shall be surprised ... If you see any way of making us busy, we should all be very thankful. It is demoralising to have to work at half-speed all the time ...[131] [Emphasis his.]

Assault landing craft moored at Folly Bridge, 1942.

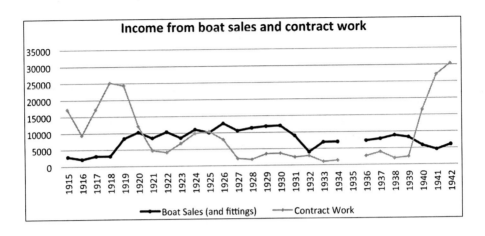

Sir Arthur Salter's subsequent letter to Lieutenant-Commander R. Fletcher MP appears to have worked because the order was subsequently placed. However, this did not appease Frank because there was no deadline, giving him the impression that the craft were not wanted. Fortunately, his spirits had been improved by an order from Thornycroft for three assault landing craft, which he described as being 'the tonic our men wanted' because, unlike the Admiralty order, they were 'required at the earliest possible moment'.[132] The landing craft were constructed in Brook Street and tested at Nuneham Courtenay. Amongst those building them was a young Arthur Salter (born 1922), who was serving his apprenticeship before being called up and transported to France in one such craft, although not one of the firm's.

Although complaints about the Admiralty were commonplace during the war, Salters' experienced a significant improvement in its turnover because of the contract work it took on. The revenue generated in this manner rose from £2,304 11s 3d in 1939 to £27,061 12s 1d in 1941. As in the earlier conflict this constituted around one-half of the firm's overall turnover at this time.[133] Nevertheless, Salters' built far fewer craft (sixty-one) than in the First World War (see the appendix) and it experienced considerable problems in sourcing suitable building material, especially timber, as the war progressed.

The boat-building department may have been supported by the rise in contract work, but crucially, its relative importance to Salters' (in terms of overall turnover), which had already declined in the 1930s, did not recover after the war. In the 1920s this side of the business tended to generate between 20 and 30 per cent of the firm's overall income, but by the late 1940s it had dropped to between 10 and 13 per cent.[134] This was partly to do with the success of other sides of the business, which is another reason why the firm's focus shifted away from boat-building after the war. This also meant that Salters' became more heavily dependent on generating income in the summer months, as spring was the busiest time for constructing craft (see p. 48).

· · ·

The number and range of craft that Salters' produced shows that it was a major inland boat-builder. It was responsible for producing around 17,000 craft between 1858 and 1980, and these included almost anything from 6ft wooden dinghies to 110ft steel passenger boats. This flexibility was vital, because different types of boat were popular at different times. The firm was not particularly innovative, but it did successfully exploit a number of emerging markets, such as the demand for children's craft and hydroplanes in the late 1920s. After the Second World War, the company focused on producing cheap 'corporation craft', which were widely distributed around the country. This change of direction was influenced by market forces, the difficulty in sourcing boat-builders and the relative success of other areas of the business. Indeed, the overall focus at Salters' shifted away from boat-building and in order to understand why this occurred, it is necessary to look at the rise of leisure on the waterway and the firm's role in promoting 'the Thames trip'.

Notes

1   F.V. Morley, *River Thames* (London, 1926), p. 78.

2   *Rowing Almanack 1863* (London, 1863), p. 113.

3   *Rowing Almanack 1865*, p. 109.

4   Email from Tony Hobbs, 16 October 2012.

5   Pollard and Robertson, *British Shipbuilding Industry*, pp. 26–27.

6   T. Moores, 'From Forest to Factory: Innovations and Mass Production', in J. Jennings (ed.), *The Canoe: A Living Tradition* (Toronto, 2002), p. 177.

7   W.G. Luscombe, *Canoeing* (London, 1936), pp. 18–19. He also recorded that one of the firm's oldest canoes was being stored in one of the yards.

8   D.I. Greenstein, 'The Junior Members, 1900–1990: A Profile', in B. Harrison (ed.), *History of the University of Oxford: The Twentieth Century*, vol. 8 (Oxford, 1994), p. 46.

9   *The Motor Boat*, vol. 32, no. 832 (18 June 1920), p. 589.

10 SA Master List of Boats 1911–36.

11 SA Inventory Book 1926–30. This included West Virginia spruce, Oregon pine, mahogany (Honduran, African and South American), walnut (Canadian and Nigerian), Alaskan silver spruce, teak, cottonwood, cypress, celery wood, as well as elm, ash and oak from England (collectively valued at over £2,500).

12 SA Records of B. Collar 1924–27. The Oxford firm originally relied upon George Ralph of Lambeth to provide its oars.

13 Data from *Rowing Almanacks*, Inventory Books and the Master List of Boats 1911–36 and 1937–87.

14 SA Carmans Boat Works.

15 C. Sherriff, *College Barges: Their History and Architecture* (London, 2003), p. 54. She estimates that there were thirty-six barges in total.

16 SA Book of Estimates 1873–1917 and Sherriff, *College Barges*, p. 58. The stern of the Keble barge is now in the Museum of Oxford.

17 Sherriff, *College Barges*, p. 46.

18 *British Architect*, 30 July 1909, p. 89.

19 *The Motor Boat*, vol. 10, no. 253 (12 May 1909), p. 322. This was ordered from Wolesey and Saunders of Cowes.

20 D. Rowntree, 'Oxford College Barges', *Architectural Review*, vol. 120, no. 714 (July 1956), p. 41.

21 *The Thames*, 8 March 1902, p. 6. It won first prize at the St Petersburg Yachting Exhibition of 1897. An unreferenced note in the archive belonging to Jim Cowan suggests that the boat may have been previously produced by another firm.

22 For a short history of the firm, see www.berthon.co.uk (accessed 12 March 2011).

23 *Oxford University Herald*, 21 April 1866, p. 8. The event was started because Cambridge held a similar event first.

24 SA The Oxford Collapsible Boat.

25 J. Arthur Bain, *Life of Fridtjof Nansen: Scientist and Explorer* (London, 1897), p. 93. The recommendation was made by J. Russell-Jeaffreson.

26 SA Inventory Book 1903. The remaining stock was sold off during the First World War.

27 An employee of the firm also lost a son on the *Titanic*.

28 Patent Number GB191210993 (A), 18 July 1918, Priority date: 7 May 1912. http:// worldwide.espacenet.com/publicationDetails/biblio?FT=D&date=19120718&DB=wo rldwide.espacenet.com&locale=en_EP&CC=GB&NR=191210883A&KC=A&ND=4 (accessed 10 October 2012).

29 SA Master List of Boats Built 1911–36. One can be seen at the Classic Boat Museum on the Isle of Wight.

30 Three military boats built in 1919 are also excluded from the data.

31 SA Master List of Boats 1911–36.

32 SA Master List of Boats 1911–36 and 1937–87.

33 P. Hartley, *The Story of Rudge Motorcycles* (Wellingborough, 1985), p. 60.

34 The houseboats were used as holiday homes and the majority of them were bought rather than built by the firm.

35 SA Master List of Boats 1937–87.

36 J.F. Robb, 'Scotts of Greenock. Shipbuilders and Engineers. 1820–1920. A Family Enterprise', vol. 1 (Glasgow University PhD Thesis, 1993), pp. xv–xvi.

37 Pollard and Robertson, *British Shipbuilding Industry*, pp. 70–230.

38 Apart from producing iron accessories for boats, like outriggers.

39 L. Lacey-Johnson, *Edwin Clark: Steamboat-Builder of Brimscombe* (Eastbourne, 2000), pp. 1–9.

40 Letters from W. Sissons to Salters', 18 December 1895, 26 October 1897 and 9 November 1897 (from archive compiled by an unnamed employee in 1976, now in the possession of Jim Cowan).

41 Census 1881 and 1891.

42 J. Betjeman and D. Vaisey, *Victorian and Edwardian Oxford* (London, 1971), photograph 39.

43 SA Agreement between Salter Brothers and Thomas Arnold Baker, 7 March 1902. The engine would have been installed after this.

44 P. Banbury, *Shipbuilders of the Thames and Medway* (Newton Abbot, 1971), p. 17.

45 'Large' is defined as more than 40ft in length.

46 SA Inventory Book 1931–37.

47 B. Stanley, *The History of the Baptist Missionary Society 1792–1992* (Edinburgh, 1992), p. 117.

48 Regent's Park College Archive (RPC) Baptist Missionary Society Western Sub-Committee Minute Book no. 12, 19 July 1904, pp. 120–21.

49 Pollard and Robertson, *British Shipbuilding Industry*, pp. 56–62 and Banbury, *Shipbuilders of the Thames*, p. 17.

50 RPC Baptist Missionary Society Western Sub-Committee Minute Book no. 12, 15 February 1905, p. 122.

51 Letter from Rev. C.T. Williams to C.T. Williams, 23 June 1906 (sent to the author by Bob Dowthwaite, grand-nephew of C.T. Williams).

52 Letter from G.L. Watson Architects to C.T. Williams, 9 June 1907 (sent to the author by Bob Dowthwaite).

53 *Oxford Times*, 22 July 1905, p. 8.

54 Ibid., 1 April, 1911, p. 5.

55 *International Marine Engineering*, vol. 15, no. 179, November 1910, pp. 461–62 and November 1911, p. 443. Their stories are recorded in W.Y. Fullerton, *The Christ of the Congo River* (London, 1927).

56 *The Motor Boat*, vol. 6, no. 148 (9 May 1907), p. 306.

57 See the Association of Dunkirk Little Ships' website: www.adls.org.uk/t1/boats (accessed 9 July 2012). These were *Hurlingham, Kingwood, Queen of England, Marchioness* and *Viscount*. One of Salters' ex-hire boats (*Wayfarer*) is also believed to have taken part.

58 Barnaby, *100 Years of Specialised Shipbuilding*, p. 48.

59 SA Letter from John Salter to T.A. Baker, 14 June 1920.

60 Steam technology predated the firm and Salters' receives little attention in E. Hawthorne's *Electric Boats on the Thames 1889–1914* (Stroud, 1995).

61 *The Motor Boat*, vol. 1. no. 13 (6 October 1904), p. 237.

62 C.S. Clark, *The Lanchester Legacy*, vol. 1 (London, 1995), pp. 8–9.

63 *The Motor Boat*, vol. 18, no. 467 (19 June 1913), p. 530.

64 *The Motor Boat*, vol. 3, no. 66 (12 October, 1905), p. 230 and *Institute of Naval Architecture*, 24 March 1904.

65 *The Electrical Engineer*, vol. 31 (1903), p. 357.

66 SA Order Book 1903–08 and *The Motor Boat*, vol. 34, no. 875 (15 April 1921), p. 356. The latter's boat was named *The Lady of the Lake*.

67 *The Motor Boat*, vol. 39, no. 993 (20 July 1923), p. 61. This had the appearance of a normal launch, but with a modified cabin.

68 Ibid., vol. 10, no. 245 (18 March 1909), p. 178.

69 Ibid., vol. 2, no. 30 (2 February 1905), p. 63.

70 Ibid., vol. 2, no. 32 (16 February 1905), p. 95.

71 Ibid., vol. 1, no. 13 (6 October 1904), p. 237.

72 Ibid., vol. 3, no. 71 (16 November 1905), p. 298 and vol. 5, no. 118 (11 October 1906), p. 221.

73 Ibid., vol. 27, no. 691 (4 October 1917), p. 270 and vol. 36, no. 924 (24 March 1922), p. 254.

74 Ibid., vol. 18, no. 456 (3 April 1913), p. 305.

75 Ibid., vol. 2, no. 50 (22 June 1905), p. 395.

76 W. Hooper (ed.), *C.S. Lewis Collected Letters*, vol. 2 (London, 2004), pp. 270–71, 486.

77 See, for example, *The Motor Boat*, vol. 67, no. 1719 (2 July 1937), p. 5.

78 *The Motor Boat*, vol. 56, no. 1443 (18 March 1932), p. 256.

79 Ibid., vol. 14, no. 345 (16 February 1911), p. 102.

80 *The Times*, 2 July 1923, p. 19.

81 *Illustrated London News*, 4 August 1928, p. 215.

82 Ibid., 30 April 1929, p. 6.

83 *The Motor Boat*, vol. 49, no. 1252 (20 July 1928), p. 58.

84 Ibid., vol. 51, no. 1305 (20 July 1929), p. 110.

85 SA Master List of Boats 1911–36.

86 *The Motor Boat*, vol. 50, no. 1287 (22 March 1929), pp. 278–80.

87 *Illustrated London News*, 7 September 1929, p. 438.

88 SA Salter Bros. Ltd Brochure (1930s).

89 Tagg and Wheeler, *From Sea to Air*, p. 11.

90 *Oxford Mail*, 30 March 1920, p. 1 and 6 May 1930, p. 5.

91 *The Motor Boat*, vol. 50, no. 1291 (19 April 1929), p. 30. See also 'Another record for Britain (1929)' on the Pathé News website: www.britishpathe.com/video/another-record-for-britain-1 (accessed 16 November 2012).

92 *The Motor Boat*, vol. 155, no. 1411 (7 August 1931), p. 12.

93 Ibid., vol. 51, no. 1312 (13 September 1929), p. 26.

94 *Oxford Mail*, 15 July 1931, pp. 3–5.

95 *The Motor Boat*, vol. 53, no. 1356 (18 July 1930), p. 69.

96 SA Order Book 1893.

97   H. Taunt, *A New Map of the River Thames from Oxford to London* (Oxford, 1872), p. 56.

98   SA Order Book 1893, 1894 and 1895.

99   SA Master List of Boats 1911–36.

100   SA Order Book 1925.

101   Wigglesworth, *History of Rowing*, p. 94.

102   *Popular Science*, October 1920, p. 58.

103   SA Master List of Boats 1911–36 and 1937–87.

104   Ibid. The other sections, which preceded them were 'Racing boats', 'Half-outrigged boats, pleasure boats, dinghies, &c.' and 'Canadian Canoes, Punts, &c.'

105   This was a modification of the pedal boat (first built in 1933), but neither sold well.

106   SA Note from W.H. Gillams to Cardigan Borough's Surveyors Office, 8 April 1952.

107   SA Master List of Boats Built 1937–87.

108   K. Norman, *Outboard Boating and Cruising* (London, 1962), p. 45.

109   Moores, 'Forest to Factory', p. 176.

110   SA Letters from Salter Bros to British Resin Products Ltd, Fibreglass Ltd, Imperial Chemical Industries Ltd (and other companies), 19 October 1956.

111   *Board of Trade Journal*, 10 January 1964, p. 58.

112   SA Master List of Boats 1937–87.

113   Patent GB19730058134 19731214, 14 December 1974, publication date: 26 May 1976. http://worldwide.espacenet.com/searchResults?compact=false&ST=advanced&lo cale=en_EP&DB=EPODOC&AP=GB19730058134 (accessed 10 October 2012).

114   SA Master List of Boats 1937–87.

115   Interview with John Salter, 20 December 2011.

116   See *Oxford Times*, 8 October 1993, p. 17.

117   Wheeler, *From River to Sea*, p. 292.

118   Interview with John Salter, 20 December 2011.

119   R.T. Rivington, *Punting: Its History and Techniques* (Oxford, 1983), p. 9.

120   SA Inventory Book 1877–79.

121   SA Inventory Book 1903.

122   Rivington, *Punting*, p. 34.

123   SA Letter from George Salter to T. Mallams Company, 5 February 1918.

124   *Oxford Times*, 19 January 1923, p. 11 and 16 February 1923, p. 15.

125   SA Salter Bros Ltd End of Year Accounts 1915–49.

126   SA Order Book 1918 and *Oxford Mail*, 1 July 1955, p. 19.

127   See R. Gardiner and R. Gray (eds), *Conway's All the World's Fighting Ships* (London, 1985), p. 100. The 40ft CMBs were numbered 50, 51, 60 and 61, and the 55ft CMBs 23, 62 and 67.

128   H. Ferguson, *Operation Kronstadt* (London, 2008), pp. 9–10.

129   Barnaby, *100 Years of Specialised Shipbuilding*, pp. 182–84. Those built by Salters' were used in Operation Z-O and Kronstadt.

130   SA Admiralty Boat Quotations 1914–18.

131   Letter from Sir Arthur Salter to Lt Commander R. Fletcher MP, 5 June 1940 (sent to author by Sidney Aster, Sir Arthur Salter's biographer).

132   Letter from Frank Salter to Sir Arthur Salter, 19 July 1940 (sent to author by Sidney Aster).

133   SA Salter Bros Ltd End of Year Accounts 1939–42.

134   SA Salter Bros Ltd End of Year Accounts 1915–42 and 1947–49.

3

Thames Pleasure Boating

> To the ordinary voyager from London, intent on 'doing the river' in the fewest
> possible days, Salter's raft is the ultimate limit and source of the Thames.
>
> Fred Thacker, 1909[1]

Throughout its history Salters' has often been described as a boat-building firm, but
this does not convey the range of activities it became involved with, as the business
also played a major role in the rise and development of pleasure boating on the Upper
Thames from the late 1850s onwards. It not only became one of the country's largest
and most significant inland boat-letters, but was responsible for popularising the long-
distance 'Thames trip' between Oxford and London.

Measuring Pleasure Boating

It has been suggested that during the Victorian period a 'minor revolution'[2] occurred
on the river that caused it to develop from a 'great commercial highway'[3] into a
'vast pleasure-stream',[4] with boats stretching in an almost 'uninterrupted procession'
between Richmond and Oxford.[5] The majority of literature on this topic has been at
the popular level, and books like Patricia Burstall's *The Golden Age of the Thames* (1981)
and R.R. Bolland's *Victorians on the Thames* (1984) have helped to propagate the notion
that the heyday of pleasure boating was at the end of the nineteenth century, at a time
when other leisure pursuits and sports were taking off.

Whilst there is a general agreement amongst authors that a transformation occurred
on the Upper Thames, they disagree about the timing. Bolland argues that many of the
things we associate with the Victorian Thames, such as boat outings, steam launch trips,
Venetian fairs, regattas, picnics and carnivals, all took off around the period between 1880
and 1900, a time in which he suggests the river 'had never been so popular before or
since'.[6] Peter Ackroyd supports this notion, claiming that the two decades 'represented
the most popular periods in the Thames' long history' and that, intriguingly, the change
on the upper part of the river can be traced 'with reasonable precision' to 1878 and
1879 (although corroborating evidence is not cited).[7] Burstall provides a slightly earlier
estimate, suggesting that the 'golden age' of boating stretched from around 1870, as this
was the period in which the Upper Thames took on a 'new character' as a pleasure

destination, which was then irrevocably lost during the First World War.[8] This timescale seems to be supported by the evidence from the river Wey, a tributary of the Thames, which experienced a twelve-fold increase in the number of pleasure boats between 1870 and 1893.[9] Yet Edwin Course suggests that the changes began earlier still: 'In the 1860s and 1870s there was an appreciable increase in pleasure traffic on inland waterways, encouraged by such publications as *The Oarsman's Guide to the Thames and other Rivers*, which achieved a second edition in 1857.'[10] The discrepancies between these estimations reflect both differing opinions of what constitutes either a 'rise' in leisure or a perceived 'golden age', as well as a lack of convenient statistical information by which pleasure use on the Thames can be measured.

There are, however, quantitative data with which to gauge levels of river use in the form of lock toll receipts (the records of which date back to the middle of the nineteenth century), boat registrations (collected from 1887) and pleasure boat returns (recorded from 1913). The former only provide an indication of the traffic on the river, however, because the charges were not always consistently applied, they only show a monetary figure (rather than the number of boats) and the fee structure was altered a number of times. Furthermore, they (and the pleasure boat returns) tend to underestimate river use, because localised boating that did not pass through a lock does not register in the data, whilst toll dodging was not uncommon. Nevertheless, the statistics can be used to show when the carrying trade declined on the Thames, when pleasure boating became popular, the types of craft that were on the waterway, and how the levels of river use varied from place to place and at different times of the year.

H.S. Davies has used the lock toll data to show that the construction of the Great Western railway through the Thames Valley, which involved building a number of bridges over the river, initially increased barge traffic (the main source of toll income). Yet once it was completed, the commercial use of the river fell sharply, with the connection of Oxford (1844) to the network and the completion of the Reading to Hungerford line (1847) being particularly damaging.[11] The change was described by *Jackson's Oxford Journal* in 1853:

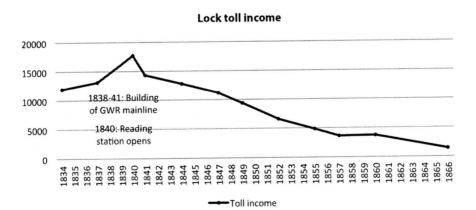

Lock toll income

Trade, prosperous trade, may be said to have taken flight from the District, and may now be seen in the heavy-goods train, whirling onwards at the rate of *12* or *14* miles an hour, whistling in derision as it passes by the Thames and Canal navigations, and by its speed mocking the drowsy barge (that emblem of the old slowness of traders and the torpid course of their commercial transactions) ...[12]

Indeed, the reduction of toll income was so great that the Thames Navigation Commission was unable adequately to maintain the waterway, which led to it being stripped of its control of the river between Staines and Teddington in 1857 and the rest of the waterway above this in 1866.[13]

Rosemary Stewart-Beardsley argues that the most significant rise in leisure activities occurred between 1879 and 1887 when receipts for pleasure boats more than doubled from £1,647 per annum to £3,805 per annum respectively (Table 3.1). This was also the period when such craft began to account for the majority of toll income, having been roughly on par with the commercial traffic in 1879. Another change was that the summer became the busiest season on the river – as at the end of the 1850s, for example, the overall toll income (including barge traffic) was relatively constant throughout the year.[14]

Table 3.1 Pleasure boat toll receipts for the Upper Thames[15]

	Amount collected (£)
1867	1,020
1879	1,647
1887	3,805
1906	4,552

The annual reports for the Thames Conservancy do not list the pleasure boat toll receipts separately until 1889 and the figures suggest that boating declined slightly in the mid-1890s, only then to increase at the end of the Edwardian period and after the First World War.[16] It is impossible to say how significant this rise was, however, because the lock tolls were increased slightly in 1910 (for steamboats and houseboats) and significantly (for all boats) in 1920.[17] Yet, it is evident that after 1921, pleasure boating was in decline, which may have been partly the result of the higher costs associated with it.

This was not the case for all types of pleasure boating, however, as the registration documents show that between 1909 and 1954, the number of small, manually powered boats on the river slowly reduced, whilst the number of launches (for which the data extend back to 1887) steadily rose. By contrast, the number of rental craft peaked in the mid-1920s and then fell more sharply than the number of privately owned small craft. The total number of (registered) boats was at its greatest just before the First World War.[18]

Yet the pleasure boat returns (dating from 1913) show that during the inter-war period the number of small boats passing through the locks fell at a much faster rate than one might expect from the gradual decline in the total number of registered craft. This suggests that they were being used much less and/or they were not travelling as far, whilst the launch traffic increased significantly only after the Second World War.[19]

Lock toll income from pleasure boats

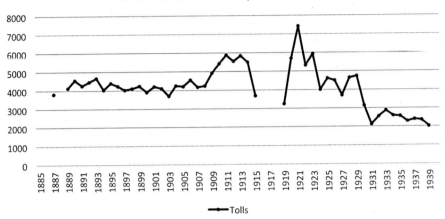

—●—Tolls

Number of Boats Registrations

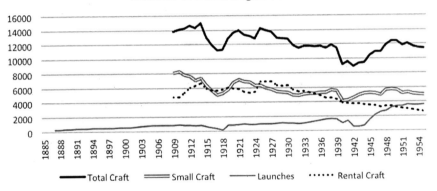

——Total Craft   ══Small Craft   ——Launches   ·····Rental Craft

There were also much greater levels of river use in certain locations, as well as at certain times of the year. The pleasure boat returns for the whole of the non-tidal Thames show that, in general, there was more traffic closer to London, with Molesey Lock (near Hampton Court Palace) being by far the busiest for small manually powered craft in 1913 and 1920.[20] This had been the case for some time; at the end of the 1880s Jerome K. Jerome described it as normally the busiest on the river,[21] whilst Elizabeth Robins Pennell claimed it was 'the headquarters of that carnival on the river which begins in June, is at its height in midsummer, and ends only with October'.[22]

Further upstream, the 'Piccadilly Circus'[23] or 'Clapham Junction'[24] of the river was Boulter's Lock, near Maidenhead, which was at its busiest on Ascot Sunday – the weekend after the horse races had finished, when spectators traditionally took to the water. In 1888 the *Lock to Lock Times* described it as being 'what the Ladies Mile is to the metropolis. It is there that the best people congregate in order that they may see

Pleasure boat returns for small craft

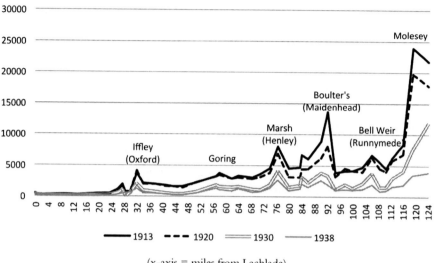

(x-axis = miles from Lechlade)

and be seen … It is at Boulter's that the cachet of the river is to be obtained.'[25] Ernest Jones (1879–1958) recalled 'the great days of Boulter's lock', which included the 'revelry at Skindles Hotel until the special late train to London', where 'crowds of actresses with their sweeping summer costumes and gay cartwheel hats obliterated the sight of all the lawns as well as most of the river'.[26] The proceedings at the lock were orchestrated by the charismatic William Turner (lockkeeper from 1881 to 1905) whose entertaining sarcasm and talent for packing in the boats 'with the closeness of barrelled herrings'[27] ensured he became a cult figure within the English-speaking world. Patricia Burstall records that 'wherever English was spoken, from the sweltering tropics to the snowy waters of Canada, from Calcutta to Calgary, there were those who remembered or knew of Turner, his prize winning lock garden and Juggins, the bull terrier with a nose for the biscuits on Salter's steamers'.[28]

So many spectators congregated at the lock that iron railings were built in 1899 to keep them back, whilst Boulter's was enlarged in 1912, which included the construction of a mechanical boat conveyor to lift smaller craft over Ray Mill Island. Although the number of small boats was declining on the river as a whole in the inter-war period, the popularity of Boulter's Lock waned in particular. By the 1930s, Marsh Lock (Henley) and Cookham Lock tended to be busier, the former being especially so at the time of the regatta, whilst Bell Weir Lock (at Runnymede) had emerged as another popular destination.[29]

Nevertheless, Boulter's was the most popular lock on the higher reaches of the river for launch traffic throughout the inter-war period, although, again, those closest to London tended to be the busiest. By contrast, there were far fewer engine-powered craft on the higher reaches, including at Oxford. There was a significant downturn in

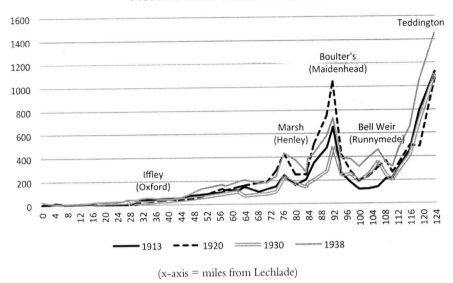

Pleasure boat returns for launches

(x-axis = miles from Lechlade)

the level of launch traffic by 1930, however, which shows that this type of boating was particularly badly affected by the Depression.[30] This also illustrates that the registration statistics can be misleading, because the number of launches on the river did not fall dramatically during this period, but their amount of use did.

The statistical information, therefore, supports the notion of there being some form of 'golden age' on the Thames with a significant rise of pleasure boating in the 1880s. The peak is more difficult to identify, but between 1889 and 1939 there were busy periods in the early 1890s and the years either side of the First World War – although there would be another more significant 'golden age' in the 1970s (see chapter 4). Yet the data also show that there were notable differences in the type and level of pleasure boating from place to place, an explanation of which requires an examination of more local sources.

The Rise of Pleasure Boating on the Upper Thames

The preamble to the Thames Preservation Act of 1885 suggested that the main reason the river became 'largely used as a place of public recreation and resort' was the 'increase of population in London and other places near the said river'.[31] The population of Greater London grew by an average of almost 20 per cent per decade between 1831 and 1901 (Table 3.2). As the city expanded outwards, some of the western boroughs by the river enlarged at a particularly fast rate. Hammersmith and Fulham, and Wandsworth, for example, both increased ten-fold in population between 1831 and 1891. By 1889, however, one commentator suggested that it was the Thames itself that had become the busiest and 'by far the prettiest' suburb of London.[32]

Table 3.2 The population of London boroughs[33]

	1831	1841	1851	1861	1871	1881	1891	1901
Wandsworth (% change)	23,000	28,000 +22%	36,000 +29%	52,000 +44%	99,000 +90%	173,000 +75%	251,000 +45%	319,000 +27%
Hammersmith and Fulham	18,000	23,000 +28%	30,000 +30%	40,000 +33%	66,000 +65%	115,000 +74%	189,000 +64%	250,000 +32%
Hounslow	22,000	25,000 +14%	27,000 +8%	32,000 +19%	41,000 +28%	55,000 +34%	68,000 +24%	85,000 +25%
Richmond-upon-Thames	22,000	25,000 +14%	28,000 +12%	34,000 +21%	48,000 +41%	61,000 +27%	77,000 +26%	95,000 +23%
Kingston-upon-Thames	8,000	10,000 +25%	12,000 +20%	18,000 +50%	27,000 +50%	36,000 +33%	45,000 +25%	56,000 +24%
Greater London	1,878,000	2,207,000 +18%	2,651,000 +20%	3,188,000 +20%	3,841,000 +20%	4,713,000 +23%	5,572,000 +18%	6,510,000 +17%

The physical changes wrought by the processes of urbanisation and industrialisation were associated with modernity, progress and vitality, but there was also a reaction against them. Lisa Tickner argues that the developing literature advocating outdoor pursuits from the 1870s was partly in response to 'the debilitating effects of "civilised" life on urban masculinity', as there was a growing appreciation for 'manly' exercises.[34] H.J. Walker suggests that a Victorian 'anti-urbanism' was propagated by authors like William Morris (*News from Nowhere*) and Robert Blatchford (*Merrie England*), who helped to popularise the idea that there was a rural utopia that people could 'return' to.[35] The search for quieter climes was certainly influential in motivating some people to take to the river. In 1891, F. Campbell Moller wrote that:

'Up the river' is a phrase most felicitously significant to the Londoner conversant with the charm and romance of boating life on the summer Thames. It means an almost idyllic phase of outdoor existence which, in manifold fascinations and picturesque surroundings, is indigenous to England and peculiar to this river. What fox hunting is to Britain boating is in its season to the Londoners – a pastime for the people of the metropolis.[36]

The higher reaches of the river were certainly more attractive than the tidal section, but boating could not become popular without the appropriate facilities being available. R.R. Bolland suggests that 'Boatyards were not slow to realize that potential customers in previously unheard of numbers were appearing on the banks of the Thames'.[37] David Blomfield's study of Thames watermen on the Upper Tidal Thames (from Teddington to Chiswick) provides an insight into how boat-letting may have first developed on the river. From 1828 watermen were required to license boats that were rented out to others and many of them operated one or two craft as small 'side-lines' (probably hired to anglers) intended to supplement their main income. As more visitors travelled to the Thames in the second half of the nineteenth century, many watermen embraced this change permanently by moving into boat-letting or boat-building, which, in turn, led to craft being designed specifically with leisure in mind (see chapter 2). There was an element of economic necessity to this transition, as the traditional waterborne carrier trades suffered from the construction of new bridges and roads, the arrival of steamboats from 1812 and the development of the railway from the 1830s. The ability to embrace the leisure market was also influenced by location and a number of boatmen were forced to move further upstream, as opportunities near London diminished. In 1828, 'most of the boat rental occurred just up river of London bridge' and only 10 per cent of the first 1,000 licences were granted to those situated on the Upper Tidal Thames. By 1860, the river had been transformed by leisure activities and the centre of gravity for boating had moved further upstream, with a third of the first 1,000 licences being granted to individuals located on the Upper Tidal Thames.[38]

Yet it was not just facilities for pleasure boating that developed on the river. Part of the appeal of the Thames was that it offered visitors a range of pastimes, which led to many organisations being formed, including canoeing, angling and sailing clubs. As Henry Wack commented in 1906:

> Facilities, whether for one day's outing or for ten, are more perfect on the Thames than anywhere else. In fact, pleasure upon this stream is conducted on the principle and in the manner of business. Alas, that so much of the business of the river should be conducted upon the principle of play.[39]

Blomfield argues that another important component in the rise of leisure on the Thames – in London, at least – was changing social attitudes to boating. Robert Chitty, a Richmond waterman (born in 1837), recalled that 'No one ever thought of rowing themselves in those days – there was always a waterman in them. For one thing their clothes were hardly suitable. Gentlemen wore top hats and kid gloves on the water, and girls were thought "fast" if they so much as touched an oar.'[40] Although Chitty conceded that watermen in those days also wore top hats – not to mention white trousers – Blomfield suggests that once it became 'à la mode for the client to take the oars or punt pole, the floodgates had opened'.[41] If this was the case, then it is likely that the sport of rowing, which is thought to have evolved from informal boating, may have helped to accelerate this process, as the accounts of many early oarsmen, such as the 'wet-bobs' of Eton College, suggest that training for contests and pleasure boating often went hand-in-hand.[42] Furthermore, the major rowing events drew large crowds to, and onto, the river (see pp. 30, 86, 107).

Chitty's remark about girls rowing is also pertinent, because 'one of the most important results of the late Victorian fashion for boating was the introduction of women to aquatics on a significant scale'.[43] They were one facet of the growing 'recreationalism' (boating for pleasure), which Wigglesworth suggests was 'merely one expression of the Victorian middle class desire to confirm social position through tasteful demonstrations of prosperity'.[44]

In terms of opening up the higher reaches of the Thames – especially to Londoners – it was the construction of the Great Western Railway (from the 1830s) that had the greatest impact. Hawthorne argues that by the 1880s the Thames Valley 'was rapidly becoming the summer resort of wealthy Londoners and, thanks to the Great Western

Railway, the day-trip playground of the growing middle-class'.[45] Similarly, Stewart-Beardsley argues that boating 'probably would not have reached the heights it did, were it not for the improved access afforded by the railways', although she points out that the relationship between the two has received little academic research.[46] Indeed, the railway played an important part in the development of a number of riverside resorts. The first section of the Great Western Railway to be completed ran from London to Maidenhead (1838), for example, and when the journalist R.D. Blumenfeld made this journey in June 1887 he estimated that there were at least 5,000 people dressed in boating attire waiting on the platforms at Paddington, which he was told was a scene that was repeated every Saturday and Sunday from eight until noon.[47] Likewise, on a normal summer Sunday in July 1888, there were almost 1,000 passengers travelling back to London from Henley-on-Thames on the last train *alone*.[48] As this suggests, the popularity of the river was dependent on the numerous attractions along its banks and the degree to which tourism was embraced varied from location to location, according to a range of factors, including the nature of the transport network and the activities of local politicians, landowners and entrepreneurs.[49]

The railway also helped to encourage leisure on the river by causing the carrying trade on the Thames to decline. By 1905 almost 90 per cent of the freight transported, in terms of tonnage, was consigned to the lowest section of the non-tidal river between Teddington and Staines (compared to only approximately 0.5 per cent above Reading).[50] The change not only paved the way for some commercial wharves to be reinvented for leisure use (see chapter 5), but also made pleasure boating faster, easier and more pleasant. Nevertheless, it was not until the second half of the twentieth century that the total quantity of freight being carried declined significantly (Table 3.3).

Table 3.3 Amount of freight carried on the Upper Thames (in tons)[51]

	Tons carried
1909	317,481
1913	397,938
1920	276,765
1930	372,808
1938	273,695
1944	606,580
1948	169,141
1956	235,992
1966	88,556
1973	10,923

Yet it was because the river was maintained for commercial traffic that it was especially well suited to leisure activities, as it was normally comparatively easy and safe to navigate (and, importantly, in both directions). In the short term, the competition from the railway caused the river's condition to deteriorate, but significant improvements were made once the jurisdiction over the waterway was transferred to the Thames Conservancy (1866), which was given greater power than its predecessor. By 1871, over £58,000 had been spent on enhancing the condition of the river (mainly on repairing and modernising the dilapidated locks and weirs),[52] which helped to improve and sustain navigation on the waterway. The Thames was also highly polluted in the middle of the nineteenth century – one guide describing the waterway in London as being 'the largest navigable sewer in the world'[53] – and the cleanliness of the river was slowly improved by the Conservancy, with help from other agencies.

The maintenance of the Thames was partly funded by the tolls collected at the locks. These charges, which were changed a number of times, played an important part in shaping the types of boating that developed on the waterway. It was a reduction of these in 1870, for example, that helped to encourage pleasure use on the upper river. Prior to that point the six locks from Teddington to Penton Hook had been free to pass through, whilst those on the higher reaches (from Bell Weir lock to Oxford) charged 6d per small craft. In a plan to raise more revenue, the Conservancy introduced a new reduced toll of 3d per craft on all of the locks, as a concession to allow it to start charging at the busiest locks, which were those that had previously been free to pass through. The initiative failed to produce additional revenue, however, because people tended to pay the lockkeepers between Teddington and Penton Hook as a 'rule of thumb' anyway,[54] but it did remove a significant financial disincentive to travel up the river.

As more people took to the water, there was also a discernible rise – from around the 1870s onwards – in the number of accounts about the Thames appearing in newspapers and periodicals, which undoubtedly helped the popularity of the river further. The difference a single publication could make is illustrated by Mr and Mrs S.C. Hall's *The Book of Thames* (1859), which was responsible for inspiring Henry Taunt to travel on the river. He then went on to produce his own range of guidebooks, as well as one of the largest photographic records of the waterway.[55] The literature inevitably helped to shape the popular perception of what travelling on the 'moving panorama' of the Thames was like. The river was seen as representing England itself (as did some of the places it ran past) and a trip on it offered the experience of an exploration into both the country's interior and its past.[56]

The Thames Valley also had considerable literary connections,[57] including its famous poets like Matthew Arnold and William Morris, but a reflection of the popularisation of the river was the number of paintings depicting the waterway. D.M. Hall's study of Goring Gap artists has shown that between 1875 and 1895 at least 300 paintings of local scenes were deemed good enough to be hung in academies, such as the Liverpool Society of Fine Arts and the Royal Academy.[58]

These changes all helped the Upper Thames to become a highly fashionable place to visit by the end of the nineteenth century, which, in turn, drew more people to the river. As one author put it in 1889, 'it is the boating throng which has made the Thames the rival of any water-way in the world and given it a character all of its own'.[59] Lisa Tickner argues that 'From the 1880s easy access to the river and hire-boats, backed up by instructional literature for those that wanted it, democratised "messing about in boats" as a leisure activity'.[60] In 1893, for example, the *Lock to Lock Times* featured a series on the different 'Up the river types' ranging from the Varsity oarsman and 'The

Canadian Canoeist', to the 'Young Lady Who Steers' and the working-class 'Arry ('to be found behind the counter in Oxford Street ... on every day except Saturdays').[61] The river was therefore like entering 'another world' where normal social distinctions were temporarily suspended as the 'rich and poor rubbed shoulders in the locks',[62] although this inevitably caused some cultural conflict, as it did in major seaside resorts in the 1870s and 1880s. The artist G.D. Leslie, for example, complained about the invasion of noisy and drunken visitors to the Goring area in the early 1880s. He suggested that 'Parties of bean-feasters out on the river for a holiday' were the worst culprits, whilst the 'country bumpkins' were 'nearly as bad'.[63] The widespread appeal of pleasure boating was partly because it was a relatively 'inexpensive amusement',[64] as those who wanted to spend longer than a day on the river could economise by camping, rather than staying in a hotel. Camping was a related activity that also became popular in the late Victorian period.

'The Thames Trip' and the Rise of Camping

In the first half of the nineteenth century there was a tradition of betting on the fastest time in which one could row between Oxford and London – the record being set in 1824 by six Guardsmen.[65] Yet it was not until the middle of the Victorian period that it became 'the "thing to do" ... to leisurely row a smart sculling skiff in easy stages to London'.[66] A key component in popularising the journey, known as 'the Thames trip', was the rise of camping as a leisure activity, which was further encouraged by the reputation of riverside hotels for being 'extortionate and crowded' by the end of the nineteenth century.[67] This can be illustrated by the twelve-day trip that Amy Gouldsmith and her brother made in 1874, which ended up costing them nearly ten times as much (around £22) as they had paid Salters' for the boat hire (£2 18s), largely because of their board and lodging.[68]

At the start of the Victorian period, 'camping out' was associated with foreign travel or the army, but by the 1870s the term was being used to describe a recreational pastime. Although it is noted briefly in D.G. Wilson's *The Victorian Thames*,[69] little attention has been given to the role that travelling on the Thames played in popularising the activity. Indeed, the majority of historians focus on land-based camping trips, of the sort which predominate today. H.J. Walker's study of the outdoor movement from 1900 to 1939, for example, traces its roots to the end of the nineteenth century, when it became an 'integral part' of the range of activities offered by organised youth groups. The Boys' Brigade, founded in 1883, was particularly influential, as it ran summer camps from 1886 onwards, which were initially in barns and halls, but were soon held under canvas. It was one of these, in 1907, that inspired Robert Baden-Powell to set up the Boy Scout movement along similar lines, which soon outgrew the Brigade.

A further development was the creation of the first holiday camp at the end of the nineteenth century. Joseph Cunningham, the superintendent of the Florence Working Lad's Institute in Toxteth, took groups on excursions in the early 1890s, which led to the rental of a permanent site on the Isle of Man. By the turn of the century there was enough demand for it to be open from May to October, and in 1909 the site boasted 2,000 visitors per year. Cunningham's enterprise, which was subsequently expanded and diversified by his descendants, was 'by far the largest single provider of camping holidays' between 1900 and 1939. It was also responsible for inspiring a number of similar ventures; amongst its visitors in the 1930s was Billy Butlin, who was looking for ideas to develop his own business empire.[70]

By contrast, Hazel Constance traces the history of camping back to the Cycle Touring Club, founded in 1878, which formed a group dedicated to the pastime in 1901: the Association of Cycle Campers. Her account is the most influential, because the Association developed into the Camping and Caravan Club, the largest organisation of its kind in the country today. The pioneer of the pastime is said to have been Thomas Hiram Holding (born in 1844), who drew his inspiration from a childhood trip across the American prairies in 1853. He was a tailor who developed a number of lightweight fabrics for tents that he used in camping trips around the country, some of which were undertaken by canoe. Yet it was a holiday to Ireland at the end of the nineteenth century that was supposedly crucial for helping popularise the activity, because it required him to produce a lightweight camping kit (weighing approximately 14lb) designed to be carried on a bicycle. In his subsequent book about the trip, published in 1898, he encouraged other enthusiasts to contact him, which led to the Association being established.[71]

Yet the activity was already popular well before the introduction of lightweight tents, and it was precisely because the equipment was initially so heavy that boats became the favoured way of transporting it. As one book from 1886 on the pastime explained, 'Camping out, as usually indulged in, means a boating trip on of our beautiful rivers; and by far the greatest favourite is of course the Thames.'[72] Another suggested that the latter was preferred because it was an ideal waterway for beginners, although there were also a 'comparatively small number' who preferred gypsy camping, which required a horse-drawn trap or caravan.[73]

It is likely that the sport of rowing may have helped to encourage the pastime too, because many events drew crowds to the river that could not all be accommodated in hotels. At the Walton-on-Thames regatta of 1872, for example, it was reported that on the Middlesex side of the river there was 'a strong *al fresco* contingent, who "roughed" it admirably well to the accompaniment of iced cup, *pâté de foie gras*, lobster salad, and other inseparable sundries of amateur camping out'.[74]

As the use of irony suggests, many of the early campers had the money (and time) to be able to do it in style. In 1878, *The Saturday Review* reported that the idea had lately arisen that 'Thames travelling is spiritless and incomplete unless what is known as "camping out" forms part of the programme', but that this often required equipment 'on a scale sufficiently elaborate for a protracted exploration of the Red River to the Congo'. It claimed that these 'psychological curiosities' (or 'amateurs of discomfort') were driven by a desire for independence and adventure, rather than economy, which meant that they could be considered the true descendants of Drake and Frobisher.[75] By contrast, Charles Dickens, the son of the author, believed that the craze of becoming an 'aquatic Beduin' (sic) was some kind of Darwinian reversion to primeval type, with those partaking in the activity wanting to return to the wild.[76] For 'R.W.S.' the appeal of the pastime lay in 'The picturesque and varying scenery about the river, combined with excellent sport both with gun and rod',[77] whilst Henry Taunt suggested that besides being '*cheap!*' (emphasis his) it was both the perfect antidote for the 'fast and energetic age' and good for producing robust health.[78] Indeed, George Wingrave, one of the *Three Men in a Boat*, recalled that they had opted for a camping craft, because 'it was a case of doing that or having no holiday. The important thing was that it cost practically nothing.'[79]

A number of sources point to the growing popularity of camping. Whilst there was no mention of the pastime in one of the earliest guidebooks to the river, Mr and Mrs S.C. Hall's *The Book of the Thames* (1859), the 1870 *Rowing Almanack* contained a feature on the trip between Oxford and Putney, because although it had 'become exceedingly popular' there was 'but little knowledge concerning the route and the halting-places on the banks'.[80]

By 1874, an 'old canoeist' from Windsor was reporting that the journey had become 'the "Grand Tour" of the fashionable boating world' and 'the favourite voyage of the Oxonian rowers in vacation, and of London oarsmen all through the summer season'. He recorded that 'The gigs, "company boats," dinghys [sic], and canoes which have ascended and descended the Thames this season nearly double those of last season, while the same was said last year of the increase over the preceding year'.[81]

Exponential growth is unlikely, but *The Pall Mall Gazette* wrote in 1877 that 'There are probably very few persons with any love of rowing who have not navigated at some time or other the wooded reaches of the Thames from Oxford to London'.[82] By the time John Salter wrote his first guide to the river (1881), he was able to say that 'The journey from Oxford to London by water has during the last few years been so widely patronised that at first sight any instructions on the subject may seem superfluous'.[83] Indeed, the Upper Thames was already the destination where large numbers of visitors had first taken part in camping for pleasure.

The activity became so popular that there were considerable tensions between the riparian land owners and those trying to use their land. In 1880 *Young England* reminded its readership that 'With many landed proprietors up the Thames, these up-river excursion parties are held in abhorrence' because of the damage they caused.[84] As this suggests, the large number of visitors harmed the very landscape they came to see, as was often the case at popular resorts.[85] By 1884 the situation was so bad that a House of Commons Select Committee was formed in order to address the preservation of the river. The owner of Bisham Abbey, E.V. Neale, explained that the problem was severe enough for some tenants to demand lower rents because they lived by the water:

> About 20 years ago boats had much increased, but it was only for ten years he had personally any cause of complaint. Latterly they had become very aggressive and inclined to do damage. They landed in his woods and did damage. There was a great deal of camping done there, and they burned his wood to make their fires. A great many of the visitors came from London and the lower parts of the river in boats and camped in different places. People in steam launches were of a better class, who landed to picnic, and litter, but did not do so much damage ... There were some eyots below Marlow belonging to Mr. Ellam, which were so infested by landing parties that the tenants said they must have their rents reduced.[86]

All kinds of groups were formed to try and protect their own interests (the Thames Anglers' Defence Association being one), and, after much debate, the Thames

Preservation Bill of 1885 was passed. This sought to control leisure on the river by defining more clearly the rights of both the river user and the landowner. Greater restrictions were placed on campers, which brought to an end the 'old days of camping at one's own sweet will on any private lawn'.[87] Furthermore, a list of designated campsites was reproduced in a number of publications (Table 3.4).

Table 3.4 Official campsites on the Upper Thames (1888)[88]

Sandford Lock island	Sutton Courtenay
Cleeve	Goring (by permission from the Swan Hotel)
Hart's wood	Mapledurham
Norcot Scours (by permit from Keel, the fisherman)	Caversham island
Sonning Lock island	Shiplake Lock island
Marsh Lock	Henley (on the aits)
Medmenham (at the Ferry Hotel)	Cookham Lock island
Walton Bridge	Sunbury Lock island

Despite the measures that were taken, the Thames had become so popular – not to mention commercialised – that some people suggested avoiding it altogether. This sentiment was summed up perfectly by *The Pall Mall Gazette* in 1886:

> For the last few years it has been gradually dawning upon us, however sad and unwilling we might be to believe it, that the Thames was not the place for a holiday. 'Arry camping in rows of tents on the lock islands, house-boats anchored against every available bank, launches destructive of peace and property rushing up and down – all these were bad enough; but the bitterest part of all was perhaps the knowledge that every respectable person on the banks of the river who did not want to make money out of you regarded you as a pest and a nuisance.[89]

It is perhaps unsurprising, therefore, that pleasure boating and camping on the Upper Thames appear to have subsequently gone into a period of stagnation and then decline.

Salters' and 'the Thames Trip'

Salters' played a vital role in popularising the long-distance trip by providing a service where a boat could be hired for a one-way journey to the capital with the cartage of the craft back to Oxford included in the rental cost. The firm was able to offer this because the Salter family already had another yard in Wandsworth (where the craft could be left free of charge), although the immediate inspiration may have come from Harry who undertook the journey in 1858. The service appealed to customers because it enabled them to take the easier downstream trip and more sights could be seen, as they did not have to retrace their journey, in order to return the hired craft. Furthermore, providing the cartage made financial sense for the firm, because it was already delivering racing vessels to many different boat clubs in the London area, and the vans (usually empty) had to return to Oxford.

By 1870, Salters' had developed some kind of formal agreement for storing craft with the boatyards of Messenger's at Teddington and Wheeler's at Richmond.[90] The firm's carts, however, were already regularly stopping at other businesses too, like Bond's (Maidenhead), Tagg's (Thames Ditton), Searle's (Stangate) and Simmons' (Putney).[91] Indeed, Joseph and Elizabeth Pennell discovered in 1891 that the storage fee of 2s 6d, paid to whoever looked after the boat, caused considerable competition between the respective yards: 'From every landing-place men cried out "Keep your boat, sir?" – for Salter has agents on the river whose business it is to take care of boats left by river travellers until his van calls to carry them back to Oxford.'[92]

In order to tap into a wider market, the firm utilised its extensive delivery network (see chapter 1) by extending the service to any waterway in the country by 1884,[93] and *any* place 'on English and Continental rivers' by 1888.[94] The family understood this clientele, as Edwin Course suggests that John Salter was amongst a small group in 1873 that travelled on a number of rivers and canals in the south of England in a week-long excursion that took them to, amongst other places, Leamington, Gloucester, Chepstow, Bristol and Reading.[95]

Writing in 1906, Henry Wack explained how the delivery and retrieval service worked:

A voyager of the Thames orders his canoe at Folly Bridge, Oxford, of Messrs. Salter Brothers, and arranges for it to meet him wherever he intends embarking. Vans haul craft anywhere along the stream, and call for those which are left by persons who have completed their cruise. In summer considerable traffic is carried on in this manner. People go to Oxford, or some other town up the river, row or paddle down twenty miles a day, leave their boat with the nearest waterman, notify Messrs. Salter by postal card and have no further responsibility in the matter.[96]

This service appears to have operated very efficiently: in the 1890s, one customer referred to Salters' as being 'usually prompt and infallible'. He said 'usually' because in this instance the boat did not show up – but he later realised that he had failed to post the request to the firm.[97]

Another reason why Salters' was significant in helping to popularise the trip is that it built up its rental fleet to an enormous size. As noted earlier, many boat-letters who rented out craft to rowing clubs moved into the leisure market, once they realised they could make more income this way.[98] Salters' continued to do both, as it had a large enough fleet to do so, although it slowly became more reliant on pleasure craft, partly because of the decline of its racing boat department (see chapter 1).

The number of craft the firm owned was constantly changing, because it kept 'a large selection of boats, both new and second hand … in readiness for sale *or* hire' (emphasis added).[99] Yet the early *Rowing Almanacks* (from 1861) provide exact figures for the size of the fleet, including racing boats, and these show that it nearly doubled in only four years from 203 boats in 1861 to 350 by 1865: an average increase of forty boats per year.

After this, it continued to expand – albeit at a slower rate – with the total reaching 483 by 1875.[100]

The overall fleet of Salters' probably peaked sometime around 1887, as this is when the firm sent a deputation to challenge the introduction of a proposed new Thames by-law that would have required all boat owners to provide a complete list of *all* of the craft they owned *every time* a new boat was registered. As the fleet was constantly changing in size, this proposed rule was, as John Salter explained, 'impossible, as they owned some 900 boats and only took stock once a year'.[101] This astonishing number was confirmed by his oldest son six years later, although the 'regular stock' had reduced to approximately 700 by this stage.[102] The higher figure would have represented around 7.5 per cent of all of the craft on the Upper Thames and one can see why in 1889 *Jackson's Oxford Journal* described Salters' as being 'gigantic' and ranking as 'one of the largest [boat companies] in the kingdom'.[103] The size can be put into context by the Maidenhead business of Harry Wilder, which Patricia Burstall argues was 'one of the largest of its kind on the Upper Thames, with over 200 boats' by 1910 – a time when Salters' still had over 600.[104]

The statistics, however, require a degree of qualification. Firstly, although the majority are likely to have been stationed in Oxford, some of them may have been elsewhere; we know that the firm was providing boats at least for Bond's of Maidenhead in the 1890s.[105] Furthermore, the rental fleet also contained a large number of racing craft (see chapter 1). One way of distinguishing between the types of boat is to identify which were outrigged, because this shows that they were designed for racing. This is not a perfect separation, however, because the speed of such craft ensured they were initially popular for pleasure boating, until they fell out of favour from around the mid-1870s, as they could easily get entangled in locks.[106] This partly explains why the skiff became more popular at this time, because it was more suited to a busy waterway (see chapter 2). By excluding the outrigged craft, one can see that Salters' had over 200 pleasure boats in its rental fleet by the late 1870s, with the absolute peak of over 400 being achieved sometime between 1887 and 1904. This was followed by a period of decline during

Boats in the fleet

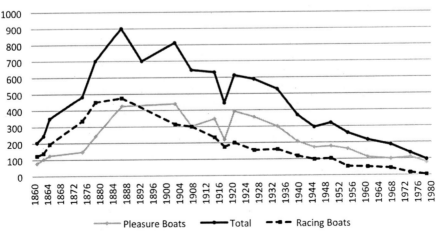

the twentieth century, although significant short-term increases were made to the fleet either side of the First World War, which was in keeping with the wider trends occurring on the river for rental craft at that time (see p. 78).

The size of the fleet meant that Salters' was able not only to supply and transport large numbers of craft for an event like the Henley Regatta, but also to offer customers a wide variety of options. One visitor in the early 1870s described the 'famed Salters' yard' as being 'a wonderful place packed all over with every imaginable kind of boat', although 'It required no little ingenuity in getting out of Salter's to avoid collisions with the countless boats moored round about. They seemed to be everywhere and all over the place, and how occupants and owners were ever found for them puzzled both of us.'[107]

By 1865, the firm was offering a list of standard rental boats with set prices, ranging from the very small, such as canoes, to more spacious craft, like four-oared gigs.[108] The former were the cheapest to hire (£1 10s) and, significantly, there was little change to the charges for over seventy years. By 1870, however, the firm had placed a time limit on the trip of one week, after which a further charge was made per day,[109] and by 1885 intermediate fares to Henley and Eton were introduced, after a local competitor had started to offer this option.[110] Yet, technically, any craft could be hired, including those that were much larger still. In 1887 *Time* reported that Salters' was one of the best places to rent houseboats from.[111] In the late 1880s Theodore Cook took one of the smallest of these, *Midge* (complete with a Canadian canoe slung on the roof), for a trip downstream to Fawley, near Henley. Cook and his two friends were on a budget, so instead of getting it towed (by horse or human)[112] or using the services of a 'competent waterman' (usually a young staff member), which Salter's offered at a 'reasonable charge' for any customers who did not want the trouble of propelling themselves,[113] they opted to negotiate the craft using only a tow rope and a punt pole, which posed a considerable challenge when it came to navigating some of the bridges.[114]

Unsurprisingly, however, most customers preferred to take smaller craft and many took advantage of the range of boats Salters' offered for those wanting a 'river tour without hotel bills'.[115] Broad gigs (typically 22ft by 3ft 9in), known in Oxford as 'Company boats', tended to be used in the 1870s. These had an awning that could be raised and a waterproof covering (attached by rings) that could be run along a line between the two masts.[116] The design appears to have been refined, as by the 1880s the shorter but wider (18ft by 4ft 6in) paired-oared pleasure skiffs had become the craft of choice. These had a ridge pole instead of a line between the masts and they provided a sleeping area of approximately 8ft 6in by 3ft.[117] By the end of the decade the masts had been replaced by three hoops, over which a green waterproof canvas could be stretched using 'a complicated arrangement of strings', enabling the craft to be 'an umbrella by day, [and] a whole hotel by night'.[118] *The Windsor Magazine* suggested that these were particularly associated with the firm, because it described such craft as being 'fitted *à la Salter*'.[119] Indeed, the firm's activities may partly explain why a number of camping pioneers, like Henry Taunt and A.A. MacDonell, came from Oxford.

Sleeping on board (the arrangement favoured by Taunt) was advantageous because suitable land to pitch a tent on did not have to be found, which not only was 'decidedly preferable in a wet season',[120] as it kept the occupants dry, but also reduced the chances of a confrontation (or charge) from riparian land owners. As *The Graphic* wrote in 1875:

Pair-oared pleasure skiff
(1880s).

> ...there is nothing cheaper or handier than a trip up the Thames, camping out,
> or better still, sleeping in, with a tent so arranged as to stretch over the boat. It is
> an existence even more independent than that of a gipsy, for if you are displeased
> with your night's resting place, you can haul up your anchors, and glide away to a
> more attractive spot.[121]

Additional comforts, each itemised on the rental card, could also be provided at a cost.
Joseph and Elizabeth Robins Pennell opted for a number of extras during their trip
in 1891:

> Salter's men at once began to load her with kitchen and bedroom furniture. They
> provided us with an ingenious stove with kettles and frying pans fitting into
> each other like the pieces of a Chinese puzzle, a lantern, cups and saucers and
> plates, knives and forks and spoons, a can of alcohol, and, for crowning comfort, a
> mattress large enough for a double bedstead.[122]

Another option was to camp *on* the riverside. MacDonell was strongly in favour of this
arrangement, as he recorded that 'Most of those who have once tried the boat-tent will
probably never use it again'. This was because the unscrewing of the thwarts to make
the sleeping area was troublesome, it did not provide much room and the enclosed
space resulted in 'a great stuffiness'.[123] There were a growing number of options for
those choosing this type of arrangement, as is shown by the variety of tents that could
be rented from the firm in the 1880s. As well as the likes of patrol tents and military
bell tents, there were even a number designed specifically with boating in mind.[124]
MacDonell described one that was intended for a canoe, for example, which measured
7ft by 5ft and weighed only 5lb.[125] As this suggests, there were lightweight options
available before Holding designed his cycle camping kit, and such innovations probably
helped to broaden the pastime's appeal, as it made carrying the equipment on land more
of a practical proposition. Although there were fewer sites that people could stop at
after the Thames Preservation Bill was passed (1885), MacDonell was still able to say that
the river offered 'excellent camping-grounds, about which information can always be

obtained by the lock-keepers' and that permission to use them was 'often granted free of charge', or else for the fee of half a crown (or 5s for a week).[126]

One can gain an idea of how popular the service provided by Salters' became from an entry in *A Pictorial History of the Thames* (1889), which recorded that 'several hundred boatloads of tourists annually' were putting out from Salters' boat-house 'on their voyage down-river'.[127] It was certainly well enough known for Jerome K. Jerome to note that it was 'common practice to get a boat at Oxford and row down' – although he personally considered this 'exercise' to be reserved for those who were either 'too constitutionally weak, or too constitutionally lazy … to relish up-stream work'.[128] In 1893, John Henry Salter claimed that the service was 'one of the most important features of the business', with between 800 and 900 boats doing the trip between Oxford and the capital in a fine season.[129] This would have meant that there was a constant stream of craft heading downstream, with new parties presumably starting the trip on most days during the boating season. This was certainly the experience of Joseph and Elizabeth Pennell in 1891. As it was pouring with rain, they chose to delay their departure from Folly Bridge, but were amazed to see that although the outlook 'looked hopeless', two or three other pleasure parties started out on their trips down river regardless.[130]

The season appears to have started relatively early, because 'Usually at Easter the boat yards were filled with luxuriously fitted skiffs, gay with carpets, cushions and canopies, with personal luggage neatly stowed in the sterns'.[131] Yet the trip was inevitably more popular during the hottest months, because in 1861 the firm recorded that its vans were travelling between Oxford and Wandsworth (a round trip that took four days)[132] twice a month and 'oftener [sic], during the summer'.[133] In 1881, G.D. Leslie noted that 'Salter's vans are in the season continually occupied in carrying back to Oxford the empty boats. These boat-vans pass my door at Remenham pretty nearly every day in July and August, with five or six boats to a load, and are the great delight of my children.'[134] They sometimes travelled in groups:

> At the height of the season, it was often an interesting sight to see a convoy of six horse-drawn boat vans laden with all sorts of river craft, from racing eights to canoes, on the roads between London and Oxford, slowly making their way back to Oxford, returning the boats after having done 'the Thames Trip'.[135]

The earliest financial data (from 1896 to 1898) do not list the profit produced by the different areas of the business, but they show that just under a third of the firm's income was coming from boat-hire, including localised journeys (Table 3.5). This was more revenue than was being generated by the sale of boats and fittings combined and it was a similar figure to that produced by the Oxford and Kingston service and the steam launches taken together. This shows that it was an important source of income for the firm. Yet although the *Lock to Lock Times* reported that large parties were departing on camping-out expeditions from Salters' almost every week at this time, which supposedly included 'thousands of Americans' annually,[136] the figure for 'down river' trips (presumably referring to the one-way journeys) was less than 9 per cent of the firm's overall total.

Table 3.5 Revenue from different parts of the business[137]

	1896	1897	1898
Boat-hire *(% of overall turnover)*	£2,937 0s 2d *22.6%*	£2,943 18s 9d *24.5%*	£3,085 2s 9d *24.3%*
Boat-hire (down river)	£1,041 5s 6d *8%*	£1,011 0s 1d *8.4%*	£827 6s 3d *6.5%*
Cartages	£191 0s 6d *1.5%*	£222 6s 0d *1.9%*	£176 19s 3d *1.3%*
Boats sold	£2,992 0s 0d *23%*	£1,685 10s 6d *14%*	£1,606 3s 3d *12.6%*
Fittings	£401 5s 7½d *3.1%*	£310 15s 3½d *2.6%*	£376 0s 4d *3.0%*
Oxford and Kingston steamers	£2,964 0s 6½d *22.8%*	£3,224 0s 1d *26.9%*	£3,168 5s 0d *25%*
Steam launches	£794 3s 0d *6.1%*	£749 0s 2d *6.2%*	£620 13s 0d *4.9%*
Other	*12.9%*	*15.5%*	*22.4%*
Total	£12,987 1s 4d	£12,001 14s 11d	£12,681 2s 4½d

Another indication of the success of the service is that it helped to shape the perception of the river. As the 1920 *Burrow's Guide to the River Thames* explained: 'For the average boating man "The Thames" is that part of the river between Folly Bridge, Oxford, and the Bridge in the Metropolitan Borough of Putney ... The Thames above Oxford is as unfamiliar as the Nile or the Amazon.'[138]

'The Thames trip', therefore, meant travelling between Oxford and London, which was further reinforced by many of the publications that only described this particular section, such as *Taunt's Map of the River from Oxford to London* (1872) and W. Senior's *The Thames: From Oxford to the Tower* (1891). Some guidebooks even expressly referred to 'Salter's Slope' (the piece of land on the island leading from the offices down to the river) or the firm's raft, as being a well-known landmark in its own right, because it represented the starting or finishing point for most of the longer journeys.[139] It seems, therefore, that Walter Jerrold's tripartite depiction of the river in 1904 did ring true: 'From the Nore to London it is the highway of commerce, from London to Oxford it is the stream of Pleasure, from Oxford to the Cotswolds it is the stream of quiet.'[140] This also shows that there were tourist 'break points' (places above which certain boats would not go), in much the same way as had existed for commercial freight on the Thames in the medieval period.[141]

There were a number of other reasons why the upstream section did not take off in the same manner as 'the Thames trip'. Firstly, by the mid-1860s, many of the locks above Oxford were in a bad state of repair and some weirs needed to be dismantled for craft to pass through, which meant that navigation was much less straightforward than on the lower sections. Secondly, even once improvements were made, there was still, as Ernest Ryan pointed out in 1938, a lingering perception that the Thames did not go through anywhere of significance once someone had passed the city.[142] William

Morris confirmed this in the 1860s when he described the river near Lechlade as being 'This little stream whose hamlets scarce have names. This far-off lonely mother of the Thames ...'[143] Furthermore, there was less to see, in terms of the immediate landscape, as the banks of the river were much higher than on the lower reaches, which restricted the view. Thirdly, the section was geographically further away (and not as easy to reach) from London. Lechlade was not linked to the railway until 1873, for example, and then only to the East Gloucestershire Railway rather than the Great Western. Fourthly, there was less to explore, as there was over a hundred miles of river below Oxford, but only approximately 30 miles above it (to Lechlade), after which only the very smallest craft, such as canoes, could navigate. Fifthly, Osney Bridge in Oxford was a barrier for tall craft and the situation became worse still in 1889, when a new iron bridge was built that was the lowest on the navigable Thames. Finally, a more prosaic reason was that the area immediately upstream of Folly Bridge was dominated by the city gas works (built in 1818 and expanded in both 1869 and 1892), and it was widely considered to be one of the ugliest parts of the Thames. It was singled out for particular criticism by a number of authors, such as W.H. Auden, who likened it to T.S. Eliot's *The Waste Land*,[144] and C. Fox Smith, who claimed it was 'one of the few sordid blots on the river's beauty', which required avoiding, if possible, or else covering 'as rapidly as may be'.[145]

Nevertheless, the beauty of the waterway was restored shortly after Osney Bridge and by the end of the Edwardian period Salters' was promoting the higher reaches of the river. This was a move to exploit more of the waterway, as well as catering for those wanting to travel the entire length of the navigable Thames, or those, like Paul Blake, who were drawn to it because of its supposed quietness and the difficulty of navigating it.[146]

Yet by this stage people were no longer travelling on the river in the same manner as they had been two decades earlier. Although there would be a resurgence in the activity during the war (see p. 96), the 1911 *Salters' Guide to the Thames* declared that 'Camping out from place to place has gone out of fashion, largely owing to the difficulty of securing suitable camping grounds'.[147] Nevertheless, the firm's reputation for promoting leisure on the river had been established, as was summed up by the *Lock to Lock Times* in its obituary for John Salter in 1890:

> ... to him is due a debt of gratitude for the steps he took towards bringing the beauties of the Upper Thames within the ken of a large section of the public, who, but for his efforts, would not have been able to enjoy one of the most delightful trips obtainable. It was undoubtedly Mr Salter's scheme of supplying boats for the voyage down stream at a modest cost that had *the greater influence than anything else in popularising the Thames*. The well-formed craft he provided and prompt manner in which he responded to the requirements of his customers, did much to revolutionise the art of tripping, and there must be hundreds of frequenters of our river who owe their first outing to his supervision. [Emphasis added.][148]

Different Types of 'Thames Trip' from 1911

A much clearer indication of both the type of boats that were being rented and the parts of the river that were most popular can be gained from the list of the advanced bookings made between 1911 and 1954. In 1911 the firm received 345 reservations, which was a much smaller number than the 800–900 boats travelling between Oxford and London in the 1890s (although it is not clear how many from the earlier figure were booked in advance). The document only lists the initials and surnames of most of the customers, but it seems to imply that the vast majority of customers ordering craft were male, as only thirteen of those booking craft (2.8 per cent of the overall total) had identifiably female names. The minority with titles show that Salters' was attracting a wide range of professionals and some from the nobility, as they included six reverends, four captains, four doctors, three majors, three lieutenants, a judge, a lady, a professor, a bishop and a baron.

Ninety-six of the bookings required the boat to be delivered outside of Oxford and 242 required its collection. Not all of these were one-way trips, however, as twenty-one boats were collected from the same places that they were delivered to, showing that the vessel did a return trip or was used locally.[149] Thirty-eight bookings were collected from a different location from where they were taken to, showing that they were a single one-way trip, although they show up on both the delivery and the retrieval list. If the figures are adjusted to take these into account, this means that there were 258 one-way trips, a total that represented about three-quarters of the overall bookings. Only eight of these did not involve the Thames at all, with excursions shown on the rivers Wye, Dee and Avon. Of the remaining 250 excursions on the river, around three-quarters (185 bookings) predictably started in Oxford, although there was also a sizeable number beginning at either Lechlade or Cricklade (thirty-nine or 15.6 per cent of the 250), showing that there was some demand for travelling on the upper part of the river.

The destination of around three-quarters of the boats was downstream of Oxford, with Windsor/Eton (13.6 per cent), Henley (11.6 per cent) and Goring/Streatley (6.4 per cent) being the most popular destinations, suggesting that people were taking advantage of the intermediate fares. The largest proportion of the trips (just under 20 per cent) ended between 60 and 70 miles from Oxford, whilst travelling to London had fallen out of fashion, as only 2 per cent of craft went beyond Richmond. Only seven of the thirty-seven boats that finished at Oxford travelled upstream, whilst a further ten came from locations on other waterways, including Newport Pagnell and Bedford.[150]

The document also shows a number of ways in which pleasure boating developed between 1911 and 1954. The first notable change was the resurgence of bookings for camping craft, which was partly owing to the popularity of the tent punt in the inter-war period. In 1911, almost two-thirds of the boats reserved were rowing craft and, although the skiff was the most popular type of boat, those that were open, like the Thames skiff and the sculling skiff, were in much greater demand (42.4 per cent of bookings) than those designed for camping (9.9 per cent). Canoes were the second most popular craft (17.3 per cent), followed by punts (11.6 per cent), gigs (11 per cent), tent skiffs (9.9 per cent, as noted above), tent punts (6.3 per cent) and dinghies (1.5 per cent).

Yet, during the First World War, the camping boats started to become fashionable once again, and by 1921, over half of the bookings were made for such craft. The tent punts were the most popular craft (31.7 per cent), followed by skiffs (22.4 per cent), tent skiffs (19.9 per cent), canoes (9.9 per cent), punts (8.2 per cent), gigs (6.2 per cent), dinghies (1.2 per cent) and tent canoes (0.6 per cent).[151]

By 1931, over half of all of the advanced bookings were made for tent punts (50.2 per cent) and this would remain the case until after the Second World War, when their popularity started to wane. Tent skiffs and canoes were the next most popular (both 13.7 per cent), followed by skiffs (11.6 per cent), punts (6.4 per cent), gigs (3 per cent) and dinghies (1.3 per cent).[152] By 1951, the tent skiffs (31.9 per cent) were almost as popular as the tent punts (36.7 per cent), which between them accounted for two-thirds of the boats that were rented in advance. Punts were the next most popular (12.6 per cent), followed by canoes (10.2 per cent), tent canoes (4.8 per cent), skiffs (1.9 per cent), gigs (1.1 per cent) and dinghies (0.8 per cent).[153]

The second notable change was that there was a surge in bookings during the Second World War. Between 1911 and 1939, typically between 220 and 320 craft were reserved in advance per year, although the numbers dropped below this range during the first half of the First World War. Yet from 1941 onwards the number of bookings rose sharply and between 1943 and 1945 the firm received nearly 600 parties per year – approximately double the peacetime average.[154]

This change was partly because of the southern and eastern coastal resorts being effectively closed for tourists from the summer of 1940 onwards. John Walton suggests that an 'important effect of this was a bottled-up longing for seaside pleasures', and although he notes that this caused large numbers to flock to those that remained open, such as Blackpool,[155] the Thames also became a popular tourist destination with agencies like Pathé News helping to promote it.[156] Indeed, the river became so busy that Salters' was used by local newspapers (alongside the likes of the Great Western Railway station) as a barometer for the levels of tourism in the city. After the August bank holiday of 1942, for example, the Oxford Mail reported that the Thames had been particularly heavy with pleasure boaters, including many families experiencing their first taste of 'camping on the river'. Salters' had a fleet of approximately fifty tent boats at this time, and a company spokesman confirmed that the number of people asking for them was well above average. The favoured direction was upstream towards Bablockhythe and Northmoor, however, which shows that people were travelling in the opposite direction to normal – that is, away from London, as one would expect.[157]

Another reason for the increase in river use was that, from July 1942 onwards, cars that might have otherwise been used for reaching other destinations were laid up owing to fuel sanctions. This put a greater strain on the public transport network, and despite the newspapers regularly encouraging people to refrain from using the trains during peak period, huge numbers still took holidays at the customary times. During the August bank holiday of 1942, for example, record crowds were reported to have travelled from Oxford, although this was accompanied by a 'particularly heavy' number of people arriving in the city too.[158]

There was also a growing 'Holidays at Home' movement, which included the involvement of the Oxford City Council, which established a special committee in 1942 to improve leisure facilities. Boating was one of the activities it specifically promoted, as thirty-seven paddle and rowing boats were bought for its recreation lakes (some of which may have come from Salters'), and these were so popular that it added a further thirteen from Littlehampton District Council.[159] The following year, the council organised a more extensive programme of entertainment that included regular concerts and a grand gala week over the August bank holiday, which was complemented by a Butlin's Amusement Park operating on the Botley Road Recreation Ground.[160]

Finally, another reason for the increased number of bookings was that it became popular to rent out a cabin cruiser with a smaller manually powered boat to accompany it. The first recorded instance of this was in 1941, when a 'tent single sculler' was shown as being hired out with the cabin cruiser *Wayfarer*. There were ninety-seven such bookings the following year and the number remained just over 100 each year until 1946, when the figure dropped back down to only four, which largely accounts for the reduction in overall bookings at this time. The reason two boats were hired at once was that the firm's eight cabin cruisers (ranging in size from two to six berths) were rendered immobile owing to the fuel restrictions. They were moored up between the Free Ferry and Iffley and let out as holiday houseboats, with the smaller boat provided so that customers were able to travel on the river.[161]

After the conflict, the firm experienced another short-term rise in bookings, which was largely owing to clients renting craft for longer periods, as a more economical way of using a boat without purchasing it. In 1948, these accounted for sixty-seven of the 497 bookings (13.5 per cent), which included thirty-two craft that went to Oxford colleges until Trinity term – a system that enabled the firm to receive them back for the busy summer period. The remaining thirty-five were let for the whole of the season, with twenty-nine going to pubs and rental businesses, mainly located upstream of the city, although nine of these (punts) went to C. Howard of Oxford, which operated on the river Cherwell near Magdalen Bridge. A further six went to organisations that wanted a single punt, like BBC Oxford and A.C. Nielsen's Sports Club.[162]

The third notable change in boating habits between 1911 and 1954 was the declining popularity of the one-way trip. In 1911, around three-quarters of the advanced rentals had been for such journeys, but this had fallen to just over a half by 1921 and just over a third by 1936. By the early 1950s they only accounted for approximately a quarter of the bookings.[163]

The main reason for this decline was probably the popularity of the firm's passenger boats, which became the most common way by which visitors travelled longer distances on the river (see chapter 4). Yet, as noted above, there was also a broader shift in boating habits away from the use of manually powered vessels towards motorised craft. The firm was part of this process, as it introduced cabin cruisers to its fleet in the 1920s, for example, which could be used for long-distance trips (see pp. 100–1).

Sir Arthur Salter, however, argued that it was another form of mechanised transportation that was responsible for impacting pleasure boating on the river: 'until the age of the motor-car, boating on the Thames was among the chief recreations of those of the professional and well-to-do upper middle-classes who were within reasonable distance of the river.'[164]

Sean O'Connell's study of the 'first era of mass motoring' (1918 to 1939), when the number of cars in the country increased from approximately 100,000 to just over 2,000,000 (or one for every five families), has shown that the new craze was blamed for taking people away from a multitude of regular destinations, from resort hotels to church services. Cars provided people with a greater freedom to be able to explore new destinations and one of the most notable developments was that the countryside was opened up to more visitors. Yet the majority of motorists continued to travel on the same well-beaten paths, as is shown by the rising traffic to and from popular destinations. O'Connell notes, however, that cars initially helped to encourage day-trips at the expense of week-long holidays, because the price of buying a vehicle was still high enough to mean that many families were required to cost-cut in other areas.[165] Furthermore, people would have had to return to their vehicles after an outing, which must have rendered a one-way trip on the river less appealing.

Another issue for river transportation was the growing 'culture of speed', owing to the rise of the motor car and the advertisement strategies of certain manufacturers that emphasised performance.[166] In 1930, the *Oxford Mail* ran an article that posed the question of whether the motor car was 'killing' boating on the Thames. Although opinion amongst local boat-letters was divided, one argument was that the river was being increasingly viewed as slow and old-fashioned.[167] The mechanisation of transport in general, including the arrival of the railway, certainly caused perceptions about travel times to change, as there are many examples of people being surprised at how long it took to travel by river. A Yale student, Minty Wright, for example, wanted to take a boat to London in 1948, but had second thoughts when he discovered it would take him two days to get there.[168] Yet whether boating was seen as old-fashioned is more difficult to establish, as part of the appeal of the Thames was that it remained relatively untarnished by modernity. Indeed, the firm made a point of emphasising this in its publicity during the 1920s, when it wrote:

> The motor car and char-a-banc have opened up the rural parts of England and their old world charm has in many cases been seriously interfered with. Not so with the river. It is still the same peaceful place that it has been for centuries and it is a relief to get away from the noisy traffic of a modern town ...[169]

Yet, on the other hand, it is clear that manually powered boats in general became less popular and slowly marginalised in the second half of the twentieth century. One commentator noted in 1951 that 'the innocent lover of hand-propelled craft' had become 'regarded as something of an oddity',[170] whilst in the 1960s the ex-lockkeeper David Blagrove described the (non-competitive) Thames oarsman as a 'dying breed'.[171]

After the Second World War, the firm made the decision to significantly reduce the publicity for the long-distance journey on manually powered craft. The 1948 edition of *Salters' Guide to the Thames* was the first for over fifty years not to mention the rowing boat as one of the three main ways of doing 'the Thames tour' (the others being the Oxford and Kingston steamers and the private launch). It is likely that economic considerations also played a part in this decision. By the 1930s, the firm was earning three to four times as much per year from launch hire, as it was from manually powered craft (although the former included income from renting out larger steam launches too).[172]

Furthermore, collecting boats from different locations became less financially viable because the decline in the number of one-way trips meant that the cartage service was required only on an increasingly irregular basis.

There were always some, as there remain today,[173] who preferred more traditional forms of propulsion for long-distance trips, but the firm finally disposed of its camping boats in the 1970s, owing to a lack of investment in both the craft and their fittings. They were replaced by a new generation of motorised cabin craft, which offered customers a greater level of comfort.

Self-Drive Motorised Rental Craft

Whilst Salters' played a significant role in popularising 'the Thames trip' on board manually powered craft, the same cannot be said for the use of self-drive motor boats. Yet according to *Thames* magazine, the firm was a pioneer in introducing such craft in the early 1920s – a date confirmed by Salters'.[174] Other yards, like Bushnell's of Wargrave,[175] were renting out self-drive craft at a similar time, but the Oxford business was certainly one of the first in its area to do so, as there were far fewer motorised boats on the higher reaches of the river. Indeed, the firm was only storing three privately owned motorised craft in the winter of 1919–20, although the number rose steadily thereafter.[176]

From the 1880s onwards, Salters' was renting out steamers 'by the day, week or for a specific trip',[177] but these would have required the expertise of an engineer to operate them safely. It was not until the invention of the internal combustion engine that self-drive craft began to proliferate. Nevertheless, the early models had a reputation for being unreliable and the first to appear in the firm's fleet (from at least 1902) appear to have been skippered by a staff member sitting in the stern away from the passengers. In 1903, Salters' had five launches, including two that were electric, and by 1915 the number had risen to seven.[178]

The first identifiably self-drive boat was the cabin cruiser *Ravensbourne* (1922), which was followed by *Pilgrim* (1923) and *Rover* (1925). These were probably introduced because of the growing demand for camping craft at this time, and between 1925 and 1927 each boat typically generated £90 of revenue per year.[179] In 1928, the *Illustrated London News* declared that 'Marine Caravanning' was a 'remarkably popular open-air pursuit' and it ran a regular feature on the pastime until 1931, although it largely focused on private craft used for offshore travel.[180] Yet the continued enlargement of the firm's fleet shows that the activity was becoming more popular on the Thames, because they numbered eight by 1939.

After the war, the firm joined the Thames Hire Cruiser Association, which was set up in 1955 to look after the interests of those in the trade. The organisation, which briefly had Hubert Salter as its chairman (1957),[181] sought to control the market by determining the pricing structure of all of its members and excluding outsiders from using its facilities. Furthermore, it regularly lobbied the Thames Conservancy or local councils over a range of issues, like the cost of operating and the need for better facilities. The list of its members shows that the majority of them were based downstream of Marlow, although there were non-members nearer to Oxford, as at Benson waterfront. The lack of competition does not appear to have translated into more bookings, however, because between 1957 and 1959 the firm's craft were being rented out an average of 22.8 times each per year, which was around the standard for members.[182]

The busiest period for the firm's cabin cruisers was in the 1970s when it operated under the Hoseasons banner, which involved providing boats from Reading and Oxford, as well as static holiday houseboats at the latter. The Suffolk firm heavily advertised its services, including using television, and this was initially a 'licence to print money' for Salters'.[183] The income enabled the firm to add a range of 50ft and 38ft canal boats to the fleet (run by a subsidiary company, Friston Narrowboats Ltd, from 1975), which were 'popular to hire and cheap to build'.[184] Yet Hoseasons did not benefit only Salters', as by 1976 it was also providing bookings for seventeen Thames firms which operated over 100 craft between them.[185]

The market collapsed spectacularly in the space of a single decade, however, when the number of holiday boats on the Thames fell from just over 800 in 1980 to just over 300 by 1990.[186] Salters' was forced to scale down its fleet of cabin cruisers during the 1980s and they were eventually disposed of in the early 1990s, owing to the running costs of operating them. They appear to have been a casualty of the development of affordable package tours to overseas destinations in the 1980s. The number of such holidays taken in the UK increased from 6.3 million in 1980 to 12.9 million by 1989, and the trend was one of further growth in the 1990s.[187] Yet not all locations were as badly affected as the Thames. On the Norfolk Broads the number of motor cruisers fell from 2,187 to 1,592 between 1980 and 1987 (although this was partly the result of some of them being reclassified as day launches), only for their numbers to recover to 1,955 by 1990.[188] This may have been because the area was considered to be a better place than the Thames for a boating holiday, as it was more remote and it offered a greater number and variety of waterways to explore.

As well as overnight craft, the firm also provided self-drive boats for shorter periods, typically by the hour. The first of these was introduced in 1927, but it was not until 1965 that their number was increased significantly with the addition of twelve small (15ft) slipper-launches, known as 'runabouts', to the fleet.[189] These were retained until 1975, when they were broken up and replaced by fibreglass models. By 1979 the firm owned five 13ft outboard runabouts and eighteen motor cruisers, which was the largest number of motorised craft it ever operated (as it also had ten canal boats). This still only constituted just over 20 per cent of the overall fleet, which was partly because manually powered craft were still favoured by customers for shorter trips and they were less troublesome to rent out, as they were not as prone to mechanical problems.[190]

The entire rental fleet was eventually disposed of in the early 1990s, as it was not generating enough money. Nevertheless, the demand for short-term localised boating in Oxford remained, and the firm subsequently re-entered the market in 2003. It began renting out small craft – punts, rowing boats and motor boats – from a platform opposite its head office (by 'The Head of the River' pub), but this time it did not offer any craft for overnight hire. At the end of the decade it then took over the other Folly Bridge rental business on the west side of the bridge, which had been run by Nigel Fisher.

Pleasure Boating in Oxford

Salters' may have helped to popularise 'the Thames trip', but its influence was inevitably greatest in Oxford. Indeed, it was the strong local market that was crucial in enabling the firm to expand its operations into other areas.

Pleasure boating was 'well-established' amongst students in the seventeenth century,[191] but it was not until the nineteenth century that it became hugely popular. One can gain an indication of the levels of river use in Oxford at the time when Salters' began operating, by a 'crisis meeting' that was called in November 1859 to discuss safety on the river. The gathering, held at the Radcliffe Library and chaired by Dr Acland, was prompted by a significant rise in the number of water-related deaths in the 1850s after nine fatalities had occurred in nine years (compared to six in the twenty-one years preceding it). G.V. Cox (1786–1875), the city coroner, suggested that the blame lay with the 'more dangerous kinds of boat lately introduced' (namely, canoes, whiffs and skiffs),[192] although the growing popularity of boating was clearly another cause, as 'he remembered when there were but few boats on the river'. He estimated that 250 boats a day were proceeding between Oxford and Sandford during the summer term and that the yearly total was in the region of 30,000.[193] This number presumably included the rowing crews that trained on this stretch of water, but this seems to be a suspiciously high figure, as fewer than 5,000 lock tickets were being sold annually at Iffley Lock in 1913.[194] Nevertheless, it does show that John and Stephen Salter started their business at a time when boating was becoming very popular in the city. Indeed, only a decade later, one commentator noted that:

> Most people who know Oxford know that of all the amusements of the place, boating is the most absorbing, and the most keenly pursued ... few understand why its influence so widely pervades Oxford life and its spirit enters so deeply into every Oxford man, whether he take part in it personally or not.[195]

The location of Salters' was also important, because Folly Bridge emerged as the centre for pleasure boating, as well as for competitive rowing, in the city during the nineteenth century. Its status may well have been briefly helped by the arrival of the railway, as the first station built in Oxford, in 1844, was just south of the river, which meant that everyone arriving by train had to cross the bridge in order to reach the city centre. The 'Boat House Tavern', situated on the island, was particularly popular,[196] and it was no coincidence that the building not only stored the city's resuscitation apparatus (as well as its drags and hooks for recovering bodies), but was also the venue for inquests into river-related deaths.[197] Salters' initially took over Isaac King's business, however, which was one of the 'humbler proprietors' that nevertheless owned a 'small kingdom' of punts and canoes.[198] Yet the firm soon accumulated most of the prominent sites around Folly Bridge (see chapter 5) and this included Hall's yard (and the 'Boat House Tavern') in 1870.

Salters' undoubtedly benefited from both its prime location and the growing popularity of pleasure boating, but it was the expansion and diversification of the fleet, as noted earlier, that enabled the firm to forge a position of dominance. It was operating over 400 pleasure boats in the latter part of the Victorian period, at a time when Oxford was 'the Mecca of all river tourists'.[199] One guide to the Thames (1889) stated that the city was the 'head of pleasure navigation,'[200] where more boating was practised 'than at any other place in the UK ... excepting ... the Metropolis',[201] and that Salters' landing stage was not only the busiest in Oxford, but was said to be '*the* busiest in the summer time on the Thames [emphasis added]'.[202] Indeed, the firm could offer visitors a whole flotilla of craft if they wished, as in 1904 when the British Medical Association was provided with fifty punts, fifty rowing boats and thirty Canadian canoes, as well as having two steamers put at its disposal to take members to Nuneham or Reading.[203]

Table 3.6 The most popular craft in the rental fleet (according to the number the firm owned)[204]

	1860s	1880s	1900s	1920s	1940s	1960s	1980s
1st	Gig	Skiff	Skiff	Punt	Punt	Skiff	Skiff
2nd	Skiff	Gig	Canoe	Canoe	Skiff	Punt	Motor boat
3rd	Punt	Canoe	Punt	Skiff	Canoe	Motor boat	
4th	Canoe	Punt	Gig	Gig	Motor boat	Canoe	
5th	Sailing boat		Motor boat	Motor boat			

The importance of diversifying the fleet is shown by the changing fashions in pleasure boating on the Thames in Oxford (Table 3.6). In the first half of the 1860s, for example, the firm owned twelve sailing boats, but by 1878 these had disappeared from the fleet. This seems to have been a testament to the growing dominance of rowing on the section of water between Folly Bridge and Iffley Lock, as well as a result of the proliferation of college barges – a process for which Salters' was partly responsible (see chapter 2) – which removed its mooring space.[205]

During the nineteenth century rowing craft were the most popular on the Thames and it was the gig, rather than the skiff, that was the favoured type of pleasure boat. Salters' had almost 200 of these in 1875, although, as noted, these would not all have been pleasure boats. By 1879, the firm had nearly eighty pleasure gigs and these were the first to be given individual names, like *Jane* and *Clara*. Their number then slowly diminished from forty-two in 1903 to nine in 1921. This seems to have been in keeping with the wider trends on the Thames, as in 1931 C. Fox Smith wrote that the once popular gig was 'now never heard of',[206] although Salters' retained four up until the Second World War (in addition to its racing gigs).

By the end of the Victorian period, the skiff was the firm's most popular pleasure boat. In 1920, *Burrow's Guide to the Thames* declared them to be 'no doubt the favourite craft among the majority of river users'.[207] W.B. Woodgate suggested that these became fashionable in the 1870s, because they were lighter than gigs, which made them more suitable for pleasure use.[208] The number of skiffs grew from thirty-two in 1861 to seventy by 1875 – the latter being slightly fewer than the number of gigs at the time. By 1903, however, they had reached a total of nearly 200, which was almost half of the entire pleasure boat fleet. The most numerous were the sculling skiffs (sixty in total), which measured 18 or 20ft long and were named after small animals, and the Thames skiffs (forty-five in total), which measured 22 to 25ft and were named after rivers. The firm also offered other sizes, ranging from the small skiff (16 or 18ft in length) to the four-oared pleasure skiff (32ft in length). There was a sharp reduction in the number of such craft during the Edwardian period, which was followed by a more gradual decline (with the exceptions of the two world wars, when there was a short-term downsizing of the fleet followed by a short-term recovery). In 1908, the firm owned approximately 100 and this had fallen to thirty-three by 1968. One reason for the initial decline, as noted earlier, was that the punt replaced the skiff as the favoured camping craft. By 1974 the 'elegant Thames double skiff' had 'effectively disappeared' from the river, except for the few in private ownership.[209] This was partly because of the introduction of fibreglass, as by 1975 Salters' had fifty-one skiffs (almost half of the fleet), but only ten were wooden Thames skiffs built in the 1920s and 1930s. By the end of the decade there were only twenty-eight skiffs in total and only five of the wooden craft remained.[210]

The second most popular craft, at least in the nineteenth century, was the canoe, which one guide to Oxford from 1811 suggested had previously been 'much used for pleasure' in the city, until the death of an undergraduate caused them to be banned by the university authorities.[211] It was the explorer John MacGregor (1825–92), who became 'the leading popularizer'[212] of modern canoe travel, owing to his accounts of international trips on board *Rob Roy*, which were best-sellers from 1866 onwards.[213] Salters' owned fifteen canoes in 1861, but this had risen to fifty-eight by 1875, which were single, double and Rob Roy craft. One estimate in 1893 suggested there were 'at least a thousand Canadian canoes on the Thames alone',[214] and in 1903 Salters' owned approximately 100. Although the number at the firm decreased sharply during the First World War, from seventy-six in 1915 to thirty-three by 1918, many more were added to the fleet after the conflict. By 1921 a peak of 115 was reached (virtually all of which were Canadian canoes), which was two years after the *Oxford Times* featured a trip made by one of Salters' employees, W.H. Gillams (and his brother), around the Midlands on board their canoe *Etukishuk*.[215] After the 1920s the canoe seems to have steadily declined in popularity, with the number reducing from sixty in 1934 to only thirteen by 1968. By 1974 canoeing in Oxford had become almost exclusively the preserve of the private club or individual, with an estimated forty owned by the Riverside Centre, sixty by the 22nd Oxford Sea Scouts and fifty by other organisations. In particular, the 'fine strip-carvel "Canadian canoe"', of which Salters' once owned over eighty (in 1903), had all but disappeared from the Thames.[216] This is supported by the firm's inventory books, which show that the company operated canoes until 1973, when the last four in stock were shown as 'write offs'.

It was not until the end of the Victorian period that the punt started to become fashionable on the Thames in Oxford. The firm had twenty in 1861 and this number had risen to thirty-one by 1875, but it is likely that the majority of these would not have been the modern type, as the earliest inventory book shows that of the thirty-four that Salters' owned in 1879, only half were 'light punts' (used for leisure), whilst the remaining seventeen consisted of eight rowing punts and nine used as ferries. By 1903, however, their number had almost tripled to just under 100, and by 1927 they were the most popular type of pleasure boat with 140 in the fleet – partly because many of them were being used for camping trips. One estimate is that there were around a thousand punts in Oxford during the Edwardian period, and 600 by 1936,[217] which would suggest that the firm owned between 10 and 20 per cent of the total.

The relatively late arrival of the craft appears to have been because in the middle of the nineteenth century punting was 'chiefly practiced [sic] on the Cherwell'.[218] During the summer term the river was said to be 'covered at intervals with punts' occupied by students, typically reclining on cushions reading a book, whilst smoking a pipe.[219] Yet although these craft were ideal for shallower waters, they were not as necessary on the larger Thames, nor as suitable on the section of river below Folly Bridge that was dominated by the rowing fraternity. R.T. Rivington suggests that the introduction of saloon punts to Oxford in the late 1880s helped to popularise punting (see chapter 2), as it made the craft a more sociable form of transport.[220] It was also comfortable for the occupants (one author described it as 'the paradise of the lazy oarsman'),[221] it had the advantage of the operator facing forward and it required a certain skill to operate. Furthermore, the boat managed to enter the popular mindset by becoming inextricably linked with Oxbridge life. Paul Deslandes suggests that many of the features associated with the university, like May balls, annual exams for degrees and the Oxford and Cambridge 'manner', only date from between 1850 and 1920, even though they are believed to be long-established traditions.[222] Although he does not mention punting, it is likely that the pastime may have been one of the 'invented traditions',[223] which became established as *the* type of pleasure boating done in Oxford, even on the Thames.

The number of punts declined sharply in the late 1950s, from seventy-three in 1955 (the most numerous craft) to thirty-two by 1961. This was a time when many Oxford rental firms were struggling, with the long-established businesses of Talboys and Harris, for example, both selling up. *Cherwell* reported that building them had become prohibitively expensive by that point, as in 1959 it featured an unnamed Salters' boatman who claimed that 'A punt costs six times more than in the thirties and a lot of firms have sold off'.[224] This problem was alleviated by the introduction of fibreglass punts in the 1970s, and although Salters' replaced the last of its (irreparable) wooden punts in 1976, other operators did not follow suit, probably because the new building material was not considered in keeping with the traditional image of the boat. A more significant problem on the Thames was the rise in the number of powered vessels, because punts could easily be swamped by the wash of these larger craft. This may explain why the pastime was more resilient on the quieter Cherwell, where motor boats could not travel. By the middle of the 1970s there were an estimated 200 punts in Oxford,[225] but Salters' only had eleven in 1975 and three by 1979.

The Oxford Waterways Actions Group suggested that one of the reasons why the rental companies were folding at this time was that maintaining the craft was becoming more expensive, as it required specialist expertise that was increasingly hard to find. This argument is supported by the data from Salters', as the number of skilled boat-builders it employed decreased after the Second World War (see chapter 6). Secondly, and linked to the first point, the group argued that boats were being damaged through carelessness and vandalism. There is no evidence to suggest that the firm's rental fleet was affected, although riverside properties were vulnerable, which is one of the reasons why Neptune and Hannington rowing clubs merged in 1968, in order to move into a more secure building.[226] Thirdly, it was claimed that the seasonal and weather-dependent nature of boat-letting meant that a constant cash flow was not ensured and that this resulted in higher rental costs. This would have been a usual part of operating, however, although, as noted, certain other costs were increasing at this time. Finally, the group argued that leisure tastes had changed and that boat-hire businesses had lost out to what they described as the demand for 'effortless entertainment and recreation'.[227] The falling popularity of manually powered craft on the river as a whole does support this, and it may also have been linked to the rise of pleasure boating for its own sake, rather than as a form of exercise bound up with the notion of 'rational recreation'. Furthermore, there is plenty of evidence to suggest that people from Oxford were spending less time boating.

What is striking about the diaries of those who used the river during the Victorian period is the length of the trips they took. Some only went on outings occasionally, like Rev. Charles Dodgson (better known as Lewis Carroll), who hired a craft from Folly Bridge 'at most four or five times a summer'[228] between 1856 and 1865, though his journeys tended to be long ones. His famous trip in 1862, during which he first told the stories to his passenger that would become *Alice in Wonderland* – which some authors believe was on a Salters' boat[229] – was upstream to Godstow. Yet his favoured destination was Nuneham, which would probably have taken over two hours to reach from Folly Bridge. Others went on the river much more often, like Alfred Gregory, who studied at Oxford from 1867 to 1872, was part of the 'reading set' who spent seven to eight hours a day in their books, and yet regularly had an afternoon 'constitutional' rowing up to Godstow.[230] John Ritson (1886–90) enjoyed trips on the river 'on most days', with his excursions taking him both upstream and downstream, as well as on the Evenlode and Cherwell.[231] Both had little involvement with the sporting side of university life, which suggests that the river provided a good opportunity for exercise.

Indeed, the popularity of boating amongst the students is reflected in the close attachment that many at the university had with Salters', which would have been added to by the firm's association with the sport of rowing. Algernon Stedman's guide to studying at Oxford (1878), for example, explained that those who boated were 'obliged' to allocate £3 3s of their estimated annual £219 8s budget to the firm. This appears to have been an integral and non-negotiable part of expenditure, as it was not amongst the items that he suggested could be cut for those wanting to exercise 'self-denial' whilst maintaining their 'gentlemanly appearance' (making £15 worth of savings).[232] In 1891, another author wrote that 'Salter's is an Oxford institution! Your undergraduate may get hopelessly "plucked" in classics or "ploughed" from mathematics, but just as dear old Perkyn Middlewick knew all about inferior "Dossit", so on this one point his knowledge is perfect, i.e. he can tell you about Salter's.'[233]

This connection still appears to have been strong three decades later. When John Salter was awarded his honorary degree in 1923 the city's public orator asked, 'For without our exercises on the river, what would become of this University? And without Mr Salter's activity how would the Thames profit us?'[234]

Although large numbers of craft continued to be hired out during major events, like eights week, the firm's close association with the university was slowly lost, as its racing boat department declined (see chapter 1) and boating habits changed. In 1927, W.E. Sherwood reported that 'Mr Salter will tell you that the old "pleasure boating" is dead ... In the old days it was crowded with boats whose occupants were reviewing the delights of a river once more untravailled by the exactions of coach or cox ... The old boating man is extinct in Oxford.'[235]

There was also a growing tension between sport and scholarship at the university during the twentieth century, because of rising academic standards from the Edwardian period onwards and a reaction against the public-school worship of organised games, exacerbated by student radicalism in the 1960s. There was less enthusiasm for sport amongst dons,[236] and Arthur Salter is an early example of an undergraduate who was dropped from his college rowing crew at the behest of one of his tutors, who did not want it affecting his studies.[237] The downsizing of the firm's rental fleet, however, suggests that even informal activities, like pleasure boating, declined in popularity. In 1959, the president of Trinity, A.L.P. Norrington, suggested that students were becoming less active, in general, as he complained about the decline of undergraduate sport and, in particular, the tendency of scholars to 'mooch in the afternoon instead of taking exercise'.[238]

• • •

Salters' became one of the most significant boat-letters in the Victorian era, not only in Oxford, but on the Thames. As Peter Chaplin suggests, 'Salter's really were pioneers of the holiday afloat game',[239] at a time when the river and a number of its resorts were becoming popular. By offering a retrieval service and by building up its fleet to become one of the largest in the country, the firm helped the one-way trip to London become the 'thing to do', which was linked to the rise of recreational camping. Indeed, the latter was well established before the Association of Cycle Campers was set up in 1901, which is thought to have popularised the pastime. Boating habits changed considerably over time, however, and the long-distance journey by manually powered craft had fallen out of favour by the second half of the twentieth century. Salters' introduced new types of craft to cope with the changing demand, but its rental fleet declined in size until the boat-letting side of the business was stopped altogether – albeit temporarily – in the 1990s. One of the main reasons for the decline was the popularity of the firm's passenger boats. Indeed, the Oxford to Kingston service was marketed as a new way of doing 'the Thames trip' and it made a significant impact on the river and the surrounding area.

Notes

1   F. S. Thacker, *The Stripling Thames* (London, 1909), p. 18.
2   R.R. Bolland, *Victorians on the Thames* (Tunbridge Wells, 1994), p. 14.
3   Burstall, *Golden Age of the Thames*, p. 7.
4   *Lock to Lock Times*, 25 August 1888, p. 16, in Tickner, 'Messing About in Boats', p. 21.
5   *The Century*, vol. 37 (London, 1889), p. 237, in Tickner, 'Messing About in Boats', p. 6.

6   Bolland, *Victorians on the Thames*, p. 17.

7   P. Ackroyd, *Thames: Sacred River* (London, 2007), p. 252.

8   Burstall, *Golden Age of the Thames*, p. 7.

9   P.A.L. Vine, *London's Lost Route to the Sea* (London, 1965), p. 210.

10 A. Farrant, *Rowing Holiday by Canal in 1873* (Blandford, 1977), p. 4 (foreword).

11 H.S. Davies, 'The Thames Navigation Commission 1771–1867' (Reading University MA thesis, 1967), p. 229.

12 *Jackson's Oxford Journal*, 2 March 1853, in Prior, *Fisher Row*, p. 292.

13 Davies, 'Thames Navigation Commission', pp. 159–61.

14 Berkshire Record Office (BRO) Thames Navigation, Bills Paid 1838–85: Tolls Received 1858–62, reference: D/EX 1457/1/43.

15 Stewart-Beardsley, 'After the Railway', p. 112. The toll charges were the same in 1879 as they were in 1887.

16 Museum of London Docklands (MLD) and RRM Thames Conservancy Annual Reports 1887–1939.

17 BRO Letter from J.H. Salter to the Conservators of the River Thames, 5 March 1910, in Thames Conservancy Minute Book 1909–11, reference: D/TC 190 and *The Times*, 4 February 1920, p. 24.

18 MLD and River and Rowing Museum (RRM) Thames Conservancy Annual Reports 1887–1939 and Thames Conservancy, *The Thames Conservancy 1857–1957* (London, 1957), pp. 77–78.

19 BRO Pleasure Boat Returns 1913–65, reference: D/TC 336/1-18.

20 BRO Classification of Tickets and Tolls received at the Different Locks 1913–38, reference: D/TC 336/1-18.

21 J.K. Jerome, *Three Men in a Boat* (London, 1889), p. 95.

22 J. and E.R. Pennell, *The Stream of Pleasure: A Month on the Thames* (London, 1891), p. 125.

23 Tickner, 'Messing About in Boats', p. 1.

24 *The Times*, 23 June 1912.

25 *Lock to Lock Times*, 11 August 1888, p. 6, in Tickner, 'Messing About in Boats', p. 7.

26 E. Jones, *Free Associations: Memories of a Psychoanalyst* (New York, 1990), p. 67.

27 *Lock to Lock Times*, 13 May 1893, pp. 1–2, in Tickner, 'Messing About in Boats', p. 10.

28 Burstall, *Golden Age of the Thames*, p. 9.

29 BRO Classification of Tickets and Tolls received at the Different Locks 1913–38, reference: D/TC 336/1-18.

30 Ibid.

31 *The Law Reports: The Public General Statutes Passed in the Forty-Eighth and Forty-Ninth Years of the Reign of Her Majesty Queen Victoria 1884–5*, vol. 21 (London, 1885), p. 393.

32 *The Century*, vol. 37 (London, 1889), p. 237, in Tickner, 'Messing About in Boats', p. 6.

33 C.R. Morrey, 'The Changing Populations of the London Boroughs', in Greater London Council, *Research Memorandum 413*, 2nd edn (London, 1978), pp. 15–16.

34 Tickner, 'Messing About in Boats', p. 7.

35 H.J. Walker, 'The Outdoor Movement in England and Wales, 1900–1939' (Sussex University DPhil thesis, 1987), pp. 8–14.

36 F. Campbell Moller, 'Boating Life on the Upper Thames', in *Outing*, vol. 18, no. 4 (1891), p. 279.

37 Bolland, *Victorians on the Thames*, p. 13.

38 Blomfield, 'Tradesmen of the Thames', pp. 3–129.

39 H.W. Wack, *In Thamesland* (London, 1906), p. 11.

40 Blomfield, 'Tradesmen of the Thames', p. 92.

41 Ibid.

42 A. Campbell, *Memories of Eton Sixty Years Ago* (London, 1917), pp. 126–31.

43 Wigglesworth, *History of Rowing*, p. 107.

44 Ibid., p. 113.

45 Hawthorne, *Electric Boats*, p. 5.

46 Stewart-Beardsley, 'After the Railway', p. 120.

47 R.D. Blumenfeld, *R.D.B.'s Diary* (London, 1930), p. 13.

48 Horn, *Pleasures and Pastimes*, p. 2.

49 See Stewart-Beardsley, 'After the Railway', G. Clark, *Down by the River: The Thames and Kennet in Reading* (Reading, 2009) and S. Townley, *Henley-on-Thames: Town, Trade and River* (London, 2009).

50 RRM Thames Conservancy Duplicate Minute Book 1905, in Stewart-Beardsley, 'After the Railway', p. 113.

51 RRM General Report of the Proceedings of the Conservators of the River Thames during the Year Ending 31 December 1973, p. 33.

52 Thames Conservancy, *The Thames Conservancy 1857–1957* (London, 1957), p. 9.

53 T.L. Wood, *The Oarsman's Guide to the Thames and Other Rivers* (London, 1857), p. 101.

54 *The Pall Mall Gazette*, 24 October 1872.

55 S. Reid, *The Thames of Henry Taunt* (Gloucester, 1989), p. 7.

56 Byerly, *Are We There Yet?*, pp. 83–141.

57 G.S. Maxwell, *The Author's Thames* (London, 1924), p. 1.

58 D.M. Hall, *Art and Artists of the Goring Gap* (Goring-on-Thames, 2006), in Stewart-Beardsley, 'After the Railway', p. 127.

59 Pennell, 'The Stream of Pleasure', p. 483.

60 Tickner, 'Messing About in Boats', p. 7.

61 *Lock to Lock Times*, 17 June 1893 in Tickner, 'Messing About in Boats', p. 14.

62 Hawthorne, *Electric Boats*, p. 5.

63 G.D. Leslie, *Our River* (London, 1881), p. 123. 'Bean-feasters' were those who attended an annual outing provided by a company for its employees, where typically beans and bacon were eaten.

64 Pennell, *Stream of Pleasure*, p. 142. For a comparison of the costs of different leisure activities, see J. Lowerson, *Sport and the English Middle-Classes 1870–1914* (Manchester, 1993), pp. 2–14.

65 *Jackson's Oxford Journal*, 15 May 1824. The time was fifteen hours and twenty-five minutes, which was not beaten until 1971.

66 H.G. Salter, 'History of Salter Bros' (*c.* 1958).

67 Pennell, *Stream of Pleasure*, p. 6.

68 Diary of Amy Gouldsmith, 9–20 August 1875 (unpublished, sent to author by Susan Pike, Amy Gouldsmith's great-granddaughter).

69 D.G. Wilson, *The Victorian Thames* (Stroud, 1997), pp. xii–xv.

70 Walker, 'The Outdoor Movement', p. 265.

71 H. Constance, *First in the Field: A Century of the Camping and Caravanning Club* (Coventry, 2001), pp. 13–165.

72 Gyp, *Camping Out or Holidays under Canvas* (Newbury, 1886).

73 A.A. MacDonell, *Camping Out* (London, 1890), pp. 10–11.

74 *Bell's Life*, 13 July 1872.

75 *The Saturday Review*, 14 September 1878, pp. 339–40.

76 *All The Year Round*, 15 September 1877, pp. 131–33.

77 Taunt, *New Map of the Thames*, p. 22.

78 Ibid., p. 30.

79 *Oxford Mail*, 25 June 1933, p. 4.

80 *Rowing Almanack 1870*, p. 102.

81 *The Dundee Courier and Argus*, 17 September 1874.

82 *The Pall Mall Gazette*, 15 August 1877.

83   Salter, *The River Thames: From Its Source*, p. 65.

84   *Young England: Kind Words for Boys and Girls*, 10 April 1880.

85   See R.W. Butler, 'The Concept of a Tourist Area Cycle of Evolution: Implications for Management of Resources', *Canadian Geographer*, vol. 24, no. 1 (1982), pp. 5–12.

86   *The Standard*, 10 June 1884.

87   Pennell, *Stream of Pleasure*, p. 145.

88   *Young Folks Paper: Literary Olympic and Tournament*, 28 July 1888.

89   *The Pall Mall Gazette*, 1 October 1886.

90   *Rowing Almanack 1870*, p. 102.

91   SA Carmans Boat Works.

92   Pennell, *Stream of Pleasure*, p. 136.

93   Salter, *Guide to the River Thames* (1884), advertisement.

94   SA Advertisement, 1888.

95   Farrant, *Rowing Holiday*, p. 4.

96   Wack, *In Thamesland*, p. 11.

97   J. Ashby-Sterry, *A Tale of the Thames* (London, 1896), p. 105.

98   Wigglesworth, *History of Rowing*, p. 53.

99   SA Advertisement, 1888.

100   SA Agreement Dissolving the Partnership between John and Stephen Salter, 21 June 1875.

101   *Jackson's Oxford Journal*, 21 May 1887.

102   *Lock to Lock Times*, 5 August 1893, p. 2.

103   *Jackson's Oxford Journal*, 25 January 1890.

104   Burstall, *Golden Age of the Thames*, p. 139.

105   MLD Thames Conservancy Minute Book 8, 26 September 1892, p. 508.

106   Woodgate, *Boating*, pp. 143–44.

107   M. Black, *Our Canoe Voyage* (Manchester, 1876), pp. 298, 356.

108   *Rowing Almanack 1865*, advertisement.

109   *Rowing Almanack 1870*, p. 102.

110   *Rowing Almanack 1885*, advertisement.

111   *Time*, October 1887, p. 405.

112   For a discussion on the decline of towing, see Bolland, *Victorians on the Thames*, p. 116.

113   See C. Eddy, *Voyaging Down the Thames* (New York, 1938), p. 118.

114   T. Cook, *The Sunlit Hours* (London, 1925), pp. 34–35.

115   *Oxford University Summer Eights' 'Blue' Race Chart*, 1923.

116   Taunt, *New Map of the Thames*, pp. 22–23.

117   Salter, *The River Thames: From Its Source*, pp. 68–69. A 25ft randan pleasure skiff used for larger parties.

118   Pennell, *Stream of Pleasure*, p. 6.

119   *The Windsor Magazine*, January 1895, p. 462.

120   Salter, *River Thames*, p. 68.

121   *The Graphic*, 2 October 1875.

122   Pennell, *Stream of Pleasure*, p. 9.

123   MacDonell, *Camping Out*, p. 47.

124   A.S. Krausse, *A Pictorial History of the Thames* (London, 1889), p. 215. A tent with ground sheets was 12s 6d for a week.

125   MacDonell, *Camping Out*, pp. 49–57.

126   Ibid., pp. 10–11.

127   Krausse, *Pictorial History of the Thames*, p. 38.

128   Jerome, *Three Men in a Boat*, p. 299.

129   *Lock to Lock Times*, 5 August 1893, p. 2.

130 Pennell, *Stream of Pleasure*, p. 5.

131 H.G. Salter, 'History of Salter Bros' (*c.* 1958).

132 *Oxford Times*, 6 March 1931, p. 24.

133 *Rowing Almanack 1861*, advertisement.

134 Leslie, *Our River*, p. 245. Vans were four-wheeled carriages, whilst the firm also used two-wheeled carts.

135 H.G. Salter, 'History of Salter Bros' (*c.* 1958).

136 *Lock to Lock Times*, 27 August 1898, p. 25.

137 SA Finance Book 1896–1900. This excludes outstanding debts on the respective accounts, as it is not clear when these related to.

138 E.J. Burrow, *Burrow's Guide to the River Thames* (London, 1920), p. 31.

139 Thacker, *Stripling Thames*, p. 18.

140 W. Jerrold, *The Silvery Thames*, (London, 1906) p. 1.

141 J. Langdon, 'The Efficiency of Inland Water Transport in Medieval England', in J. Blair (ed.), *Waterways and Canal-Building in Medieval England* (Oxford, 2007), p. 120.

142 E. Ryan, *The Thames from the Towpath* (London, 1938), p. 193.

143 W. Morris, *The Earthly Paradise: A Poem* (London, 1867), p. 454.

144 M. Prichard and H. Carpenter, *A Thames Companion*, 2nd edn (Oxford, 1981), p. 56.

145 C. Fox Smith, *The Thames* (London, 1931), p. 153.

146 *The Boy's Own Paper*, 21 April 1883.

147 Salter, *Salter's Guide to the Thames* (1911), p. 242.

148 *Lock to Lock Times*, 25 January 1890, p. 50.

149 Later examples of this include supplying craft for the boating lake at Blenheim Palace (for use during different events).

150 SA Hire Fleet Bookings 1911–36.

151 Ibid.

152 SA Hire Fleet Bookings 1911–36.

153 SA Hire Fleet Bookings 1937–87.

154 SA Hire Fleet Bookings 1911–36 and 1937–87.

155 Walton, *The British Seaside*, p. 86.

156 See 'River Folk (1943)' on the Pathé News website: http://www.britishpathe.com/video/river-folk (accessed 16 November 2011).

157 *Oxford Mail*, 3 August 1942, p. 1.

158 *Oxford Times*, 7 August 1942, p. 5.

159 *Oxford Mail*, 2 July 1942, p. 4.

160 *Oxford Times*, 9 July 1943, p. 7.

161 *Oxford Mail*, 3 August 1942, p. 1.

162 SA Hire Fleet Bookings 1911–36 and 1937–87.

163 Ibid.

164 Salter, *Memoirs of a Public Servant*, p. 16.

165 S. O'Connell, *The Car in British Society: Class, Gender and Motoring, 1899–1939* (Manchester, 1998), pp. 86–179.

166 K. Möser, 'The Dark Side of Automobilism, 1900–1930', *Journal of Transport History*, vol. 24, no. 2, p. 242.

167 *Oxford Mail*, 6 May 1930, p. 5.

168 O. A. Pease, 'Splendid Summer: Yale Students in Oxford and Britain 1948' (unpublished).

169 Salter Bros, *Down the River from Oxford to Nuneham and Abingdon* (Oxford, 1923), p. 19.

170 *Thames*, April–June 1951, p. 67.

171 D. Blagrove, *The Quiet Waters By* (Kidderminster, 1998), p. 50.

172 SA Salter Bros Ltd End of Year Accounts 1936–49.

173 One of the more recent accounts is Mark Wallingham's *Boogie Up the River* (Oxford, 1988).

174   *Thames,* July 1949, vol. 1, p. 17.

175   See www.bushnells.co.uk/index.php/about-bushnells-marine-services (accessed 2 November 2012).

176   SA Winter Storage Book 1919/20–1948/49.

177   *Rowing Almanack 1885,* p. 2.

178   SA Inventory Book 1903 and 1915.

179   SA Private Party Boats List 1925–27. The other motor boats were *Vioelle, Swiftsure* and *Dabchick.*

180   *Illustrated London News,* 29 September 1928 (and subsequent editions).

181   SA Minute Book of the Thames Hire Cruiser Association 1956–64, April 1957, p. 5a. He served for just over four months before resigning.

182   Ibid., 30 October 1959, p. 35a.

183   Interview with John Salter, 20 December 2011.

184   Ibid. These were Salters'-built, although the firm only fitted out the craft, having bought the hulls from another firm.

185   SA *Come Boating with Hoseseasons on the Beautiful River Thames* (1976).

186   River Thames Alliance, *Thames Waterway Plan 2006–2011* (2005), pp. 56–62.

187   W. Barnes and R. Smith, 'Travel Trends' (Office for National Statistics, 2010), p. 19.

188   M. George, *The Land Use, Ecology and Conservation of Broadland* (Chichester, 1992), pp. 370–71.

189   These were all named after birds.

190   SA Inventory Book 1979.

191   N. Selwyn, 'Social and Cultural Activities', in Crossley, *The Victoria History of the County of Oxford,* vol. 4, p. 428.

192   G. V. Cox, *Recollections of Oxford* (London, 1868), p. 428.

193   *Oxford University Herald,* 26 November 1859, pp. 10–11.

194   BRO Pleasure Boat Returns 1913, reference: D/TC 336/1-18.

195   Anon., *Boating Life at Oxford* (London, 1868), pp. 1–2.

196   Sherwood, *Oxford Rowing,* p. 4.

197   *Jackson's Oxford Journal,* 28 August 1820, 27 January 1827, 25 April 1835, 3 February 1849.

198   Cook, *Eliza Cook's Journal,* pp. 263–64.

199   Pennell, 'Stream of Pleasure', p. 483.

200   Krausse, *Pictorial History of the Thames,* p. 39.

201   Ibid., p. 62.

202   *A New History of the Thames VI,* in *Lock to Lock Times,* 27 October 1888, p. 5.

203   *British Medical Journal,* 9 July 1904.

204   Data from *Rowing Almanacks* and the firm's inventory books.

205   Sherwood, *Oxford Rowing,* p. 89.

206   Fox Smith, *The Thames,* p. 7.

207   Burrow, *Burrow's Guide to the Thames,* p. 7.

208   Woodgate, *Boating,* pp. 143–44. This is because they had tapered gunwales, which provided the leverage without too much extra weight.

209   Oxford Waterways Action Group, *Oxford Waterways* (Oxford, 1974), p. 34.

210   SA Order Book 1965–79.

211   *The Young Travellers or a Visit to Oxford* (London, 1811), p. 50.

212   J. Benidickson, *Idleness, Water, and a Canoe: Reflections of Paddling for Pleasure* (Toronto, 1997), p. viii.

213   E. Hodder, *John MacGregor ('Rob Roy')* (London, 1895), pp. 207–13.

214   Benidickson, *Idleness, Water and a Canoe,* p. 115.

215   *Oxford Times,* 7 November 1919, p. 5.

216   Oxford Waterways Action Group, *Oxford Waterways,* p. 34.

217   Ibid., p. 36.

218   *The Leisure Hour*, vol. 10 (1861), p. 767.

219   *Belgravia*, vol. 2 (March–June 1867), pp. 477–78.

220   Rivington, *Punting*, p. 34.

221   G. Rixon, *Rowing and Sculling* (London, 1904), p. 58.

222   Deslandes, *Oxbridge Men*, p. 7.

223   See E. Hobsbawn and T. Ranger (eds), *The Invention of Tradition* (Cambridge, 1983), p. 4.

224   *Cherwell* (undated) in Rivington, *Punting*, pp. 145–46.

225   Oxford Waterways Action Group, *Oxford Waterways*, p. 36.

226   Wigglesworth, *History of Rowing*, p. 225.

227   Oxford Waterways Action Group, *Oxford Waterways*, p. 36.

228   C. Hargreaves 'Alice's Recollections of Carrollian Days', in *Cornhill Magazine*, no. 433 (July 1932), p. 7.

229   J.E. Jones and J.F. Gladstone, *The Alice Companion* (London, 1998), pp. 260–61 and Davies, *Alice in Waterland*, p. 39. His diaries (E. Wakeling, *Lewis Carroll's Diaries*, vols 3 and 4 (Luton, 1995)), however, do not state where he hired the boat from, although Salters' was one of two large boat-letters based at Folly Bridge at the time.

230   B. Gregory, *Consecrated Culture: Memorials of B.A. Gregory, MA* (London, 1885), pp. 86–91.

231   J.H. Ritson, *The World is Our Parish* (London, 1939), p. 19.

232   A.M.M. Stedman, *Oxford: Its Social and Intellectual Life* (London, 1878), pp. 42–47.

233   W.F.F., *The Thames Trip* (Oxford, 1891). Perkyn Middlewick was a character in the well-known play *Our Boys* by Henry James Byron.

234   *Oxford Chronicle*, 25 May 1923, p. 13.

235   W.E. Sherwood, *Oxford Yesterday: Memoirs of Oxford 70 Years Ago* (Oxford, 1927), p. 24.

236   D. J. Wendan, 'Sport', in B. Harrison (ed.), *The History of the University of Oxford: The Twentieth Century*, vol. 8 (Oxford, 1995), pp. 519–20.

237   Salter, *Memoirs of a Public Servant*, p. 31.

238   *Oxford Magazine*, 29 January 1959, p. 206, in Wendan, 'Sport', p. 520.

239   P. Chaplin, *The Thames from Source to Tideway* (Hong Kong, 1982), p. 144.

4

Thames Passenger Services

… for really seeing the Thames valley and absolutely appreciating the beauties of its scenery, there is nothing like one of Salter's Steamers.

Colonel Torneywayne in *A Tale of the Thames*, 1896[1]

There has been little academic research on Thames passenger boat operators. John Armstrong and David Williams argue that steamboats played a pioneering role in the development of popular tourism in the first quarter of the nineteenth century, although they 'merely served coastal areas and in that sense could never provide a nation-wide stimulus'.[2] Their study of the earliest services from London to Margate and Gravesend, the first of which began in 1812, shows that the trips evolved in three stages. Initially, the time taken for the journey and the cost of travelling restricted the use of the steamboats to those from the middle and upper classes. Yet as the technology advanced, faster craft were introduced and this led to the next significant development, which was the day-trip from the capital. Once the demand for these became apparent, this led to the third development: the start of special excursion trips with significantly reduced fares. A trip from London to Margate was priced at 15s in 1820, for example, but by 1835 it was only 7s.

Although there was a range of operators that targeted different social groups, Williams and Armstrong suggest that 'it was in providing recreational activity for the lower orders that the steamboat's greatest impact lay'. By operating on Sunday (the only day off for many employees), a number of the companies came to rely heavily on the working classes. Some of the craft were regularly carrying over 500, with the largest able to accommodate over 1,000, and the popularity of the services is shown by the burgeoning passenger numbers. In 1830–31, 292,000 visitors arrived at Gravesend by steamer and this had reached over 1.1 million by 1841–42. As the services predated the railway, Williams and Armstrong argue that the steamboat would have been the first taste of commercial transportation for many people. Furthermore, the novel experience was enhanced by a range of facilities which operators laid on for their customers, including on-board refreshments, like alcoholic beverages, and entertainment, such as live music. As a result, 'The day trip and the excursion, largely down river, became an element of London life and set a long-term pattern for the ordinary Londoner's relationship with his river and the sea'.[3]

By contrast, there has been very little written about steamboats operating on the Upper Thames. The most exhaustive popular work is Frank Dix's *Royal River Highway*, which attempts to trace the use of the whole waterway from Roman times to the present. He argues that the first documented steamboat to travel between Kingston and Oxford was *Shell* in 1838 (although *Jackson's Oxford Journal* records it as 1839),[4] but that there is no record of a regular service between the two, as the owners had planned.[5] Whilst he does not mention some of the other early steamboats operating in Oxford, like *The Richmond Steamer*, which could accommodate up to 300 passengers and was operating during the 1840s,[6] and the 88ft *Enterprise*, which was running between Oxford, Nuneham and Abingdon in the summer of 1852 (with shorter trips to Iffley conducted on a Sunday),[7] he points out that long-distance services did not take off until the 1870s. The early ventures included *Julia*, a 'diminutive' 'steam yacht' that was travelling between Kingston to Oxford in 1875,[8] *Isis*, which operated between Oxford and Richmond in 1876 and 1877,[9] and another *Isis* (possibly the same craft), which operated between Oxford and Kingston from 1878 and was then replaced by *Thames* in 1879 by the operators (The Thames and Isis Steamboat Company) which ran the service until 1882.[10]

Dix argues that the late arrival of steam-driven passenger boats 'was almost certainly due to the difficulty of operating paddle steamers through the narrow locks' and that it was not until the 1870s that screw propulsion became a practical proposition, owing to the Conservancy's efforts to improve the condition of the river with initiatives like clearing weeds.[11] The locks were probably the main reason why steamboat trips were not as popular on the Upper Thames, but for a number of different reasons. Firstly, boats using them had to pay a toll, which meant that operators could be burdened with significant running costs, especially if the service covered a long distance. Secondly, the locks limited the size of craft that could travel on the river (as did the depth of the water and the height of the bridges), which meant that boats could not carry the number of passengers who were being transported on the tidal Thames. Thirdly, they could be very slow to pass through, which made the higher reaches of the river less suitable for the day-trip market from London. Furthermore, commercial barges had the right of way over pleasure craft, which was another potential source of delays. Although the number of craft carrying freight decreased significantly once the Thames Valley was connected to the railway in the 1840s (see chapter 3), the passenger boats also had to compete with trains, which were a faster and cheaper form of transportation.

The Oxford and Kingston Steamers (1888–1939)

Salters' started operating passenger boats between Oxford and Kingston on 21 May 1888 (Whit Monday) and the service would continue to run for almost a century. This section examines why the firm was able to make a success of the longer-distance trip, when others before it had failed. Salters' was able to use the service to open up the already popular 'Thames trip' to a much wider customer base, including those wanting a day-trip from the capital. It was the enlargement of the passenger boat fleet and the firm's association with the Great Western Railway (and agents) that enabled Salters' to establish a monopoly over the long-distance journey and to increase both the number and variety of customers who used its services.

Initially, Salters' used horse-drawn barges, rather than steamers, to carry large groups.[12] There may be an interesting early example of this way of transporting large numbers of people: Alan Wykes records that in 1555 William and Elizabeth Bates from Abingdon organised a package tour up to Oxford, complete with refreshments served on board, for those wanting to watch the burning at the stake of bishops Latimer and Ridley.[13] Salters' played a significant role in increasing the number of such craft moored at Christ Church Meadow in the nineteenth century (see chapter 2), and by 1885, one guidebook was recording that a 'Great and many barges are towed down to Nuneham, and there merry people dance round Carfax, and float up again to Salter's in the heavy purple dusk, trolling snatches of songs'.[14]

The firm was offering small steamers for hire by the mid-1880s, but the catalyst for entering the long-distance passenger boat market was becoming an agent for what became the Thames and Isis Steamboat Company. The service was a five-day round trip between Kingston and Oxford, which departed on Monday and took three days to reach Oxford (with overnight stops at both Windsor and Reading) and two days to return to Kingston (with an overnight stop in Henley). The full journey (single) was initially £1, reduced to 18s the following year, with intermediate fares for shorter distances.[15] It is unclear what proportion Salters' kept as agents, but after a slow start of only five tickets sold in 1879 (with sales amounting to £2 14s), the firm sold 270 in 1880 (£165 19s 3d), 215 in 1881 (£148 13s 6d) and 245 in 1882 (£152 3s 9d).[16] Despite this revenue, the service was unable to make a profit – it was costing Salters' over £300 per boat per year to operate the same trip a decade later (see p. 120) – and the company was wound up in 1883.

Salters', as a former agent, continued to receive 'numerous' enquiries about the trip, 'especially from people who did not want the trouble of taking a rowing boat and waterman', and it was these that eventually prompted the firm to launch its own service.[17] As this suggests, the decision was made partly because there was demand for a different way of doing the long-distance journey on the river, which the firm had already helped to popularise with its manually powered craft (see chapter 3). Indeed, continuity with this other side of the business was maintained by marketing the steamer service as 'the Thames trip', whilst the firm also retained the same stop-off points and pricing structure as the Thames and Isis Steamboat Company (although the craft started its journey on Monday in Oxford rather than Kingston). Salters' was certainly well positioned to judge the market, because it already operated small steamers and it shared an island with James Porter's business, which ran passenger boats between Oxford and Abingdon from the early 1880s onwards.

The craft the firm used to launch its service was the 60ft *Alaska*, a propeller-driven steamer bought from Walton-on-Thames with a certificate for sixty-two passengers. There is no reason to suggest that the clientele at this time was significantly different from those observed by G.D. Leslie on the earlier Thames and Isis Steamboat Company's service: 'The passengers on board are chiefly composed of a class of people who would not otherwise see the river in any way; quiet middle-aged townsfolk, many of them, perhaps, taking the trip on their only holiday, mixed with a few old ladies and invalids.'[18] Salters' was certainly trying to attract a particular type of customer, because it recorded in a 1902 brochure that 'the comfortable and stylish character of the boats and their

Alaska, the first steamer used by Salters' on the Oxford and Kingston service.

capable and intelligent management have won for them a class of passengers decidedly above the average'.[19]

There were a number of reasons why the trips would only have had a fairly narrow customer base, at least initially. Firstly, the steamers appealed to a different type of passenger (and age group) from the manually powered craft. They were ideal for the 'old', 'infirm' or 'the very tired', according to Paul Gedge,[20] or those 'deterred by nervousness' from other forms of activity, as G.D. Leslie put it.[21] Secondly, unlike the Gravesend and Margate steamers, the Oxford and Kingston service did not run at all – at least initially – on a Saturday or a Sunday, even though these were 'the great boating days' for Londoners.[22] This would have excluded many of the working classes from being able to use them, because the majority of those employed in factories, for example, would only have had a full day off work on Sunday and a half-day on Saturday – the latter being established in many industries by the Factory Act of 1867. Nor was a day-trip from London possible, anyway, unless the trip was combined with a different form of transportation. Thirdly, the fares were considerably higher than many other excursion options. A single from Kingston to Henley (10s), for example, was almost three times more than the *return* journey from London by train on a special third-class ticket (3s 6d).[23] It was also much higher than the steamer fare from London to Gravesend (1s 4d single or 2s return) and it was even possible to do a return day-trip from the capital to Calais for the same price (10s) with South-Eastern Railway (second class).[24]

The key to the long-term success of the Oxford to Kingston steamers was the way in which the firm developed the service in order to increase the number and type of passengers it was able to carry. The most important part of this process was the expansion of the fleet through the purchase and construction of more steamers, which was linked to a partnership the firm forged with Great Western Railway (see pp. 120–1). By 1907, Salters' had fourteen large passenger boats in its fleet, which ensured that it was not only the biggest operator on the non-tidal Thames,[25] but also one of the most significant on any river in the country. The growth continued after the Second World War, when the company took over the Reading business of E. Cawston in 1945 (an amicable sale, two decades after Salters' had first been offered it for purchase),[26] thereby acquiring its craft. E.J. Maynard's *Queen of the Thames* was then added to the fleet in 1948 and the peak of seventeen craft was reached when the Dutch boat *Kagerplas* was purchased in 1956 (renamed *Mary Stuart*).

The enlargement of the fleet was significant because, firstly, it enabled the firm to carry more passengers. Indeed, this was the reason why Salters' started to buy more steamers (from Edwin Clark of Brimscombe). Despite both a relatively inauspicious start to the service, consisting of thirty-five passengers being carried on the first week's round trip (generating ticket sales of £10 16s 6d) and twenty-five on the second (£7 7s 6d),[27] as well as a summer when the weather was described as the most 'disappointing to the pleasure seeker' and 'ruinous to the trader' in living memory,[28] the trips were successful enough for the firm to require a larger boat, because *Alaska* was deemed too small.[29] Furthermore, by the end of the following season, *Lock to Lock Times* reported that river trips were booming thanks to a *Daily Telegraph* report, and that those operated

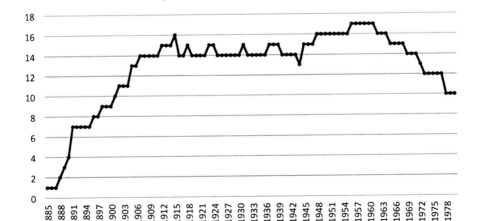

Large Passenger Boats in the Fleet

Passenger boats

('Large' is defined as a craft measuring more than 40ft in length)

by Salters' had been 'well patronised during the season', requiring a further expansion to the fleet.[30]

It was not just the number of craft that increased, but also the size of them. When the 72ft by 12ft *Oxford* was introduced to the service in 1889, it was 'the largest launch on the river above Teddington with a licence to carry 120 passengers'.[31] The firm then added three more generations of successively larger steamers, with the first of each being in 1896 (85ft by 13ft 6in), 1912 (90ft by 14ft 6in) and 1927 (105ft by 16ft 6in, although this was intended for the private hire market). Furthermore, those built by Salters' (from 1901) had a flat roof, rather than a lower section on either side, which was a design change intended to provide further space for both passengers on the top deck and in the saloon. By 1903 the firm could carry almost 1,500 passengers daily,[32] and the capacity would be increased further by slowly replacing the older craft with the newer larger vessels. Out-going steamers were sold away from any immediate competitors, with *Kingston* and *Windsor*, for example, going to the Euphrates and Tigris Navigation Company, where they were used to ferry troops during the war.[33] The size of the craft was important, because the number of passengers could fluctuate hugely owing to a variety of factors, like the weather, the day of the week, the time of the day, the month of the year, and whether or not parties were booked on. It was important, therefore, to maximise income during the busiest periods, especially as space on board was not always occupied by fare-paying customers. In 1896, for example, the firm was allowing people to bring with them a 'moderate quantity of luggage' for free (a necessity for those travelling overnight), whilst there was a charge for bicycles brought on at the owner's risk (6*d* for up to 12 miles, 9*d* for 25 miles, etc.).[34] Dogs were not allowed on board, but by the 1920s special permission could be sought for small ones 'under control' (subject to a charge), and a limit of 1 hundredweight had been imposed on baggage (112lb or 51kg).[35]

Secondly, the fleet enlargement enabled the firm to increase the profitability of the service, because the additional cost of running extra steamers was proportionally lower than the increase in revenue it produced. When Salters' doubled the fleet from two to four in 1892, for example, the income from the ticket sales rose by 74.6 per cent from the previous year, whilst the running costs only increased by 48.4 per cent (Table 4.1), which ensured a profit of more than twice that of 1891. Yet the service appears to have been growing in popularity anyway, as in 1895 the steamers were carrying approximately 50 per cent more passengers (13,345) than they had been in 1892 (9,127), without any new craft being added to the fleet. Furthermore, despite fluctuating yearly results, the Oxford and Kingston steamers were posting consistent and sizeable profits during this period. Indeed, the company was even able to widen the appeal of the steamers further by introducing a series of small price reductions. By 1900, for example, the cost of travelling from Oxford to Kingston was 14*s*, which was 4*s* cheaper than it had been when the service started.

Table 4.1 Revenue generated by the steamers[36]

Year	Steamers	Passengers	Receipts (% change)	Payments	Profit
1890	2	5,059	£1,384 14s 11d	£647 6s 10d	£737 8s 1d
1891	2	–	£1,309 7s 5d (−5.7%)	£676 3s 4d (+4.5%)	£633 4s 1d (−14.2%)
1892	4	9,127	£2,285 14s 11d (+74.6%)	£1,003 16s 5d (+48.4%)	£1,281 18s 6d (+102.4%)
1893	4	–	£2,741 13s 5d (+20%)	£1,061 3s 7½d (+5.8%)	£1,680 9s 9½d (+31.1%)
1894	4	–	£2,465 5s 7d (−10%)	£1,083 3s 6d (+2.1%)	£1,382 2s 1d (−17.7%)
1895	4	13,345	£3,048 6s 7d (+23.7%)	£1,099 4s 2d (+1.5%)	£1,949 2s 5d (+41%)
1896	4	13,572	£2,964 0s 6½d (−2.8%)	£1,326 12s 3d (+20.7%)	£1,637 8s 3½d (−16%)
1897	5	–	£3,260 13s 11d (+10%)	£1,408 12s 11d (+6.2%)	£1,852 1s 0d (+13.1%)

Thirdly, the enlargement of the fleet enabled the firm to offer a greater range of trips, which not only was important for attracting more customers, but also enabled Salters' to establish a monopoly over the long-distance journey. As well as doubling the firm's capacity, the introduction of a second craft in 1890, for example, enabled the service to operate in both directions simultaneously. Another important change was made in 1891, when the upstream journey was reduced to two days, which meant that Salters' could fit three return trips in per boat each week (with the service also running on a Saturday). The most significant development came in 1892, however, when the operational fleet was doubled to four, which not only allowed the firm to have craft travelling in opposite directions between both Oxford and Henley, and Kingston and Henley, but also enabled the firm to enter into a partnership with the Great Western Railway (see below). This meant that Salters' could run a range of return day-trips from different locations, such as to Abingdon, Clifton, Day's Lock and Wallingford from Oxford. In 1902 the timetable was enhanced further when two more vessels were added, allowing the firm to operate twice daily services, using six craft, from the different locations – a morning and an afternoon cruise. This helped to ensure that each section of the river became well patronised, as in 1905, the firm's publicity recorded that it was only 'within the past few years that the whole of the ninety-one miles can be said to have become a popular pleasure resort'. August was the busiest month, followed by July, June, September and May, in that order.[37]

Fourthly, the expansion of the fleet enabled the firm to join forces with the Great Western Railway in 1892 to offer combined river and rail journeys between many locations. Indeed, it was this relationship that was 'responsible for the building of the passenger boat fleet',[38] because it enabled the firm to tap into the excursion market. Trains were not only faster, meaning that people could be brought from further afield, but also operated at a wider range of times, enabling the steamer service to be linked into a whole variety of 'circular tours'. By 1896, the stations selling combined river and rail tickets were Paddington, Westbourne Park, Ealing, Maidenhead, Windsor, Staines, Marlow, Henley, Reading, Pangbourne, Goring, Wallingford, Abingdon, Oxford, Banbury, Leamington, Birmingham, Bath, Bristol, Cheltenham, Newbury, Wycombe and Basingstoke (a list that would be subsequently expanded). Furthermore, Salters' also had three agents in London (Thames Boating Agency, Thomas Cook and A. Hays), two in Kingston (Sun Hotel and W. Drewett and Sons) and one in Manchester (Thomas Cook), Birmingham (Thomas Cook), Reading (Farrer and Sons) and Windsor (J. W. Weight) respectively.[39]

Each trip was numbered separately and signs would direct customers to the boats from the relevant stations. In 1911, for example, tour number one involved carrying passengers from Paddington to Henley on the 8.48 a.m. train and then from Henley to Kingston on the 9.50 a.m. steamer, which would reach its destination at 7.10 p.m., with an hour's stop at Windsor for lunch. The fare ranged from 10s (third-class train ticket) to 13s 2d (first class), although there were also cheaper half-day tours available from London starting at 5s 6d.[40] The variety of trips ensured that the firm provided 'as complete an up-river service as could be desired',[41] and Salters' became a convenient 'one-stop-shop' for travel providers wanting to book trips on the river. It was not until 1911, however, that the firm began to promote the tours more heavily in its new-look guide to the river,[42] and it was during the inter-war period that they became particularly popular. In 1929 the *Oxford Mail* ran an article on the imminent 'invasion of Oxford' by thousands of excursionists taking advantage of the tours, which offered integrated transport by rail, road and river. A spokesman for Salters' claimed that the combined trips had 'taken off wonderfully' and that enquiries about them were at an unprecedented level. A typical tour consisted of a group arriving from the West Midlands at 9.00 a.m., morning sightseeing in the city (courtesy of Oxford Motor Services), a steamer trip to Abingdon at 2.00 p.m. (with guides on board) and time to spend there, until they boarded the 7.00 p.m. steamer to get back to Oxford in time for the 9.20 p.m. train.[43] Other locations were also busy at this time: excursion trains and motor coaches brought thousands of day-trippers to Bourne End in the 1930s, for example, where they would 'frequently board a river steamer at Townsend's Yard and travel to Windsor or Henley to complete their rail or road journey'.[44] By 1955 the western region alone was putting on 133 'special trains' for Salters'.[45]

A crucial part of the popularity of the tours was the attractions near the places that the steamers stopped at. Salters' exploited some of these by combining the river trips with land-based sightseeing, as in Oxford, where they were pioneers of walking tours in the 1920s. Indeed, two of the staff used for the tours became founding members of the Guild of Guides.[46] One of the favourite long-term destinations from the city was Nuneham House, at which Salters' had permission to stop on Tuesday and Thursday from 1905 onwards. Writing in 1910, Charles Harper claimed that 'everyone' knew of Nuneham House because of Salters' and thousands of people had travelled there by steamer.[47] The firm regularly added new attractions to its tours, including the Morris Motor Works in the 1930s. By the mid-1960s, the three main destinations favoured by its customers were, in order of popularity, London Airport, Windsor Castle and

Large numbers of passengers on board two steamers at Windsor in 1929.

Blenheim Palace, whilst the firm also sold tickets for the Oxford colleges, Bekonscot Model Village and London Zoo.[48]

The tours also helped to establish the steamer trip as an integral part of the sightseeing itinerary, rather than having to compete with road- or rail-based transportation. Indeed, the train journey was part of the overall excitement of going away on holiday,[49] and, similarly, as the passenger boats plied the 'glorious' Thames (as the river was described in much of the firm's marketing), they offered much to stimulate the senses.

The firm's formal relationship with the railway petered out in the post-Beeching era. The train drivers' strike of 1982 and a lack of rolling stock meant that 'within a few years' the business was lost,[50] resulting in Salters' finally removing the option of rail and river trips from its passenger services brochure in 1988.

Promotional photograph of the tour of Oxford and the Morris works (1930s).

Whilst the railway was vital for the service in the first half of the twentieth century, it was coach companies that became the firm's most important clientele after the Second World War. As mentioned earlier, some of these relationships were forged prior to the conflict. In 1937, for example, GWR and Salters' combined forces with the Thames Valley Traction Company.[51] Yet it was not until after the war that the road replaced rail as the most common way by which passengers travelled to holiday destinations.[52] Indeed, by the mid-1960s Salters' was receiving twice as much revenue from non-rail special parties as it was from rail parties.[53]

The firm promoted a range of tours in its brochures, which were provided in partnership with a coach operator – the arrangements of which could change from year to year. Salters' also had links with numerous other travel providers from around the country, because many of them organised trips on board the Oxford and Kingston steamers. The importance of coach companies can be illustrated by looking at the variety of customers who booked groups onto the service on the busiest day of the year in 1965 (Sunday, 22 August). Twenty-nine of the forty-two groups (69 per cent) were part of tours arranged by coach/travel companies (Table 4.2) and this included six bookings from Southland coaches (Bromley), three from Timpson and Sons (Catford), and two from Eastern National (London).

Table 4.2 Bookings on the service, 22 August 1965 (bold type denotes travel/coach company)[54]

Abbey Panels Ltd	Ancient Order of Foresters	**Barton Transport (Chilwell)**
Berry's Coaches (Taunton)	**Bristol Omnibus Company**	**Bourne and Balmer (Croydon)**
CANUSPA Watford branch	**Chivers Motors (Oxted)**	**Coliseum Coaches (Southampton)**
Cosy Coaches (Parkstone)	J.H. Cotton Ltd	**Eastern National Coaches (London)**
Evan Evans (London)	**Frames' Tours (London)**	**S.M. Ementon Coaches (Cranfield)**
Epsom Coaches	Mrs T. Ham	**Frank Harris Coaches (Grays)**
Harris's Coaches (Bromsgrove)	Heelas of Reading	**Kendricks Transport (Walsall)**
Midland Red (Birmingham)	Ministry of Defence	**Newland Coaches (Ringwood)**
Popular Coaches (Barking)	RACS	Royal Hampshire Regiment Assoc.
Southdown (Brighton)	**Southland Coaches (Bromley)**	**A. Timpson and Son (Catford)**
Williams Coaches		

The firm was certainly well connected in the industry, and from the mid-1960s it even advertised a 'Salters Travel Group', which offered, amongst other things, a passport service, 'air–sea tickets', school and group travel, and yacht cruises.[55]

Marketing

The most successful businesses tend to be those that are good at manipulating the commercial culture to their advantage. In the leisure market, guidebooks are sometimes described as a prerequisite for popular travel,[56] because they not only influence where people travel to, but also shape the prevailing perceptions about destinations.[57] Visual marketing was used by a number of British seaside resorts, for example, to help to popularise an idealised image of what the holiday experience was like.[58] Although it is difficult to summarise over a century of advertising by Salters', one can see that the firm was not only very active in publicising itself, but also influential in promoting both the river and the Thames Valley. Furthermore, it benefited from a large amount of free advertising, owing to the range of services it offered and the partnerships it forged.

Salters' advertised in many specialist publications, often ensuring that different aspects of the business were showcased, so as to appeal to as many people as possible. This enabled the firm to exploit, as well as to build up further, its existing reputation. Salters' also had representatives who would canvas travel operators (with trade discounts offered), whilst money-off vouchers were distributed to schools. Furthermore, advertisements were also regularly placed in a range of national and local newspapers.

A significant development in the firm's marketing came when John Salter wrote *The River Thames: From Its Source to Wandsworth* (1881). Containing both images and fold-out maps of the waterway (as Henry Taunt's earlier publication had done), the *Salter's Guide to the Thames*, as later editions were known, became 'perhaps *the* standard guide'[59] with fifty-seven editions printed (the last being in 1968). This not only added to the river experience by providing information about the sights, thereby helping to shape people's perception of the waterway, but also strengthened the firm's overall brand. Indeed, Salters' became known as a leading authority on both the Thames and its valley, as it offered visitors comprehensive information about holidaying in the area, which included providing lists of campsites and hotels.

In terms of using visual images, the early advertisements for the Oxford and Kingston steamers in guidebooks tended to feature a monochrome silhouette of a passenger boat underneath the words 'Delightful steamer trips on the Thames'.[60] Around 1905, the firm commissioned a series of watercolours of the steamers, each depicted in the location after which it was named, which were used to produce a set of postcards. The artist of five of these was William Matthison, whose paintings were already widely used in the postcard industry in Oxford,[61] whilst R. Murdoch Wright produced a further two. During the inter-war period, the firm used a range of photographic images and after the Second World War much of the publicity was devolved to the Thames Valley Art Company, a business set up by Arnold and Frank Salter in conjunction with an employee, George Cox. This had an office on St Aldate's and was responsible for producing a number of short sight-seeing guides, such as *The Thames Valley in Pictures: From Source to Tideway* and *Windsor, Eton and the River*, both written by Maxwell Fraser in 1953. Another marketing tool was film productions like *Sweet Thames Run Softly ...* (1949) and *See How They Fly* (1950s). The former was a programme, narrated by BBC broadcaster Freddy Grisewood, produced in conjunction with British Railways Western Region, which showcased the steamers and the main attractions between Oxford and

Kingston; the latter was produced by Isis Recording Studios and featured both a river trip and a visit to London Airport.

The firm also used its waterside offices for advertising. When Salters' acquired Hall's yard (1870) it erected a large arching banner between two buildings on the island that was clearly visible to those approaching the city by river (from downstream), and this was later accompanied by a sizeable wall-mounted notice, which is still there today, to target those passing by on the main road. The firm's offices were also emblazoned with billboards and notices, whilst nearby businesses were used to display advertisements in return for complimentary tickets. Furthermore, if a steamer was not needed on a particular day then the crew would be sent out to do leafleting.

The steamers themselves were also important for marketing purposes, as the large fleet was conspicuous on the river and *The Thames* suggested that their arrival on the waterway was seen as a 'sure sign of the recognised starting point of the tourist season'.[62] They were 'the largest and most prestigious craft' above Kingston[63] and their iconic status was further enhanced after the Second World War when many other operators started to use modern passenger vessels (see p. 139).

Advert in C. Dickens, *Dickens' Dictionary of the Thames 1891* (London, 1891).

W. Matthison's watercolour of *Oxford*, with Folly Bridge in the background.

Aldershot & District Traction Company advert (1954).

As well as actively marketing its own services, Salters' was also able to rely on a huge amount of free publicity from outside agencies. In 1891, when the service was only in its fourth year, *Lock to Lock Times* wrote that 'Salter's Thames trip has now become really famous. Scarcely a week has passed lately without one or other of the illustrated journals coming out with pictoral accounts of the voyage.'[64] This may explain why the firm introduced dark rooms on the craft in 1892,[65] for the 'ubiquitous amateur photographer'.[66] It was the amount of river that Salters' covered and its monopoly over the long-distance trip that ensured that most Thames guidebooks included both a written account of the Oxford and Kingston service and a reproduction of the timetable. Furthermore, the partnerships that the firm forged with other transport and excursion operators ensured that it was able to benefit from the marketing activities of other businesses. These could be considerable, when it came to firms like the Great Western Railway and Thomas Cook.

Perhaps the best indicator of the firm's success is the degree to which the service managed to enter the popular consciousness, on both a national and an international level. By 1896, *Lock to Lock Times* wrote that the service was 'fully recognised as a necessary part of the programme of foreign and colonial tourists in England'.[67] As this suggests, the river was part of the 'critical terrain' for tourists wanting a quintessential British experience. In 1905, the firm claimed that 'it is becoming the usual thing for travellers from all parts of the world – especially from America and our colonies – to do the Thames trip, just as it has been the correct thing to make a trip up the Rhine'.[68] By 1920 *Burrow's Guide to the Thames* was able to record that 'Probably the majority of tourists travel by Salter's Oxford to Kingston Steamers',[69] whilst the *Oxford Times* reported that the steamers were:

> … known in most parts of the civilised world, for no traveller or tourist from America, Australia or the Continent can consider he has 'done England' until he has had a trip over at least some portion of the one hundred and ten miles that separate Oxford by water from Kingston-upon-Thames.[70]

Indeed, the firm established the reputation for being *the* operator that one associated with the river, which undoubtedly helped it to dominate the market, as well as making it more difficult for competitors to challenge. Furthermore, it did so without ever putting much emphasis on its own history in its marketing. This may seem surprising, but the management wanted the business to be viewed as a modern enterprise, rather than as a relic from an earlier age. Yet the fame of Salters' slowly waned in the second half of the twentieth century as it lost its dominance on the river (see pp. 128–41), which also reduced the amount of publicity it received from outside agencies.

Measuring the Success of the Oxford and Kingston Steamers (1915–1970s)

The Oxford and Kingston service may have become famous, but the financial record (from 1915) shows that ticket sales declined in the inter-war period, before the popularity of the steamers rose to unprecedented levels during the Second World War. After the conflict the firm struggled to make a profit from the service, although the passenger numbers probably peaked in the 1970s.

The service produced annual revenue of just over £5,000 in the early years of the First World War, but this more than doubled in two years from £5,322 10s 4½d in 1916 to £12,117 19s 10d in 1918.[71] This was a time when firms on the river 'reaped a golden harvest' as the waterway's 'old rivals' in the tourist trade were adversely affected by the lack of railway facilities, sanctions on petrol and the closing of many seaside resorts.[72]

During the inter-war period, however, there was a slow reduction in the revenue generated by the steamers. It was not until the Second World War that there was a significant rise in the popularity of the service, when takings nearly quadrupled in only four years. In 1939, the Oxford and Kingston Steamers produced £7,007 6s 9d of revenue, but this had increased to £27,676 11s 8d by 1942. The reasons for the river being so popular during the conflict were discussed earlier (see chapter 3), but the trip did particularly well, because the firm was able to run a full service despite the fuel rationing, although the engines ran on briquettes rather than coal. Bill Dunckley was one employee to recall the exceptionally long queues stretching across Folly Bridge during the latter stages of the war.[73] These were predictably large during the main holidays, such as the Whitsun weekend of 1944, when 'hundreds of people' had to be turned away because the firm could not cope with the demand.[74] Another indication of the popularity of the service is that the firm took the unusual step in 1944 of extending the season until the end of September.

The period immediately after the war was also a busy time for the firm and ex-employee Alan Smith recalled that coach firms like Midland Red became 'prodigious customers', whilst the railway brought many more.[75] The revenue generated

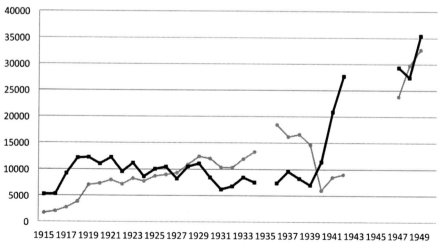

Income generated from the steamers

---●--- Boat and launch hire (and private hire steamers)   ──●── Oxford and Kingston Steamers

by the steamers rose from £35,419 14s 6d in 1949 to stabilise at approximately £60,000 per year by the mid-1950s.[76] The firm was considered to be an important leisure provider at this time, as it even received employees on National Service in the 1950s.[77] The steamers were carrying approximately 350,000 people per annum by the middle of the decade[78] and this increased to approximately half a million per year in the mid-1970s, although this figure may have included those carried on private hires too.[79] The latter was the equivalent of just over 4,000 people per day over the four-month season, which was probably the largest number Salters' ever carried. Between 1961 and 1966, the firm carried over 1,100 booked parties per year on the Oxford and Kingston steamers, as well as over 300 private hires. This meant that the service was carrying an average of just under ten pre-booked groups per day, although on the weekends in July and August there were often two to three times the number, with Sunday being the busiest day.[80]

Yet Salters' struggled to make a profit from the Oxford and Kingston steamers after the Second World War, as is shown by the discussions held at a steamer meeting in 1954. The situation was serious enough for those present to admit that the shareholders 'rightly expected interest on their valuable property' and that if the firm 'continued without showing a profit they might be tempted to sell the business'. The steamers were the most important part of the business by that point and therefore their faltering performance was a particular concern. The cost-cutting measures that were discussed in the meeting included saving wages by employing more female pursers (as the job was not attracting men) and reducing services on the less lucrative sections, by only running a 'skeleton service' between Abingdon and Reading – a route that had already been discontinued for a year in 1951 – and the Marlow to Reading trip at peak time. Revenue-generating measures that were discussed included raising all fares by one penny (thereby raising additional revenue by an estimated £1,500 to £3,000), diverting more craft to the busier sections or the places where they had notable competition (at Windsor), and converting more steamers to 'press-the-button' (diesel) boats. In the meeting Arnold Salter reaffirmed that the company's most important source of revenue was from the 'Corporations, the Railways and Coach Companies', rather than the casual passenger.[81]

Operational Challenges

The long-term success of the Oxford and Kingston steamers depended on the firm's ability to overcome several different challenges. Many of the operators faced these together, through the Thames Boating Trades Association (founded as the Thames Boat-Builders Protection Association in 1887), which was an organisation that looked after its members' interests, by lobbying the river authorities for lower charges (a particular priority for the majority of the businesses), promoting the trade (by running boat shows, for example), and providing subsidised services (including legal advice and insurance). John Henry Salter was particularly influential in this respect, as not only was he the president of the Association, but he also briefly served on the Thames Conservancy, having been elected by the Ministry of Transport in the mid-1920s. These were important positions to hold as they gave him influence over the promotion, protection and upkeep of the waterway, all of which his livelihood depended on. Yet, although the different firms worked together at the Association, they were also in competition with one another, and each operated under distinctive circumstances, which meant that they were affected by and reacted differently to the changing conditions in the market.

A particular challenge for Salters' was that the second generation of the family imposed certain restrictions on the steamers because of their religious convictions. For many years alcohol was not served on the boats and the scheduled services were not run on a Sunday, which would have had financial ramifications for the business (discussed in more depth in chapter 7), not least because it potentially helped its competitors.

Operating the passenger boats safely was always a prime concern for Salters', especially as the firm initially had unlimited liability. Nevertheless, like many forms of new transportation, steamboats were initially considered to be a nuisance[82] and one of the firm's first skippers, William Gillams, was charged by the Thames Conservancy for navigating *Oxford* at an excessive speed on a number of occasions during the early years of the service.[83] This issue was not one that was unique to Salters', but persistent offences could have significant consequences. In 1907, the licence for *Windsor* was revoked after its second conviction that season, although it was at the end of the year and the Conservancy agreed to re-instate it after the captain had been dismissed.[84] Skippers continued to be cited from time to time throughout the history of the service, but the ex-lockkeeper David Blagrove suggested that it was during the 1960s that the navigating got progressively worse, owing to the deteriorating standard of employee.[85] There is evidence to suggest that discipline at the firm, as a whole, was declining at this time (see chapter 6), but employee Bill Dunckley does not recall that this affected the handling of the steamers. Although some employees were inevitably more conscientious than others, skippers tended to be trusted members of staff who had 'graduated' from smaller craft.[86] Nevertheless, it became harder to keep to a timetable after the Second World War (see pp. 132–6), which must have put pressure on the staff to try to make up time.

The safety record of the firm appears to have been high, although serious accidents involving passenger boats were relatively rare on the Upper Thames.[87] Although crew members fell in the river from time to time, a company spokesman suggested that the first time this occurred to a passenger was in 1929 when a choirboy fell from *Henley* near Radley and had to be resuscitated.[88] The firm had been involved with some isolated incidents before this, however, including the capsizing of a gig that was being towed by *Alaska* in Oxford in 1893 (causing the death of a passenger), when towing was common practice and not illegal,[89] and a punt being swept between two stationary steamers moored at Folly Bridge in 1913 (causing the drowning of one of the occupants).[90] In the 1960s, one author claimed that dramas on the 'tranquilising vessels' were still rare, because the worst incidents reported to him were an attempted suicide in a steamer's dark room at the end of the nineteenth century (if true, this perhaps explains why they got rid of that facility), and a happy drunk who jumped off the boat in 1913, only to be rescued (suggesting that the 1929 incident may have been the first time a passenger *accidentally* fell in).[91] There had been some more serious accidents by that point, however, and the worst was in 1963, as the result of a malfunctioning primus (paraffin) stove, which caused an explosion in the saloon of *Reading*. The fire injured eight passengers and caused the death of two staff members, Samuel and Gwendoline Fuller. The stoves on the other steamers were all subsequently removed and destroyed.[92] The reputation of Salters' does not appear to have been tarnished by the incidents, probably because the most serious were tragic accidents, rather than the fault of the firm.

Another on-going challenge for Salters' was coping with the changing weather conditions, as extreme conditions could make it unsafe to operate. In June 1903, for example, the Thames Valley experienced the greatest amount of rainfall in any summer month since 1880,[93] and this caused the firm to take the unprecedented step of suspending the steamers for just over a week, owing to the flow of water. This would also have prevented manually powered craft from using the waterway.[94] Similarly, in times of drought, the river was sometimes affected by a lack of water, which could make navigating in shallower sections a challenge. In August 1899, the river was so low that the steamers could not get any further upstream than Wallingford, which required passengers to be transferred onto smaller craft.[95]

Even if the steamers were able to operate, the changing weather conditions also affected the number of casual passengers, despite two of the three decks on board being covered. This can be seen by comparing the revenue collected over consecutive years when the weather conditions were significantly different. The summers were particularly poor in 1920 and 1922 – the latter being slightly worse in terms of rainfall – whilst it was exceptionally hot and dry in 1921.[96] As one would expect, the steamer takings rose and fell accordingly (Table 4.3), which shows that although the firm's primary focus was on travel operators, the income from casual passengers was also important.

Table 4.3 Revenue from two areas of the business[97]

Year (type of summer)	Oxford and Kingston steamers (% change from previous year)	Launch and boat hire
1920 (bad weather)	£11,028 16s ½d	£7,327 1s 2 ½d
1921 (good weather)	£12,241 6s 3d (+11%)	£7,956 10s 4d (+8.6%)
1922 (bad weather)	£9,561 14s 4d (−28%)	£7,170 14s 9½d (−11%)

The same was the case for launch and boat hire, although the proportionate change was not as pronounced, suggesting that certain areas of the business may have been more affected than others. Boat-letters had a 'reputation for grumbling at the weather and proclaiming their imminent ruin',[98] but after a relatively bad summer in 1924, for example, a representative from Salters' said that 'Camping parties on the river have not been less, for they have been well protected with covers'. Nevertheless, a poor season meant that the firm had to practise 'every economy' in the winter.[99]

Keeping the steamers adequately maintained was another challenge, which required considerable on-going investment. The firm had the advantage of its own slipway where the craft could be worked on over the winter, in order to pass the annual safety check. The passenger boats also regularly required parts of machinery to be replaced, but it was not until 1944 that Salters' began converting its vessels from steam to diesel – a process that took twenty years to complete, with one craft modernised each winter.[100] A steamer would typically get through between thirty and forty hundredweight bags of coal per week, but the boats were not adapted earlier because the technology was deemed unsuitable for larger craft, following a test on *Phoenix* in 1925.[101] The immediate catalyst, however, was the soaring cost of coal, which affected many businesses during (and after) the Second World War. Between 1942 and 1947 the company's fuel bill rose by nearly 80 per cent, whilst the revenue generated by the steamers only grew by 6 per cent.[102] Significant price rises like this had previously occurred, such as during the strikes of the 1920s – although, unlike the Great Western Railway[103] and John Allen and Sons (which operated steam ploughs),[104] it had been able to continue operating a full service.

The conversion also meant that Salters' did not have to employ a steam engineer, at a time when recruiting them was becoming more difficult (see chapter 6), and it freed up space on the front deck, meaning that there was more room for passengers on board. It also relieved the staff of the duty of shovelling fuel into the bunkers (a dirty business for the individual and boat alike) and having to lower the funnel to pass under certain bridges, which could cover those on the top deck in soot or ash. The disadvantages, however, included greater noise and vibration from the engine, exhaust fumes and the absence of an obvious indication of the level of fuel on board. The craft's appearance was not altered significantly (the removal of the steam funnel being the most obvious change) and the firm subsequently tried to brighten up the 'steamers', as they continued to be known, by repainting the black hulls white to match the wooden craft that had been acquired from other operators.[105] Although the appeal of the craft was irrevocably lost for some people,[106] passenger numbers do not appear to have been adversely affected, as they probably peaked in the 1970s after the conversion process had been completed.

The mechanical parts of the boats had to be regularly replaced, but it was the condition of the hull that often determined how long a steamer would be kept for. The wooden craft were particularly vulnerable to problems and the last of these were

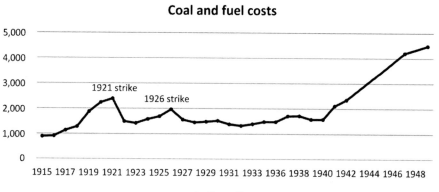

Coal and fuel costs

1921 strike

1926 strike

1915 1917 1919 1921 1923 1925 1927 1929 1931 1933 1936 1938 1940 1942 1944 1946 1948

Expenditure

sold between 1962 and 1972, causing a reduction of the fleet at this time. The steel boats were hardier, but the hulls still had to be patched up once they reached a certain age. If they were beyond easy repair, they were either laid up or sold away from competitors.

If there was a reduction in the fleet then this inevitably affected the number of passengers the firm could carry, which could help its competitors. At the beginning of the twentieth century, there was at least one other operator in Oxford, three in Reading, one in Pangbourne, two in Henley, one in Bourne End, five in Maidenhead, two in Windsor, one in Staines, one in Chertsey, one in Weybridge and one in Sunbury.[107] Yet it is difficult to assess the challenge that other firms posed, because they ran a different type of service. These tended to be shorter localised trips, although some were inevitably in direct competition with those provided by Salters'. In 1895, for example, Cawston's was operating a service from Caversham to both Pangbourne and Streatley with cheaper fares than those of the Oxford firm.[108]

The Salter family was acutely aware of the challenge posed by other businesses and they regularly discussed ways of trying to gain a greater market share, ranging from introducing new services and making timetable changes, to finding better sites to operate from and allocating more steamers to certain areas. Nevertheless, the firm's focus remained on the long-distance trip between Oxford and Kingston, which was not only a different kind of service from those of its competitors, but also one it had a monopoly over. By contrast, the shorter trips operated by Salters' brought in relatively little income. The Oxford to Iffley trips, for example, typically produced between 1 and 2 per cent of the revenue generated on the longer service (although they did well during events like eights week), whilst a brief attempt to run between Oxford and Eynsham (1932–40) produced even smaller returns.[109]

Yet the firm's large fleet and its central focus on the long-distance service meant that it could be burdened with significant additional costs, if the charges for passing through locks were increased (as they were from time to time). Salters' therefore had regularly to evaluate how many steamers to keep operational, as well as the number of passengers for which the craft were licensed, based on predictions about the levels of expenditure and income that the service would produce. The Oxford and Kingston passenger boats were also particularly vulnerable to increased traffic on the river, and it was this that eventually forced the firm to cut down its long-distance service in the 1970s, which brought it into more direct competition with other operators.

The 1970s

As mentioned earlier (see chapter 3), a number of authors view the end of the nineteenth century as the 'golden age' of the Thames, but the 1970s could also be considered as such, because a number of indicators show unprecedented levels of river use (Table 4.4). From 1956 to 1973, the number of both 'locks made'[110] and registered vessels operating on the river more than doubled, whilst the number of craft travelling through the locks more than tripled. This is why the Thames Conservancy abolished tolls in 1967, 'in order to accelerate the passage through locks'.[111]

Table 4.4 The number of boats on the Upper Thames and the traffic through the locks[112]

Year	Registered vessels	Locks made	Craft through the locks
1956	11,881	206,714	358,855
1966	17,345	297,276	642,587
1973	25,213	447,196	1,080,938

The busiest period in the history of the Upper Thames, in terms of traffic on the waterway, was from 1973 to 1981, when the number of craft passing through the locks remained over 1 million per year.[113] Boating on the river had changed significantly from the earlier 'golden age', however, because, by 1909, small manually powered boats (12,803 of the 13,824 registered vessels) outnumbered launches (861) by almost fifteen-to-one. By 1973, there was almost twice the number of registered craft on the river (25,213) and almost two-thirds of these were launches (15,871, a figure that may have been greater than the total number of boats at any time during the earlier 'golden age').[114] One study calculated that there was one motor boat for every 43ft of river.[115]

There are a number of reasons why the river became particularly busy during the third quarter of the twentieth century. Firstly, there was sustained economic and population growth during the 1950s and 1960s, which was accompanied by a rise in average incomes and a decline in working hours, with the widespread adoption of the five-day week helping to promote weekend leisure.[116] Secondly, this was a period when outdoor recreation was becoming more popular,[117] and by the early 1970s, water sports of all types were amongst the fastest-growing activities in the leisure sector.[118] Thirdly, there was a significant increase in the number of foreigners visiting the country. In 1960, for example, 1.7 million came to the UK (including those arriving for business), but by 1970 this had risen to 5 million. Consequently, the Development of Tourism Act (1969) was passed, in order to improve facilities.[119] Oxford was a particularly popular destination and in 1971 it attracted more foreign visitors than any other city in the country, except London.[120] Finally, this was followed by a significant reduction in the number of British people taking package holidays abroad during the 1970s, owing to the oil crisis and the recession. It was not until the economic revival of the 1980s and an 'epic struggle for market share between the major tour operators'[121] that the number of people travelling internationally during the summer rose significantly. Thus 'Freddie Laker and the advent of cheap foreign flights' helped to curtail the 'glory days of mass public pleasure boating on the Thames'.[122] By 2004, the number of both craft passing through the locks and the registered private boats had reduced by approximately 40 per cent and 25 per cent, respectively, from the levels they had reached during the 1970s.[123]

Although the firm carried large numbers of passengers during this time, the second 'golden age' of the river was also a particular problem for the Oxford and Kingston service, because the steamers had to cover a long distance. The greater number of launches on the river caused inevitable bottlenecks, because they tended to be much larger than the manually powered craft, meaning that fewer boats could fit in the locks (although the time taken to pass through them was reduced, as the majority of locks were mechanised during the 1960s). As early as 1967, J.H.B. Peel noted that a 'summer's

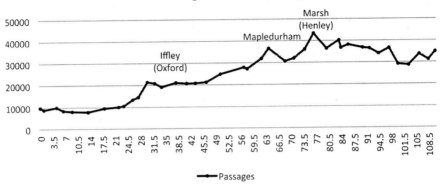

voyage in search of the Thames too often defeats its own purpose' and that Britons 'so far as ruling the waves, are defeated by a tideless backwater'.[124] The section between Henley and Boulter's Lock was the busiest, where, by the end of the 1970s, there were 'long lock queues on summer weekends, occasional conflict between anglers and motor launches, and regular use not only by rowers, but by canoeists and sailing boats'.[125] The higher reaches were not as badly affected, but even in Oxford there was more than a threefold increase in the number of craft using Iffley lock between 1958 and 1976 from approximately 6,000 boats per annum to over 20,000.[126]

The firm had had to contend with the problem of traffic in the past – in 1907, a letter from John Salter was read out in Parliament complaining about the delays caused by barges.[127] However, these issues tended to be isolated incidents or prevalent only on the lower sections of the river. In any case, they were not too much of a problem, because Salters' was the beneficiary of an unofficial arrangement with the lockkeepers that gave its craft precedence over other river traffic (barges aside). The lockkeepers knew the timetable well and they would try to have their lock ready for the arrival of the passenger boat, but if the steamer appeared at an unusual time, it was still allowed to bypass the waiting traffic. This system, as Bill Dunckley explained, was mutually beneficial for both parties: 'At the end of the season Salters' always used to give the lockkeepers a little bonus. If you were trusted you'd get all these envelopes to give out to all the lockkeepers. They used to look forward to it.'[128]

Although this arrangement was very much at the 'nod and the wink of the lockkeeper', it was vital for ensuring the boats kept to their timetable. Yet as the number and size of other craft on the waterway increased from the 1950s onwards, so did delays at the locks, which 'soured' the firm's relationship with the navigation staff.[129] There was also a growing intolerance from other river users to this system of preferential treatment and the Conservancy ceased to give the steamers priority.

On a number of occasions Salters' sought and failed to establish the arrangement on an official basis, but the issue was a divisive one, as can be illustrated by a meeting of the Thames Hire Cruiser Association in 1959. The Thames Conservancy had asked the firm to build a new landing stage above Chertsey Lock to prevent crowds congregating at the lock. Yet because this would slow the service down, Salters' had raised the question of preferential treatment for its steamers. The Conservators suggested referring the matter to the two associations representing river businesses (the other being the Thames Boating Trades Association), in order to gauge the opinion of other users. In the meeting, Hubert Salter reminded the others that the service was famous all over the world and that it attracted large numbers of visitors both from overseas and Britain in conjunction with the railway. Captain Munk agreed that the steamers brought considerable prestige and publicity to the river and that the arrangement would not seriously inconvenience the hirers of craft.[130]

This was a significant point to make, as the firm was important for the wider river economy. There was a daily rhythm of steamers arriving and departing at different points along the Thames, which provided a regular source of income for local businesses. Many parties required refreshments at their embarkation or disembarkation points, which ensured that pubs, tea rooms and hotels did very well out of the firm, with some offering discounts for steamer customers. There were also numerous opportunistic attempts to derive income from the services, ranging from rival organ-grinders targeting passengers at Wallingford in 1907,[131] to children running alongside the boats in a number of locations trying to elicit money or food from those on board.[132]

L. Bushnell also supported Salters', as he suggested that there was already an unwritten rule that the steamers had priority. Yet, despite the positive comments – and bearing in mind that this was a group representing hire craft (rather than those they were navigating themselves) *and* that traffic on the river would grow much higher still over the next two decades – the result went only narrowly in the firm's favour, by seven votes to five, with the provisos being that private parties would not get any special attention and that lockkeepers should only have the locks ready just before the scheduled time of arrival, so that other river users were not affected.[133]

Those writing about the Thames were similarly polarised. Some, like Roy Curtis, questioned why preferential treatment should be given,[134] whilst others, like the Oxford Waterways Action Group, argued that the system was vital 'to ensure that the many who enjoy these services are not prevented by the few'. It estimated that cabin cruisers carried an average of 3.6 people, whilst the steamers often transported 100 to 125.[135]

Assistance from the river authorities was not forthcoming and, as ex-lockkeeper David Blagrove put it, 'the once proud service steamers were relegated to the bottom of the earnings league and had to wait their turn at locks along with hire cruisers and launches'.[136] Indeed, the lack of action may partly have been a reflection of the declining financial importance of Salters' to the river authorities, at least in relative terms, as the latter was receiving a lot of additional income from the burgeoning number of private craft at that time.

In 1971 the *Surrey Comet* ran an article entitled 'Congestion on the Thames: Steamer service may die from boating boom', in which Arthur Salter made another appeal for help. He claimed that the firm had tried to keep the tradition going, but that it could not continue to do so for much longer, because it had been 'running at a loss for some years'.[137]

Many lockkeepers remained sympathetic to Salters' and tried their best to let the steamers through quickly, but the inevitable delays 'wrought havoc' with the timetable.[138]

The Oxford to Kingston journey was a through-service and therefore a delay to one leg of a journey could mean that people missed their connecting boats. Although the firm adjusted the timetable to try to take account of some of the delays, the problem was particularly acute at weekends. Bill Dunckley recalls that:

> You were due in at 7 and you were getting in at 10, half past 10 at night. It just wasn't viable you know. I remember turning up at Kingston … 10.30 quarter to 11 at night, when you were supposed to be in at 7! I mean people are going squirmy … the timings were very tight to start with.[139]

Salters' finally conceded defeat in 1974 and the full service between Oxford and Kingston was discontinued. The firm no longer covered the three least successful sections of the river, including between Staines and Kingston, whilst Reading to Wallingford was only operated in the peak summer months. There were still some who continued to champion the firm's cause, however, including Frank Dix, who ended *Royal River Highway* with a *cri de cœur* for an influential body of people 'to bring to pressure to bear on the problems affecting today's passenger services'. Yet he admitted that:

> … it is difficult to see how such a useful and once very popular timetabled service can ever be restored, and it seems probable that the new Authority [the Thames Water Authority], with its very much wider interests than the old Board, may be even less sympathetic to the introduction of such a rule.[140]

Short Trips

It had partly been the dominance of the Oxford to Kingston steamers that forced other operators to concentrate on shorter round trips and private hires, but once the long-distance service was divided into smaller sections, Salters' was drawn into more direct competition with other passenger boat companies. The trip inevitably lost some of its unique appeal, although the firm still had the advantage of a large and historic fleet. A further problem was that shorter round trips were not only more suited to a busy waterway (as travelling through locks could cause delays), but also ideal for what Dix described as 'the age of speed, when time is precious'.[141] As John Salter explained, 'After the war, day trips were popular, but the trend's gone. Now you might spend four hours, but you're not going to spend a day – and for some people visiting Oxford, even an hour is too much.'[142] Shorter round trips could also be run more often, which not only gave customers a greater variety of times to choose from, but also meant that the operator was highly visible in their locality.

Salters' provided this type of service in Oxford from at least 1915, but it was not until 1986 that it started to advertise regular 'out and back' trips from other locations, having previously run them on an *ad hoc* basis. The firm did not focus on this market earlier because, firstly, the longer one-way journeys were still favoured by tour operators (its most important clients) and they were what Salters' was known for; secondly, the steamers were less suited to this type of service, as they were cumbersome to turn around; thirdly, only a few locations were considered good for 'tripping'; and historically, it had not proved to be very lucrative. The latter explains why the short trips were given the lowest priority by the firm, as they were only operated 'subject to demand and boat availability'. This inevitably meant that Salters' struggled to get them established, because the services did not run on a consistent basis, unlike those of its competitors.

The introduction of cheap fibreglass passenger boats in the 1970s also made it easier for passenger boat companies to start up. Thames River Cruise at Reading (in 1974) and French Brothers at Windsor (1978) were two firms launched by former employees of Salters'.[143] Although there were still far fewer operators than at the start of the century, the new companies were able to tailor their services to a busy waterway by focusing on short trips and the private hire market. If a firm had a good location, it was relatively straightforward to expand the services. Hobbs and Sons, for example, already had a prime site by the bridge at Henley, and once the firm re-entered the passenger boat market in 1981, with a single fibreglass passenger boat called *Maratana*, it was able slowly to build up its fleet.[144]

The emergence of new companies and the growing popularity of short trips posed a considerable challenge for Salters', because of the territorial nature of operating localised services. Covering such a large distance had once been the firm's key strength, but it now became a weakness, as it was unable to compete with its competitors at the different places on the river. Yet if it stopped running from a particular section of the Thames, it was potentially ceding territory to a rival that might then expand to pose a greater threat in the future. The solution the firm came to was to maintain offices in the two busiest locations, Windsor and Oxford,[145] and to deploy its craft to cover the more lucrative sections of the river, whilst trying to protect its 'core' section of the river near its headquarters by under-cutting would-be competitors. By the mid-1990s, however, the firm's fleet had reduced to such an extent that it was not able to run daily services on some of the lower sections of river. Instead, different routes were covered on different days. This inevitably meant that, like other passenger boat companies, Salters' became increasingly reliant on (and associated with) its home city, where it had no major competitor. Nevertheless, even before the Oxford to Kingston route was discontinued, the service was being subsidised by the revenue generated by the more lucrative private hires.

Private Hire Market

The transition of Salters' to focusing more heavily on the private hire market was a gradual one, but it was an important shift that ensured the longevity of the passenger boat operation in the second half of the twentieth century. The change in priorities, however, meant that the scheduled services were run less consistently and the demand for modern craft to meet this specialised need would slowly undermine the uniqueness of the firm's fleet.

When Salters' began operating between Oxford and Kingston, the steamer *Alaska* (licensed for seventy) was used,[146] whilst the steamer *Isis* (licensed for thirty-four) was reserved for private parties. The policy of using the largest vessels for the long-distance service and the smaller craft for short trips or private work out of Oxford continued until the 1920s. This meant that the service boats had to be used for private work from other locations, as in 1921 when *Wargrave*, the newest vessel at the time, was used as a royal tender for George V when he opened the Royal Albert Dock Extension.[147] A significant change of direction was signalled in 1923, when the firm commissioned the first of three large craft designed with the private hire market in mind. *Hampton Court* was the same size as the largest service boats (90ft by 14ft 6in), but it had an enlarged saloon, in order to carry more people inside. This was followed by *Mapledurham* (1927), which could accommodate 112 seated inside and was licensed for 368 passengers (making it the largest-capacity craft on the Upper Thames), and its sister ship *Cliveden* (II) (1931), which had the same dimensions (105ft by 16ft 6in), but had a slightly different design that meant it was only licensed for 360. As a result of these additions, the number of craft the firm allocated to private work increased from four to six and the overall passenger capacity almost tripled (Tables 4.5 and 4.6).

Table 4.5 Private hire craft in 1912[148]

Steamer	Location	Licensed capacity	Carrying capacity
Marlow	Oxford	250	130
Oxford	Oxford	132	90
Alaska	Oxford	70	50
Swan	Oxford	44	25
Total:		**496**	**295**

Table 4.6 Private hire craft in 1931[149]

Steamer	Location	Licensed capacity	Carrying capacity
Henley	Oxford	240	140
Alaska	Oxford	70	50
Swan	Oxford	44	25
Cliveden	Reading–Richmond	360	250
Mapledurham	Reading–Richmond	368	250
Hampton Court	Reading–Richmond	300	150
Total:		**1,382**	**865**

Although the number of craft allocated to Oxford was reduced – *Henley* being the only larger vessel left – the firm's three biggest steamers were assigned to the lower section of river (between Reading and Richmond), which enabled private hires to be offered from most locations on the Upper Thames. This was partly a logistical decision, as it was easier to navigate large craft on the lower parts of the river, but it also shows the growing importance of excursion parties at this time, many of which were sightseeing in the Windsor area.

In 1927, over three-quarters (76.8 per cent) of the revenue generated by private work came from craft operating between Reading and Richmond. *Hampton Court* and *Mapledurham* accounted for 47.3 per cent of the total between them, as they were the largest and most expensive to hire, whilst *Hurley* produced 13.8 per cent. In addition to this, 15.7 per cent of the income went to the 'foreign boats' of Cawston of Caversham (eleven bookings), Bond of Maidenhead (eight), Clark of Sunbury (three), Mould of Kingston (six) and Mears of Richmond (seventeen).[150] Salters' used boats from other companies – having received the full rental charge – because its three steamers had to cover almost 60 miles of river and they could not cope with the demand. In 1929, for example, 1,293 passengers from the Failsworth Co-operative Society were transported between Reading and Windsor, which required eight craft to be used, six of which were run by other firms.[151] This association with other companies petered out after the Second World War. In 1936, 35.9 per cent of the overall revenue generated by launch hire was earned from other firms, but this dropped to less than a half of 1 per cent between 1947 and 1949.[152]

The private hire market grew steadily during the inter-war period, at a time when the revenue generated by the Oxford and Kingston steamers was falling. The importance of this source of income was recognised in 1936 when the company accounts began to list the revenue derived from the launches separately from other forms of rental craft. By this stage, they were already producing three times the amount of income of the day-boats, cabin cruisers and houseboats combined.

Private hire work was particularly susceptible to the fluctuations of the economy,[153] and during the Second World War, a number of the steamers were requisitioned by the Admiralty and used on the tideway. *Mapledurham* and *Cliveden* became ambulance ships for the Thames Hospital Emergency Transport Division (a fleet which included many of the craft Salters' had built for Mears) until 1942, whilst *Grand Duchess* and the smaller launch *Leander* were used for transporting passengers.[154] The larger steamers (classified as 'A' craft) were intended to carry between 100 and 120 casualties, with the ambulatory cases on the top deck, the minor casualties on the front deck and the major casualties in the saloon where the medical supplies were kept.[155] Christian Brann suggests the firm's biggest steamers were chosen because the government was expecting large casualties,[156] although the majority of the other boats were being used on the Oxford and Kingston service anyway, and they had considerably smaller saloons, which would have rendered them unsuitable for accommodating many inside. Unlike the craft they built for Mears, the firm's steamers were not able to participate in the Dunkirk evacuations, however, because their engines were cooled by fresh water and their range was limited by the special water tanks that had to be fitted to them to enable them to operate on the tideway.

After the Second World War, private work assumed even greater importance to Salters', because the firm struggled to make a profit from the Oxford and Kingston service. Another challenge at this time was the proliferation of a new generation of craft designed to meet this specialised demand. Dix estimates that on the whole of the Thames, seventy-seven modern boats appeared in passenger boat fleets between 1960 and 1984, whilst a further fifteen 'traditional' passenger boats (including some that had been built by Salters' for other operators) were modernised by extending the saloon and enclosing the top deck. This 'radical change in the appearance of the fleets' affected all parts of the river, although it was particularly pronounced on the tideway, where, from the late 1970s, all-the-year-round services became possible.[157]

By contrast, Salters' did not modify its steamers to make them more enclosed, because it did not operate during winter. Furthermore, the conversion costs would have been considerable, and the alterations would have made navigating through low bridges, many of which were on the higher reaches of the river, more difficult. Another reason was that the change would have compromised the look of the steamers and rendered them less appealing for day-time use, as the steamers were favoured by many clients not only because of their appearance, but also because they were preferable if the weather was nice.[158] This was an important consideration because, as the firm's fleet reduced in size from the 1950s onwards, more of the boats had to be used for both scheduled services and private work, and thus be suitable for both. This flexibility ensured that the firm could maximise its income, but it also meant that the boats received heavier use, and therefore that maintaining their condition and appearance was more of a challenge.

In 1980, Salters' followed the lead of many of its competitors by buying the first of a number modern craft that it would add to its fleet (*Lady Ethel*),[159] although financial constraints meant that the firm did not finish fitting it out until 1988. The new boats were more enclosed, making them ideal for evening cruises, which were already popular on the tideway by the time Salters' introduced them in 1978. Night parties enabled the firm to generate more income from its fleet, although passenger numbers were capped to below the figure carried during the day, in order to try to ensure comfort and safety. Furthermore, the modern craft also had on-board heating, which opened up the possibility of extending the season. This enabled Christmas parties to be offered, for example, although the river was prone to flooding over the winter (which could prevent the passenger boats from operating) and long-distance trips were not possible since many of the locks were closed for maintenance.

The decision to add modern craft was intended to bolster the private hire side of the passenger boat operation, but it also helped to erode the exclusiveness of the firm's fleet. Salters' had the largest collection of 'traditional' craft on the Upper Thames, as it still does today,[160] but the newer boats were more like those operated by its competitors. Furthermore, a number of its ex-craft (*Nuneham*, *Alaska* and *Streatley*) were restored to steam by rivals from the 1980s onwards, which helped to undermine the uniqueness of the fleet further. Salters' chose not to follow suit, however, owing to the cost of conversion and the complications of operating such engines.

The transition towards focusing more on private hires was important for a number of reasons. Firstly, it widened the firm's customer base further, by catering for those who wanted exclusive use of a steamer and/or those who wanted to dictate the timings and route of an outing. By the mid-1920s this included operating the boats on a Sunday, which was not sanctioned on the scheduled services until 1933. In 1927, for example, there were fifty-two bookings between 28 May and 17 September for *Mapledurham* (which had replaced *Queen of the Thames* that year), and this included being rented out on every Sunday from 12 June to 28 August.[161] As this suggests, there were more private parties in the middle of the summer (July being the busiest month, followed by June and August) and the weekends were always particularly busy.

Secondly, the private work provided a guaranteed level of income, because those booking the craft paid a flat rate for the hire of the boat, whereas travel companies using the service boats were only charged according to how many turned up on the day. Furthermore, privately hiring a vessel by the day (as was standard initially) was generally a more expensive option, unless the customer wanted the craft for a long journey and was willing to fill it to close to its carrying capacity.

Thirdly, the private work was significant because there was a lot of scope for gaining further revenue from the extras that some parties wanted, like catering and entertainment. The firm only provided light refreshments on its boats (although customers could make their own arrangements) and it was not until 1945 that Thames Catering Company, a subsidiary, was set up to specialise in this side of the business. A range of menus was developed for different types of party, although they all had to be suitable for serving on the boats, because there were no cooking facilities on board and everything had to be transportable. The company continued to produce catering until the 1970s when Salters' moved to using external firms.

Similarly, the firm also introduced new forms of entertainment for its passengers. By 1929, customers were able to rent a piano from Salters',[162] for example, and in the 1970s 12v record players (running off the boat's batteries) were introduced, which meant that disc jockeys could be hired to play music. The latter became increasingly popular, although an inevitable result was complaints about noise. The options for entertainment were further increased once inverters were fitted to the boats in the late 1990s, which enabled different forms of entertainment that required 240v power to be provided, like karaoke and background music played on a sound system.

It was the amount of money that they generated that led to private hires being considered the most important source of income from the passenger boats, although it was not until 2000 that Salters' produced its first brochure targeting this market. Yet this change of priorities ultimately undermined the scheduled trips. If the demand for private boats was particularly high, then the service had to be sacrificed, because in such an unpredictable market the firm had to direct its resources to where there was a guaranteed income. Operating passenger boats remained the most important leisure service the firm provided, and this was recognised in 2002, when a rebranding exercise saw this side of the business (including the boat-building department) run under the banner of Salter's Steamers Ltd, as Thames Catering Company had been renamed.[163]

• • •

The impact of the railway in transporting people around parts of the UK is well documented, but there has been much less research on carrying passengers by river. This chapter has shown that Salters' were 'pioneers of launch excursions on the [Upper] Thames'[164] and one can see why employee W.H. Gillams claimed in the 1950s that 'Millions of people must have had their first glimpses of the lovely river from the decks of those veteran steamers'.[165] By expanding its fleet and by forging a close association with the railway (and subsequently with coach operators), the firm became *the* major operator on the Upper Thames with a monopoly over the long-distance trip and a range of well-marketed journeys unmatched by any competitor. Indeed, this legacy was recognised in 2012, when four passenger boats that had once been connected with the firm were part of the twenty-four-strong royal squadron at the Thames Diamond Jubilee Pageant.[166] Yet the firm's dominance slowly waned during the second half of the twentieth century, as it struggled to make a profit from the Oxford and Kingston service. Salters' became more reliant on the private hire market, as increased traffic on the river forced it to cut the long-distance service into shorter sections (in 1974). There was also a growing demand for short round trips and by catering for this market the firm was drawn into direct competition with other operators. As the fleet declined in size, Salters' became more heavily dependent on and associated with Oxford.

Notes

1   Ashby-Sterry, *Tale of the Thames*, p. 97.
2   Armstrong and Williams, 'Steamboat and Popular Tourism', pp. 61–76.
3   Williams and Armstrong, 'Thames and Recreation', pp. 25–36.
4   *Jackson's Oxford Journal*, 8 June 1839.
5   Dix, *Royal River Highway*, p. 67.
6   *Jackson's Oxford Journal*, 13 August 1842, 27 August 1843 and 14 April 1848.
7   Ibid., 31 July 1852. It had previously been operating between London and Richmond.
8   Ibid., 15 May 1875.
9   Ibid., 8 April 1876.
10   E.C. Alden, *Alden's Oxford Guide* (Oxford, 1879), p. 114.
11   Dix, *Royal River*, p. 91.
12   *Oxford University Herald*, 21 July 1860, p. 9.
13   A. Wykes, *An Eye on the Thames* (London, 1966), p. 117. He does not cite a reference.
14   Cassell and Company Ltd, *The Royal River: The Thames From Source to Sea* (Henley, 1885), p. 59. Services to Nuneham were stopped in 1950.
15   *Jackson's Oxford Journal*, 31 May 1879.
16   SA Fare Book 1880–83 and 1888.
17   *Lock to Lock Times*, 9 June 1888, p. 2.
18   Leslie, *Our River*, p. 261.
19   *Summer Trips on the River Thames*, May and June 1902, p. 5. This may have been related to some of the rowdy behaviour that was occurring on passenger boats at this time (see chapter 7).
20   P. Gedge, *Thames Journey* (London, 1949), p. 21.
21   Leslie, *Our River*, p. 261.
22   C.E. Pascoe, *London of To-day: An Illustrated Handbook* (London, 1890), p. 191.
23   *The Standard*, 18 May 1888.
24   *The Pall Mall Gazette*, 17 May 1888.
25   The firm also had smaller 'tripping' boats (see appendix).
26   SA Letter from George Salter to Mrs Harris, 5 July 1923.
27   SA Fare Book 1880–83 and 1888. There are no further records after that point.
28   *Lock to Lock Times*, 1 September 1888, p. 3.
29   Ibid., 5 August 1893, p. 1.
30   Ibid., 7 September 1889, p. 149 and 14 September 1889, p. 161.
31   Ibid., 27 April 1889, p. 234.
32   *Reading Mercury*, 27 June 1903, p. 7.
33   The renamed *Cliveden* also joined them there, having been sold by Mears.
34   SA *Summer Trips on the River Thames* (1896).

35 SA *Summer Trips through 90 Miles of Thames Scenery Oxford to Kingston Steamers* (1926).

36 SA Oxford and Kingston Steamer Takings 1890–97.

37 *Summer Trips on the River Thames*, May and June 1902, p. 4.

38 Interview with John Salter, 20 December 2012.

39 SA *Steamer Trips on the River Thames* (1896). The agents took 10 per cent of the ticket sale.

40 Salter, *Salter's Guide to the Thames* (1911), p. 136–37.

41 *The Thames*, 18 May 1901, p. 1.

42 Salter, *Salter's Guide to the Thames* (1911), p. 140.

43 *Oxford Mail*, 12 January 1929, p. 1.

44 B. Brenchley Wheals, *Theirs Were But Human Hearts* (Bourne End, 1984), p. 149.

45 SA Minutes of Steamer Meeting, 9 August 1954.

46 *Guild of Guides*, Newsletter no. 14 (Summer 1991).

47 Wilson, *Victorian Thames*, p. 35.

48 SA Rail Party and Non-Rail Party Ledgers 1964–66.

49 Walton, *The British Seaside*, pp. 83.

50 Interview with John Salter, 20 December 2011.

51 P. Lacey, *A History of the Thames Valley Traction Company Ltd 1931–1945* (Wokingham, 2003), p. 83.

52 Walton, *The British Seaside*, p. 86.

53 SA Rail Parties Ledgers 1961–66, Non-Rail Special Parties Ledgers 1962 and 1964–66.

54 Ibid.

55 *Thames Holidays with Salters of Oxford* (1965), p. 22.

56 Armstrong, 'Steamboat and Popular Tourism', pp. 73–74.

57 Byerly, *Are We There Yet?*, pp. 104–10.

58 D. Crouch and N. Lübbren (eds), *Visual Culture and Tourism* (Oxford, 2003), pp. 3–8.

59 Gedge, *Thames Journey*, p. 18.

60 C. Dickens, *Dickens' Dictionary of the Thames: From Oxford to the Nore 1891* (London, 1891), advertisement.

61 www.headington.org.uk/history/famous_people/matthison.htm (accessed 14 April 2012).

62 *The Thames*, 13 June 1899, p. 8.

63 Blagrove, *Quiet Waters By*, p. 86.

64 *Lock to Lock Times*, 29 July 1891, p. 95.

65 Ibid., 9 January 1892, p. 2.

66 W.F.F., *The Thames Trip* (Oxford, 1891), p. 11.

67 *Lock to Lock Times*, 16 May 1896, p. 3.

68 *Summer Trips on the River Thames*, 1905, p. 5.

69 Burrow, *Burrow's Guide to the Thames*, p. 43.

70 *Oxford Times*, 24 August 1923, p. 8.

71 SA Salter Bros Ltd End of Year Accounts 1915–49.

72 *Oxford Times*, 10 June 1921, p. 6.

73 Interview with Bill Dunckley, 4 December 2010.

74 *Oxford Times*, 2 June 1944, p. 5.

75 Letter from Alan Smith to Brian Hillsdon, 2 November 1992 (passed on to author).

76 SA Salter Bros Ltd End of Year Accounts 1949 and Minutes of Steamer Meeting, 9 August 1954.

77 *Canal and Riverboat*, November 1981, pp. 39–41.

78 Ibid.

79 COS Radio interview with Arthur Salter (1971), reference: OXOHA: MT 536.

80 SA Rail Parties Ledgers 1961–66, Non-Rail Special Parties Ledgers 1962 and 1964–66.

81 SA Minutes of Steamer Meeting, 9 August 1954.

82　See Tickner, 'Messing About in Boats', p. 7.

83　*Jackson's Oxford Journal*, 9 August 1890.

84　MLD Thames Conservancy Minute Book 1907–09, 31 October 1907, p. 162. Reference found through the (unpublished) work of Iain MacLeod (sent to author).

85　Blagrove, *Quiet Waters By*, p. 89.

86　Interview with Bill Dunckley, 3 March 2010.

87　See M. Foley, *Disasters on the Thames* (Stroud, 2011). Safety regulations were not significantly tightened until the *Marchioness* disaster in 1989.

88　*Oxford Mail*, 21 May 1929, p. 1.

89　*Jackson's Oxford Journal*, 29 April and 6 May 1893.

90　*Oxford Times*, 3 May 1913, p. 11.

91　Wykes, *Eye of the Thames*, pp. 109–10.

92　*Oxford Mail*, 10 June 1963, p. 1 and *Oxford Times*, 14 June 1963, p. 11.

93　Data from the Meteorological Office's website: www.metoffice.gov.uk (accessed 10 June 2010).

94　*Reading Mercury*, 20 June 1903, p. 7 and 23 June 1903, p. 7.

95　*Jackson's Oxford Journal*, 26 August 1899.

96　Data from the average monthly high and low temperatures and total rainfall figures recorded at Benson's weather station by the Meteorological Office: www.metoffice.gov.uk (accessed 10 June 2010). Summer is defined as being June to August (the peak months for the steamers).

97　SA Salter Bros Ltd End of Year Accounts 1920–22.

98　RRM Thames Conservancy Cuttings, May 1913–December 1934, *The Morning Post*, 1934 (excerpt from paper, but exact date not recorded).

99　*Oxford Times*, 26 September 1924, p. 13.

100　Two of the steam engines (from *Cliveden* and *Queen of the Thames*) are now on loan at Markham Grange Steam Museum in South Yorkshire.

101　SA Arthur Salter correspondence to Frank Dix in preparation for the book *Royal River Highway* (postmarked 1980).

102　SA Salter Bros Ltd End of Year Accounts 1915–49.

103　*The Times*, 19 May 1926, p. 18 and 22 May 1926, p. 9.

104　G.T. Launchbury, 'John Allen and Sons (Oxford) Ltd, 1863–1952', in *Allen's Activities*, vol. 4, no. 16 (Summer 1953), p. 14.

105　These were returned to black hulls in the twenty-first century.

106　John Davis, 'Memories of Salter's Steamers', in *The Funnel*, no. 148 (Spring 2011), p. 56.

107　Dix, *Royal River*, pp. 113–14.

108　Stewart-Beardsley, 'After the Railway', p. 125.

109　SA Salter Bros Ltd End of Year Accounts 1932–40. This was known as Eynsham Motor Boat Services and was on *Leander*.

110　This refers to the number of times the lock is operated (i.e. filling or emptying).

111　RRM Thames Conservancy Finance Committee Letter to Thames Conservancy, 22 April 1965.

112　RRM Thames Conservancy General Report of the Proceedings of the Conservators of the River Thames during the Year Ending December 1973, p. 4.

113　*Thames Water Statistics* 1976, p. B6.1 to 1983, p. C5.1.

114　RRM Thames Conservancy General Report of the Proceedings of the Conservators of the River Thames during the Year Ending December 1973, p. 4.

115　Oxford Waterways Action Group, *Oxford Waterways*, p. 48.

116　J. Burchardt, *Paradise Lost: Rural Idyll and Social Change in England since 1800* (London, 2002), p. 178.

117　Ibid.

118   M. Dower, 'Planning for Leisure', in M.A. Smith, S. Parker and C.S. Smith (eds), *Leisure and Society in Britain* (London, 1973), pp. 311–12.

119   Ibid., pp. 314–15.

120   C.G. Smith and D.I. Scargill (eds), *Oxford and Its Region*, p. 84, in Day, 'Modern Oxford', p. 223.

121   R. Bray and V. Raitz, *Flight to the Sun: The Story of the Holiday Revolution* (London, 2001), pp. 199.

122   *Classic Boat*, August 2010, p. 52.

123   *Thames Waterway Plan 2006–2011*, p. 56.

124   J.H.B. Peel, *Portrait of the Thames* (London, 1967), p. 14.

125   Townley, *Henley-on-Thames*, p. 173.

126   Oxford Waterways Action Group, *Oxford Waterways*, pp. 40–41.

127   *Papers by Command*, vol. 3, part 1 (London, 1907), p. 342.

128   Interview with Bill Dunckley, 21 August 2004.

129   Blagrove, *Quite Waters By*, p. 90.

130   SA Minute Book of the Thames Hire Cruiser Association 1956–64, 9 December 1959, p. 34a.

131   *Berkshire and Oxon Advertiser*, 26 July 1907, in J. and S. Dewey, *Window on Wallingford 1837–1914* (Wallingford, 1989), p. 196.

132   *Oxford Times*, 19 June 1915, p. 9 and interview with Bill Dunckley, 4 December 2010.

133   SA Minute Book of the Thames Hire Cruiser Association 1956–64, 9 December 1959, p. 34a.

134   R. Curtis, *Thames Passport* (London, 1970), p. 40.

135   Oxford Waterways Action Group, *Oxford Waterways*, p. 40.

136   Blagrove, *Quiet Waters By*, pp. 90–91.

137   *Surrey Comet*, 31 July 1971, p. 1.

138   Blagrove, *Quiet Waters By*, pp. 90–91.

139   Interview with Bill Dunckley, 21 September 2004.

140   Dix, *Royal River*, pp. 212–13.

141   Ibid., p. 210.

142   Interview with John Salter, 20 December 2011.

143   Tim Deaton set up Thames River Cruise (the operating name for D. and T. Scenics Ltd), whilst Keith and Chris French set up French Brothers.

144   *Thames Guardian*, spring 1998, pp. 16–17.

145   The office in Reading was retained, but was dormant.

146   It was also used for private parties on the Saturday.

147   *The Times*, 9 July 1921. Reference found through the (unpublished) work of Iain MacLeod (sent to author).

148   Salter, *Salter's Guide to the Thames* (1912), p. 140. The licensed capacity was the legal limit that could be carried on board (based on weight), whilst the carrying capacity was what the firm deemed to be the maximum number of passengers that could be carried comfortably.

149   Salter, *Salter's Guide to the Thames* (1941), p. 140.

150   Ibid.

151   SA Receipt Book 1928–29, 12 June 1929. The trip was on 25 May and the charge was 7s 6d per person with lunch included.

152   SA Salter Bros Ltd End of Year Accounts 1936–49.

153   Dix, *Royal River*, p. 211.

154   See 'Thames Nursing Auxiliary Service at Practice (1939)' on the Pathé News website: www.britishpathe.com/video/thames-nursing-auxiliary-service-at-practice (accessed 16 November 2011).

155 *British Medical Journal* (London), 4 March 1939, pp. 93–94.

156 C. Brann, *The Little Ships of Dunkirk* (Cirencester, 1990), p. 197.

157 Dix, *Royal River*, pp. 202–10.

158 Ibid., p. 202.

159 *Oxford Mail*, 6 June 1980, p. 3.

160 Many of them are listed in the National Register of Historic Vessels: www.nationalhistoricships.org.uk (accessed 12 December 2012).

161 SA Private Party Boats List 1925–27.

162 SA Salter Bros Ltd End of Year Accounts 1929.

163 Companies House, Cardiff (CHC) Certificate of Name Change from Thames Catering Company to Salter's Steamers Ltd, 3 December 2001.

164 *The Thames*, 18 May 1901, p. 1.

165 *Thames and Medway*, March 1952, p. 28.

166 See www.thamesdiamondjubileepageant.org (accessed 3 June 2012). These were *Connaught*, *Nuneham*, *Henley* and *Streatley*. Six other craft associated with the firm also took part in the celebrations.

5

Property

There are few, if any, lounging places on the Thames where there is more to interest and amuse than here … Just beneath the bridge a number of men were engaged in repairing and painting a fleet of steamer launches, and in the midst of a delicious reverie, the combined result of a poetic temperament, animal food, and tobacco, it suddenly occurred to me that I was idling in the heart of a little kingdom of activity – in brief the kingdom of 'Salter Brothers', Oxford.

Lock to Lock Times, 1893[1]

Commercial Property: Oxford

At the beginning of the Victorian era the major rivers and canals of Britain were thriving arteries of trade. In Oxford, Folly Bridge was a flourishing centre of waterborne commerce, surrounded by numerous working wharves. Although the arrival of the railway forced the closure of many of these yards in the 1840s, some would have new life breathed into them by the rise of leisure activities on the river and in particular through the expansion of Salters'.

John and Stephen's business was initially based at the former site of Isaac King's firm on the north bank of the Thames next to the Trill Mill Stream (the address being '43½ St Aldates').[2] In order to increase their commercial activities the brothers acquired further sites to operate from, which involved taking over many of their nearby competitors. By 1867, they were renting the adjacent plot (once the Oxford and Burcot Commissioner's wharf) and the two properties became collectively known as St Aldate's Yard.[3] In 1870, the firm took over the historic boat-building business of Thomas Hall, which had yards on both the south-east side of the bridge near Isis House (later known as Grandpont Yard), as well as the east side of the island that was once a 'Rodd Eyott'.[4] This not only ensured that Salters' had a much larger premises to build boats from, but also gave it the prestige of owning the University Boat House, which was used by many oarsmen. The firm shared this part of the island with James Porter, who operated passenger boats from the stage nearest to the bridge until 1905, when this too was taken over by Salters'.[5]

In order to provide additional services, the firm added a number of new buildings on the island. These included one in the early 1880s that provided services for oarsmen, such as dressing rooms, storage and washhouses,[6] and another in 1900 (on the former site of the 'Boat House Tavern') that offered facilities for steamer passengers, such as a waiting room and a luggage and ticket office.[7] The latter was designed by Stephen Salter (1861–1954), the son of the co-founder, who was not connected with the boating business, but who was significant to the city as 'the most eccentric of Oxford's turn-of-the century architects'.[8] He championed 'beautiful' buildings[9] and was responsible for a number of notable landmarks in the city, including the Lloyd's Bank building at Carfax, where his office was based, and Wesley Hall on Cowley Road, of which John, James and George Salter were committee members (see chapter 7).[10] He also designed a number of villas in Boars Hill, the Isle of Wight (where he went to after Oxford), and Pangbourne (the so-called 'Seven Deadly Sins' by the Thames).

The firm continued to accumulate property on the south side of the river with the acquisition in 1884 of 'land, warehouses, shops and timber drying sheds at Buckingham and Brook Street'.[11] This was followed by the purchase of 5 Brook Street and the neighbouring workshops in 1891, owing to the liquidation of the Oxford Building and Investment Company. In 1906, Salters' also leased from Brasenose College a cottage, yard and stables belonging to Grandpont House (where John Henry Salter had briefly lived), which was next to the firm's Grandpont Yard. Furthermore, two properties on the north-west side of the river on Thames Street were added in 1895 and 1896 respectively, which included Charles Bossom's boat-building shop and yards.[12] It is not clear what happened to these, but the firm was using a yard in a similar area at the end of Isis Street, for storage, until the end of the 1940s.

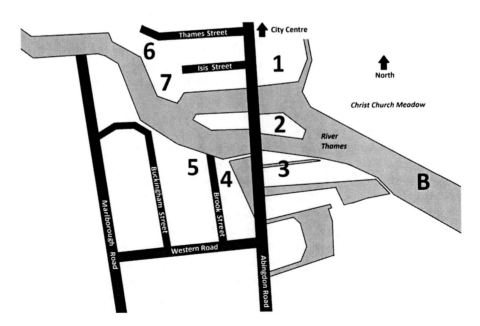

Sites occupied by Salters' at Folly Bridge (c. 1900, plan not to scale): 1. St Aldate's Yard; 2. The Island; 3. Grandpont Yard; 4. The Red Shops; 5. Brook Street Yards (backing on to Buckingham Street); 6. Thames Street Yard; 7. Isis Street Yard; B: Site of the green barge.

The company insurance book (1887–1945) shows what the buildings on the east side of the river were used for. On the island there were offices, stores, boat-building workshops, a dressing room and an upholstery works-room, whilst at Grandpont Yard there was a private dwelling, a boat-building sawmill, a barge-building sawmill, a punt-building shop, an engineer's workshop, a timber store, a cart shed, a scull-maker's shop, a general store and stables.[13]

By the late 1940s, St Aldate's Yard housed a racing boat-builder's workshop, 'Shop thirteen', used for overhauling the rental fleet engines, and stores. The Red Shops at Brook Street were used for storage, whilst the yard on the opposite side of the road (now Jean Marguerite Court), housed an engineer's shop on the ground floor and a carpentry workshop and awning shop, which made upholstery and cordage, above it. The ground floor of the yard next to it (now Arthur Salter Court) was used for punt- and skiff-building, whilst the second floor was the paint shop, where the colours were mixed and where the varnish and enamel were stored.[14]

The commercial property in Oxford was not confined to Folly Bridge. In 1892 land near Iffley was acquired, so that the firm could build a slipway dedicated to handling larger passenger craft. Salters' appears to have been very adaptable in this respect, as in 1888 it had asked the Thames Conservancy for permission to build one at Folly Bridge,[15] before considering a larger site near Osney lock in 1891.[16] The Iffley building was roughly doubled in size in 1900, with a second channel added, so that the firm could start building its own passenger craft, after its supplier stopped operating (see chapter 2). It also provided additional space in which to store and maintain the existing fleet, as it could accommodate six steamers at once. Furthermore, the firm also inherited property in Benson Place on the river Cherwell (near Lady Margaret Hall), but this was not held for long (1919–21) as the lease was not renewed by St John's College.[17]

The numerous sites managed to survive the years immediately preceding the First World War intact, after the Women's Social and Political Union, a radical wing of the suffragettes, burned down a number of buildings in the area. Although an attack on Nuneham House, home of Lewis Harcourt MP, was foiled in 1912 (with Salters' boats used for reconnaissance),[18] the following year Councillor Basson's timber yard on Marlborough Road and Rough's boatyard at Long Bridges were both destroyed.[19] The latter may have been considered an easy target, as it was situated on the towpath in a relatively quiet location, but it is possible that it may have been specifically chosen because Rough was the leading racing boat-builder at the time. The sport of rowing was an almost exclusively male pastime and some at the university believed it to be intrinsically bound up with the masculine ideal of an Oxbridge man.[20] By contrast, Salters' may have been spared, as James was a vice president of the Oxford Women's Suffrage Society from 1913 to 1915, and the firm was closely associated with women's rowing at the university (see chapter 1).

The business did, however, experience two large fires at its workshops in 1920 and 1953 respectively, both of which appear to have been accidents. The first of these affected the Iffley slipway on 24 May 1920 (during eights week) and caused an estimated £30,000 worth of damage to the partially insured building. Two launches that were being built were destroyed, but the hull of the *Caucase* remained intact and the firm was able to use this to produce the fittingly named *Phoenix* (later renamed *Hurley* and deployed in the steamer fleet).[21] The workshop was subsequently rebuilt to a new concrete design with electric rather than gas lighting. The second major fire affected the saw mill at Grandpont Yard on 12 November 1953. The building was completely gutted, but four fire engines managed to save the neighbouring workshops and the firm was particularly indebted to a student who dived into the river in order to cut loose three launches.[22]

The firm's ability to adapt to the changing conditions is shown by the redevelopment of many of its properties, which occupied prime waterside locations, at the end of the twentieth century. The long-term lease of St Aldate's Yard expired, resulting in its conversion in 1977 into 'The Head of the River' pub (a name chosen by residents). This was costly for the business, as the full repairing lease led to a protracted dispute over the standard to which the buildings needed to be 'restored'.[23] In 1982, to avoid the same thing happening again, the firm, despite not being in a strong financial position at the time, bought its offices on the island, as well as the Red Shops on the east side of Brook Street, for £175,000.[24] By that point, the many workshops were not only being used less, owing to the decline in certain areas of the business (see chapters 1–4), but also becoming a drain on resources, as they were costing a significant amount in rates. As a result, all of the yards in Brook Street were subsequently converted into flats. The first were the Red Shops in 1989, which were sold, partly to pay off some of the mortgage that had been taken out to purchase the site and the main offices. Grandpont Yard was then sold to Hertford College for a new student accommodation block that was opened in 2000; the firm retained six flats. The last two yards in Brook Street were retained, but were converted into residential apartments (now Jean Marguerite Court and Arthur Salter Court) in 2005 and 2008 respectively. In this respect Salters' was similar to a number of other Oxford businesses that altered their activities because of the rapidly rising property prices between 1996 and 2007. In the twenty-first century, for example, W. Lucy and Co., which was based at the Eagle Ironworks near Jericho and had a workforce of over 800 in the 1960s, moved its manufacturing overseas in order to reduce production costs.[25] Part of its diversification was the redevelopment of its former sites on either side of the canal into an office block and over 250 homes, which established the firm's property division as one of the city's largest private landlords.[26]

By 2010 Salters' was left with only two 'working' sites in Oxford: the headquarters on the island, from which the passenger boats operated, and the slipway located at Iffley, where the boat-building, maintenance and winter storage was carried out. The only visible reminder of Folly Bridge's once-thriving boat-building industry are two of the firm's cranes that remain, one at the end of Brook Street and one in the grounds of 'The Head of the River' pub.

Commercial Property: Outside Oxford

The commercial activities upon which the firm embarked required the acquisition of further properties on the Thames. One of the earliest was a second boatyard in Eton, which Salters' operated from 1870 to 1875, before it was sold following the departure of Stephen from the business (suggesting that the brothers may have operated from different premises). Furthermore, Salters' purchased property in Pangbourne in 1929, which included two boathouses and forty-nine boats, but this was sold the following year to the proprietor of the neighbouring 'Swan' pub.[27]

It was the firm's decision to start running a passenger boat service between Oxford and Kingston in 1888 that required the accumulation of the greatest variety of new sites, as the steamers had to use landing stages and mooring facilities at many of the different locations on the approximately 90-mile route. Some permanent bases were also needed: by the First World War, Salters' was renting a satellite office in Windsor, from A. Maynard,[28] which was subsequently bought and is still owned today (1 Thames Side). Furthermore, in the 1920s Salters' acquired a small office in Kingston near the pier (retained until 1974), and in 1945 a larger yard at Reading from the acquisition of E. Cawston's. The latter housed a working office until 1973, and was leased to a riverside restaurant in the early 1990s, as it is today.

The Thames Catering Company, the business that was set up to provide food and drink for the steamers (see chapter 4), also required a number of sites and by the late 1940s it had premises in Reading and Windsor, as well as a car park in Maidenhead.[29] In the 1960s it produced Salter's ice-cream and crisps from sites in Reading and Wallingford respectively, whilst it also ran a tea room on Nag's Head Island in Abingdon until the early 1970s.

The family also sought out other business opportunities further afield. The archive contains an undated plan of a yard in Cambridge (20–24 Chesterton Road), suggesting that Salters' may have considered acquiring it, whilst negotiations to purchase Aylestone Boathouse in Leicester were entered into in 1927, although the sale was not pursued after the quotation the firm received was deemed too high.[30]

The largest venture the family was involved with outside of Oxford was the lease of waterside property around the 70-acre reservoir at Rotton Park in Edgbaston. This was run under the auspices of the Edgbaston Reservoir Company (one of the Salter enterprises) and used as a pleasure resort. The site attracted around 10,000 visitors during the family's first Whitsuntide in charge (1892)[31] and the facilities included approximately seventy rental boats, many of which were built by the Oxford firm. Three of these were Una boats used in the first-ever race (on 18 May 1894), which led to the formation of the Midland Sailing Club,[32] whilst the passenger boat *Mayflower*, licensed for forty-eight passengers, was used for regular steamer trips. The firm posted operating profits of over £400 in 1892 and 1893, with the largest sources of income being admissions to the regular firework shows that were held from April to September (£1,062 9s 2d in 1893), general admissions to the site (£554 14s 4½d), boating charges (£475 0s 6d), admissions to skating (£280 0s 1½d), season tickets (£201 2s 6d), payments for using the rink (£171 7s 3d), general sales (£111 12s 4d) and steamer trips (£72 1s 11½d). Smaller amounts of money were generated by the use of the swings and automatic machines, rents, refreshments, and fees from those going bathing or fishing.[33]

The site was not without its potential problems, however, as during the drought of 1893 the water levels dropped to such an extent that the firm was unable to operate its steamer from 12 August onwards and its smaller craft from 13 September onwards. This caused Salters' to claim compensation from Birmingham Canal Navigations for loss of income.[34] Yet the firm was able to exploit the extremely cold winter of 1894–95, as the lake became the 'principal attraction in the district' for nearly three weeks with an average of 2,000 people using the rink every day, and more on the weekends. The normally sabbatarian family (see chapter 7) even allowed ice skating on Sunday, with the profits being donated to charity.[35]

By 1911 the business was making a loss, however, and the firm agreed to sell it for £3,500 on a hire purchase scheme to Fred Millin, the manager of the site (and the brother-in-law of John and James Salter). Part of his business model included opening on Sunday, which he believed would contribute an additional £500 a year, thereby ensuring an estimated profit of £445 annually.[36] Yet the war appears to have put paid to this arrangement, and after posting further losses, which required loans from the Oxford business and Frank Salter to keep it going, the property was eventually sold in the 1930s.[37]

Residential Property

In addition to its commercial sites, the family and firm amassed a large amount of residential property. This consisted of, firstly, the homes of the Salter family, some of which were used for generating further income in the form of farm produce; secondly, buildings that were used as a source of rental income; and thirdly, houses that were used as subsidised accommodation for the staff.

The family came to reside by Folly Bridge, but by the mid-1860s they had started to accumulate properties outside of Oxford on Boars Hill. By 1869, Stephen owned Pickett's Heath Farm, whilst John owned Middle Farm in Wootton by 1883.[38] The family often spent their summers in Boars Hill, but the properties also had some commercial use. By 1893 one of the farms (of 320 acres) was needed to 'keep up the supply of horses used in carting the boats back from Oxford to London',[39] whilst produce was regularly sold from both Boars Hill and Folly Bridge, ranging from prize-winning animals and eggs for sitting, to hay and straw.

Table 5.1 Property owned by John Salter in 1890 (as shown in his will)[40]

38, 39, 40 and 49 St Aldate's
8 Isis Street (House, Boathouse and Shed)
Isis Lodge and Cottage
Shop at Brook Street
1, 2, 3, 4 and 5 Brook Street
Yard and Shed, Buckingham Street
23, 25, 27, 29, 31, 33 and three other 'unfinished' houses in Buckingham Street
1, 2, 3 and 5 Pipemaker's Yard
4 Pipemaker's Yard (Warehouse)
4 acres of ground in Wells Close
Allotments, Wootton, Berks
Three Cottages on the Green, Wootton

Cottage, Wootton
One blacksmith's shop, Wootton
Eight cottages (Henwood Cottages) in Wootton
Gross total capital: £7,728. Rents and interest: £86 6s 8d. Total: £7,814 6s 8d

John bought his brother's stake in the business in 1875 (see chapter 1) and his will (Table 5.1) shows how wealthy he had become by the time of his death on 21 January 1890. It lists a large number of freehold properties, the majority of which were residential, in an overall estate valued at £31,221 0s 7d[41] (almost £9,000 more than his eldest son's estate was worth forty years later).

The 'unfinished' houses on Buckingham Street show that Salters' was building up its accommodation for the workforce at this time (probably on the land it had purchased in 1884). The properties were built by the firm's employees out of shuttered concrete, which also provided a source of out-of-season work, as they were constructed in the autumn (see chapter 6). This not only provided subsidised housing, with the surplus rented out to the public, but was also a useful source of year-round rental income. In 1921, for example, a house in Buckingham Street was being rented for £2 10s per annum.[42]

At the beginning of the twentieth century a number of prominent businessmen on the local council were also property developers.[43] Amongst them was John Henry Salter, who became involved with a much bigger housing project than he had worked on previously. In 1899, he bought 4 acres from Brasenose College for £2,563, which he divided into 105 lots on Abingdon Road, Whitehouse Road, Kineton Road and Chilswell Road.[44] He then presided over the construction of the houses (as well as the

Salters'-built houses on Buckingham Street. (Photo by author in 2011)

sale of some undeveloped lots), which included ten that were retained and added to the stock of staff accommodation.

The firm's Statement of Rents from 1911 shows that although the blacksmith's shop in Wootton and the land on Wells Close had been dispensed with, over thirty new houses had been acquired since 1890 (Table 5.2), which brought the overall total to more than seventy. Few private individuals would have owned such a number at this time, as the most significant landlord from the building trade in 1905 was the 'colossus' T.H. Kingerlee, who owned 186, whilst the major figure from the retail sector was the grocer G.W. Cooper, who had sixty-five.[45]

Table 5.2 New properties that had been acquired by Salters' between 1890 and 1911[46]

	Insurance dates
4, 5, 6 and 7, 8a and 8b Isis Street	1879–1920
7, 9, 11, 13, 15, 17, 19 and 21 Buckingham Street	1892–1920
40, 40a, 42, 44, 46, 48 and 50 Marlborough Road	1897–1920
House by Grandpont Yard	1901–1920
4, 6, 8, 10, 12, 24, 26, 28, 30 and 32 Chilswell Road	1906–1914
Fulham Villa (Folly Bridge)	1906
14 and 15 Thames Street	–
1, 3 and 5 Cobden Crescent	–

The residential property was sold when the business needed additional funds, as in 1935 when 38–40 St Aldate's and 1–4 Pipemaker's Yard were purchased from the firm by the Corporation of Oxford for £1,650.[47] According to David Nutt and Merlyn Coates, whose parents lived in the firm's housing, Salters' eventually sold off most of this property *en masse* in the 1950s, when it was experiencing financial difficulties. They recall that their parents were offered the opportunity to purchase their houses and that 1 Brook Street, for example, was priced at £400.[48] The firm retained a small amount of housing for key workers, but it was not until the twenty-first century that it began to build up its residential property once again, through the development of some of its yards, although this was rented to private tenants rather than the workforce.

Significance of the Property

The property was important to the firm because the location of the business affected what commercial activities were possible and occupying water frontage kept out competitors. Furthermore, the sites were not only used for other forms of enterprise, but were a crucial reservoir of capital, which Salters' relied upon for its survival.

David Blomfield has shown that on the Upper Tidal Thames the location of a yard was critical in determining whether a waterside business was able to make the transition into the leisure market.[49] It is significant, therefore, that Salters' came to occupy a number of the yards most accessible from Oxford's city centre, which is why its property was used for notable events such as the Lifeboat Day (see chapter 2). The importance of a good location was shown by the decision of Howard and Sons, now the largest boat-letter on the river Cherwell (under the new name of Magdalen Bridge Boathouse Ltd), to move its location four times in the twentieth century, in order to secure a better position.[50]

Finding strategic sites in all of the places on the Thames from which Salters' operated passenger boats was a particular challenge, because gaining mooring rights to the most prominent locations tended to be expensive. The firm tried to find places that were easily accessible for those arriving by rail, but it could not afford to secure all of the prime locations at the many places it operated from. A site's suitability could also change over time. The firm's office in Windsor (just east of Windsor bridge) was well positioned to receive visitors from the nearby Riverside Station (London and South Western Railway), for example, but it was not so convenient for those arriving by road. The Promenade (west of Windsor bridge), where its competitors operated, not only had the advantage of being closer to the rival Central Station (Great Western Railway), but also was where much of the parking would eventually be situated. Furthermore, the Promenade was also a more visible site, which made it a good location from which to run short trips, because casual passengers could find it easily. This was significant because this type of service became increasingly popular at the end of the twentieth century (see chapter 4).

Nevertheless, Salters' was able to introduce short trips from Windsor, whilst it also started them from Henley, Marlow and Runnymede, which were locations deemed especially good for attracting casual passengers, because the landing stages were in parks where many people congregated. The firm was well aware of the need to adapt to the changing topography and it entered into many negotiations to try to secure better sites to operate from. These were not always successful, however, such as in 1920, when Christ Church turned down the firm's request to open a yard in Oxford by the mouth of the river Cherwell, which would have provided access to the Thames (via Jackdaw Lane) from the rapidly expanding eastern suburbs of the city.[51]

Occupying a good location was also important because it could keep out competitors. Unlike in Cambridge, where the large amount of river frontage led to 'punt wars' breaking out between numerous rival operators in the twenty-first century,[52] there were a relatively small number of prominent waterside sites in many of the places on the Thames. This is why securing the main yards around Folly Bridge in Oxford, for example, was particularly strategic.

The firm's properties were also important because they could be used for subsequent forms of commercial exploitation. Many of the waterside sites had mooring facilities, for example, which could be rented to clients, whilst Salters' also offered winter storage for boats in its yards. Amongst the shorter-term initiatives the firm tried was a café on the island, which operated from 1934 to the mid-1940s, serving 'Dainty teas, ices, light refreshments, fruit luncheons' and 'picnic supplies at shortest notice',[53] and a campsite by the slipway that opened in 1982 and was closed two decades later.[54] The latter was not without precedent, as Salters' had caravans on the 2-acre site in the late 1940s, which were presumably used as temporary housing for its workforce (see chapter 6).[55]

Finally, and most importantly, the property was a reservoir of capital that was 'absolutely vital' for undergirding the company's finances.[56] One of the main challenges for Salters' was trying to maintain a cash-flow during the winter and spring months, when the vast majority of income was accumulated in the summer. This was a problem for even the most popular outdoor tourist attractions, like Oxford Zoo (based in Kidlington from 1931 to 1937), which in 1932 attracted 160,000 visitors and yet was forced to close temporarily because of insufficient takings in the winter.[57] The normal way in which Salters' dealt with the problem was relying upon its overdraft facility, although keeping this down was a recurring challenge. During the Great Depression the company's turnover dropped by approximately 40 per cent between 1930 and 1932,[58] and its overall debt to the bank reached almost £20,000, which threatened its ability to pay the wage bill.[59] As a result, Sir Arthur Salter sought to negotiate directly with W.M. Goodenough, a board member of Barclay's, about how to resolve the matter. The measures they agreed upon included paying the interest on the joint accounts separately every six months to prevent it accruing, and the setting up of a directors' joint loan account to lend the business funds in the spring time, when money was running low, and to then repay a certain amount in the autumn, once most of the income had been received.[60]

The directors' loans provided the flexibility that was crucial in maintaining the firm's liquidity in the short term, although the amount that was borrowed and repaid was dictated by the financial situation at the time, which was dependent on the wider economy and whether or not it had been a good summer. Yet the loans and the overdraft needed to be secured against something and it was the firm's property that was generally used for this. In February 1913 and May 1915, for example, Salters' had to deposit the deeds for a number of its buildings with Barclay's bank in order to receive additional funds. The former was a difficult time for the business because a 'further loan' of £1,500 that had been taken out four months earlier proved insufficient and Salters' had to resort to mortgaging one of the passenger boats it was in the process of building (Royalty) for another £1,500 to cover the wage bill.[61] If the financial situation was particularly bad, then the firm resorted to selling off its property to raise funds, which is what happened in the 1950s. This was only a short-term solution, however, and by the start of the twenty-first century, Salters' was favouring the conversion of its commercial property into residential flats, as a way of creating more sustainable year-round income.

Indeed, the increasing importance of this side of the business was officially recognised at the beginning of the twenty-first century when John Salter, who had his own lettings firm,[62] presided over a restructuring of the company that established property management as the focus of Salter Bros Ltd.[63] This was much more profitable than the riskier and seasonal activities relating to water-based leisure, which were devolved to the newly separated Salter's Steamers Ltd.[64] A good illustration of this is Jean Marguerite Court, a development that cost the equivalent of £35,000 for each of the thirteen one-bedroom flats built in 2005. The expense of almost the entire project was covered by the (required) sale of some of the properties for social housing, leaving the firm with eight flats that not only provided rental income, but were each valued at over £200,000.[65]

· · ·

Salters' began operating from a single site at Folly Bridge, but in order to expand the business the firm accumulated a large amount of property, which included numerous commercial sites in Oxford and other locations. It also built up a large amount of residential housing that provided subsidised accommodation for the workforce, as well as year-round rental income. Although this side of the business was less apparent to customers, it was crucial for the long-term survival of Salters'. Indeed, it is a testament to the early success of the firm that it was largely property, both commercial and residential, accumulated in the first fifty years of its existence that provided the assets with which it overcame some of the major financial challenges of the following 100 years. This was especially important in the twentieth century, as the firm went through some difficult phases, which was partly caused by the transformation of the employment market in Oxford.

Notes

1   *Lock to Lock Times*, 5 August 1893, p. 1.
2   *Hunt's Oxford Directory*, 1861, p. 4. John Salter lived at 45 St Aldate's and Stephen lived at Isis House.
3   SA Letter from Henry Galpin to George Salter, 14 August 1943 (summarising the legal history of the property the firm owned).
4   *Jackson's Oxford Journal*, 15 October 1870. Thomas Hall died in 1869 and the archive contains paperwork relating to his family's business dating back to 1773.
5   SA Arthur Salter correspondence to Frank Dix (undated) in preparation for the book *Royal River Highway* (published in 1985).
6   SA Lease for Property at Folly Bridge, 25 March 1884.
7   *Jackson's Oxford Journal*, 10 November 1900.
8   G. Tyack, *Oxford: An Architectural Guide* (Oxford, 1998), p. 269.
9   *Jackson's Oxford Journal*, 25 January 1902.
10 J. Boylan, *Cowley Road Methodist Church Centre, Oxford* (Oxford, 2004), p. 93.
11 SA Conveyance from Mrs R. H. Barrett, 24 June 1884.
12 SA Letter from Henry Galpin to George Salter, 14 August 1943.
13 SA Insurance Book 1887–1945.
14 Interview with Bill Dunckley, 2 February 2012.
15 MLD Thames Conservancy Minute Book Z, 6 February 1888.
16 MLD Thames Conservancy Minute Book 7, 2 November 1891.
17 SA Abstract of the Title of F.M.O. Ogilvie (deceased), 28 February 1903 (the lease passed to Salters' when Ogilvie died in 1919).
18 *Oxford Times*, 6 July 1912, p. 9 and 26 October 1912, p. 10.
19 *Oxford Times*, 7 June 1913, p. 16, 29 November 1913, p. 16 and K. Bradley 'The Suffrage Movement in Oxford, 1870–1920' (Oxford Polytechnic MA thesis, 1993), p. 53.
20 Deslandes, *Oxbridge Men*, p. 168.
21 *Oxford Chronicle*, 28 May 1920, p. 11.
22 *Oxford Times*, 12 November 1953, p. 1.
23 Interview with John Salter, 20 December 2011.
24 *Oxford Star*, 29–30 April 1982, p. 16.
25 *Oxford Times*, 11 January 2002.
26 *Oxford Times*, 10 August 2004 and 9 November 2005.
27 SA Folder relating to the Pangbourne Property (1929).
28 SA Letter from A. Maynard to A. Chamberlain (Salter Bros), dated 31 March 1917 (discussing renewing the lease).

29 SA Thames Catering Company Ltd, Balance Sheet, 31 December 1949.

30 SA Letter from Gordon Biggs to John Salter, 4 March 1927.

31 *Birmingham Daily Post*, 7 June 1892.

32 J. Storer, 'Memoirs of the Midland Sailing Club', in *The Midland Sailing Club Journal* (unpublished, 1922), p. 4 (sent to author by Alan Birch).

33 SA Edgbaston Reservoir Company Accounts 1892 and 1893.

34 SA Letter from Clerk of Birmingham Canal Navigations to Messrs Salter Bros, 18 January 1894.

35 *Birmingham Daily Post*, 12 February 1895.

36 SA Letter from Fred Millin to John Salter, 1 December 1911.

37 There is also an unreferenced note in the archive belonging to Jim Cowan that suggests that Salters' also briefly ran Blackroot Pool in Sutton Courtenay after the First World War.

38 *Jackson's Oxford Journal*, 1 May 1869 and 6 October 1883.

39 *Lock to Lock Times*, 5 August 1893, p. 2.

40 SA Inland Revenue Document, 21 January 1890. Pipemaker's Yard was close to the present police station.

41 Ibid.

42 SA Rental Agreements, 25 December 1920.

43 M. Graham, 'The Suburbs of Victorian Oxford: Growth in a Pre-industrial City' (Leicester University PhD thesis, 1985), pp. 316–17.

44 Ibid., p. 116.

45 Graham, 'Suburbs of Victorian Oxford', pp. 314–15. Graham defines a 'major landlord' as someone owning eleven or more properties (seventy-seven individuals in total).

46 SA Statement of Rents (1911) and Insurance Book 1887–1945.

47 SA Letter from C.M. Moon (manager of Barclay's) to George Salter, 13 April 1935.

48 Emails to the author from David Nutt, December 2005, and Merlyn Coates, February 2005.

49 Blomfield, 'Tradesmen of the Thames', p. 100.

50 Rivington, *Punting*, p. 140.

51 SA Letter from the Treasurer of Christ Church to J.E. Salter, 22 October 1920.

52 *The Guardian*, 21 August 2009.

53 *Oxford University Summer Eights 'Blue' Race Chart 1934*, advertisement.

54 *Oxford Times*, 23 April 1982, p. 1.

55 SA Letter from Oxford City Council to Salter Bros, 1 October 1947 (granting a year's licence for six caravans).

56 Interview with John Salter, 20 December 2011.

57 *Oxford Mail*, 24 April 1933, p. 5.

58 SA Salter Bros Ltd End of Year Accounts 1930–32. This excludes the revenue from catering, as this was recorded differently (a profit was given).

59 SA Letter from C.M. Moon to G. Salter, 9 February 1932. Barclay's intransigent attitude to the overdraft eventually resulted in the firm changing banks in the second half of the twentieth century.

60 SA Letter from C.M. Moon to G. Salter, 15 July 1933.

61 SA Letter from G.H. Sides to Salter Bros, 20 June 1913.

62 The firm is Kidlington Property Management Ltd.

63 CHC Articles of Association Adopted, 1 December 2008.

64 CHC Certificate of Name Change from Thames Catering Company to Salter's Steamers Ltd, 3 December 2001.

65 Interview with John Salter, 20 December 2011.

6

The Workforce

I have always envied those lucky people who find their life's happiness in messing about in boats with pots and paint and yards of intractable rope.

S.P.B. Mais, referring to Salters' workforce in 1955[1]

This book has so far shown how Salters' focused on five areas of commercial activity, each of which changed significantly over time. Yet the firm's economic performance was also dependent on the work of a host of employees. Indeed, the employment structure of a business can have a significant bearing on whether or not it is able to succeed. The collapse of the Thames shipbuilding industry, for example, was partly caused by a rigid system of wages, the presence of powerful unions that kept levels of pay high and an absence of a reservoir of skilled labour.[2]

Size and Composition

The 1881 population census records that the firm was employing '43 men and boys'. The 'Great Salter' may not have been 'every bit as important among Oxonians as Baron Rothschild among financiers', as one visitor claimed,[3] but the firm would have been a large employer in the area, even though it was inevitably much smaller than the London shipbuilding yards, which were employing on average between 400 and 500 employees in 1871.[4] As the census was taken in April, it is likely to refer mainly to the full-time and year-round staff rather than the seasonal workers. Unlike smaller firms in the city, Salters' had a Sick Club, which provides a conservative estimate of the number of this type of employee. The document lists fifty-five original members in 1906 and this figure remains around the fifty mark until the end of the book (1940),[5] which suggests that the core workforce remained fairly constant in size, despite the fluctuations in the firm's economic performance.

The year-round employees were joined each summer (from the end of May to the end of September) by those working with the firm's pleasure boats. By August 1893, Salters' had 100 to 110 employees (eighty of whom were in Oxford), which was roughly double the size of the winter workforce.[6] The firm was therefore a significant employer in the city as there were few large (non-university) employers at this time. By 1911, 26.9 per cent of the employed population of Oxford worked in domestic service, whilst only 16.5 per cent was engaged in industry (compared to 73.7 per cent in Coventry, for example).[7] By far the largest employer was the University Press, which had a workforce of around 750 by 1911,[8] whilst another major firm was John Allen and Sons (previously the Oxfordshire Steam Ploughing Company), which had 200 by 1900.[9]

The number of seasonal staff that the firm needed to recruit grew during the twentieth century, as the fleet of passenger boats was enlarged (see chapter 4). By the 1950s and 1960s, the company was employing between 110 and 140 workers during the summer, in addition to the part-time catering staff of Thames Catering Company. On the eve of the Second World War, the higher figure would have ranked Salters' as the tenth largest non-university employer in the city,[10] although there would have been considerably fewer staff in the winter. By this stage, however, the city had acquired a major industry and the firm's workforce was dwarfed by the numbers employed at Pressed Steel (5,250) and Morris (4,670), whilst the University Press, Oxford's largest industry thirty years earlier, had approximately 840.[11]

The workforce at Salters' did not grow in a linear fashion, as is shown by the wage bill between 1914 and 1949. The most significant increases occurred during the two world wars, and in both the late 1920s and late 1940s, suggesting that additional staff were taken on during the busy periods. From 1917 onwards, for example, more employees were required to build military craft (see chapter 2) and by the end of the summer in 1918 there were 167 workers on the firm's books – the greatest number shown in any of the records.[12] The wage bill was higher still in 1919, reaching £21,683 3s 8d (having been only £7,416 9s 7d three years earlier),[13] as the firm benefited from a post-war rise in both leisure activities on the river and orders for boats. Conversely, the wage bill fell considerably in both the early 1920s and the early 1930s, showing that staffing levels were reduced during the quieter periods. The latter was the result of the Great Depression, when the firm tried to generate more work for its workforce by constructing canoes in-house, instead of importing many of them from Canada. Nevertheless, some employees still had to be dismissed in order to save money, although some were subsequently rehired when business picked up again.[14]

It was not just the size of the workforce that changed significantly over time, but also its composition. The employment of a sail-maker in 1859[15] suggests that the firm had

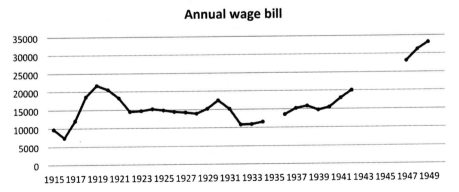

Annual wage bill

─■─ Wage bill

specialist employees from the outset, although it is not until March 1916 that there is a detailed breakdown of the overall employment structure at the company, as the firm had to collect details of its staff members to assess their eligibility for war service.[16] Oxford had a high proportion of craftsmen and unskilled labourers,[17] and Salters' was no exception. Over half (54.4 per cent) of the employees whose jobs were graded were classed as skilled, whilst 13.9 per cent and 31.7 per cent were listed as semi-skilled and unskilled respectively.

The firm did some recruitment from within families (see p. 164), as there were thirteen addresses containing one or more employee with the same surname, whilst there were thirty-five surnames in total shared by more than one staff member. There were no female employees until 1917, when a Miss Taylor joined the firm as a typist and junior clerk – a minor example of women entering the workforce during the First World War.[18]

Although the data cannot account for any staff member who left for military service in the early stages of the conflict, it can be used to show roughly what the workforce would have looked like before the outbreak of war. Sixty-eight of the employees listed in March 1916 were working there two years earlier. This included the four directors from the family, as well as the three foremen from the boat-building department (T. Arnold Baker, E.J. Shaw and Robert Tedd) who were in charge of the Iffley Slipway, wood-working and sail-making respectively. A very wide range of trades was represented and, again a high proportion of the workforce was classed as skilled (66.2 per cent, including clerical staff). The three foremen were also in this group, as were all but one of the painters, including the brothers, Edward and Roland Butterfield, who had been heraldic decorators prior to joining the firm.[19] A further 17.6 per cent, consisting mainly of launch drivers, were classed as semi-skilled, whilst the remaining 16.2 per cent, which included the watermen and the carter, were listed as unskilled. Boat-builders were predictably the largest occupational group with fourteen employees, although David Nutt, the sole 'punt and barge builder', was classed separately. There were also five steel workers on the company pay roll (two riveters and three platers), suggesting that the foreman (Baker) no longer had to 'provide and superintend' all of his labour, as had been the case at the beginning of the century (see chapter 2).

As would be expected, many of the employees were given new roles during the war. In March 1916, the sawmill staff, most of the boat-builders and the blacksmiths were deployed on cutters, whilst the platers and riveters produced buoys. Two of the boat-builders made collapsible craft, whilst one of the joiners and a number of painters were assigned to the construction of pontoons. Those who retained their previous jobs included the majority of both the launch drivers and the watermen (although some of the latter were assigned secondary roles, like labouring), whilst only one director remained (Frank Salter).

A card index of all of the employees who left the firm in the 1950s and 1960s shows that the workforce was involved in a more varied range of occupations than in 1914. The number of seasonal employees appears disproportionately large, but it shows that by the 1950s the boat-building department had declined since the earlier record, whilst the steamer department had grown. Almost two-thirds of the staff members had jobs associated with the passenger boats, which included deck hands (the most common

Jobs in March 1916

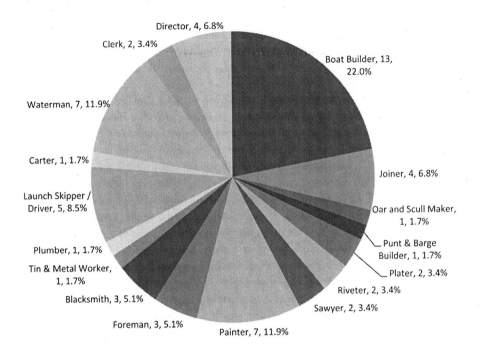

Director, 4, 6.8%

Clerk, 2, 3.4%

Waterman, 7, 11.9%

Carter, 1, 1.7%

Launch Skipper / Driver, 5, 8.5%

Plumber, 1, 1.7%

Tin & Metal Worker, 1, 1.7%

Blacksmith, 3, 5.1%

Foreman, 3, 5.1%

Painter, 7, 11.9%

Sawyer, 2, 3.4%

Riveter, 2, 3.4%

Plater, 2, 3.4%

Punt & Barge Builder, 1, 1.7%

Oar and Scull Maker, 1, 1.7%

Joiner, 4, 6.8%

Boat Builder, 13, 22.0%

occupation) and a number of 'onshore' roles, like the twenty-four guides (4 per cent of the workforce) based in Windsor, who took passengers on walking tours around the town and castle. There were also specialist employees who were the only ones assigned to their particular role, including a blacksmith, bricklayer, cabinet-maker, coalman, electrician, fitter, handyman, petrol-pump attendant, rigger, sail-maker, scull-maker and plumber's assistant.[20] The job titles give an indication of the level of skill needed, but the experience of ex-employee Derek Bromhall suggests that they cannot all be taken at face value. Whilst studying at Balliol College during the 1950s, he had approached the firm for a summer job and after confirming he could drive a car he was told 'Right, you're an engineer then'.[21] Nevertheless, there had been a reduction in the number of skilled employees, as only approximately a third of those listed were in jobs that were classed as such (including those in clerical roles).[22]

Family associations with the workforce persisted, with seventy-six of the 247 surnames mentioned in the First World War list (30.8 per cent) reappearing in the 1950s data set. Although a proportion of these may have been coincidental, this suggests that some had continued to work for the firm since the conflict. Moreover, there were fourteen addresses providing more than one employee for Salters' and, for the first time, this included three couples who were husband and wife. The employment of more female staff was a major change from the First World War period, as there were fifty-nine women recorded in the 1950s, a figure that represented 8.9 per cent of the total number of workers listed. The jobs, however, were all those traditionally associated with

Jobs at the firm (those who left Salters' in the 1950s)

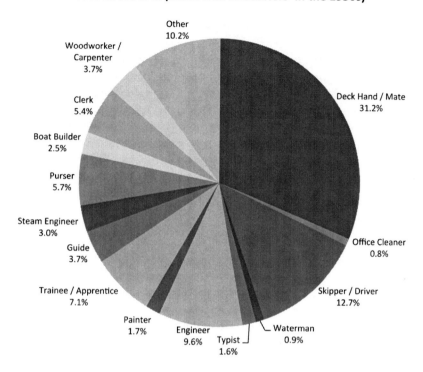

women at the time, with the vast majority employed in administrative roles (74.1 per cent) and none crewing on the boats (although there would have been female caterers on board working for Thames Catering Company).[23]

By the 1960s the workforce still covered a wide variety of occupations, the deck hands again accounting for the largest proportion of staff, with a similar figure (35.2 per cent) to the previous decade (31.2 per cent). The major difference, however, was in the boat-building side of the business, as the number of carpenters and boat-builders (including shipwrights) had declined dramatically. In the 1950s they only accounted for 6.2 per cent of those listed (thirty employees), but by the 1960s, the decade in which the firm constructed the fewest craft, this had fallen further to only 2.3 per cent (seventeen employees). Indeed, only approximately a fifth of those recorded in the latter decade were in jobs that could be classed as skilled (including those in clerical roles). There were also fewer employees being trained, as the apprentices accounted for only 3.6 per cent of those listed (twenty-seven employees) compared with 7 per cent (forty-six employees) in the previous decade. There had also been a reduction in the number of steam engineers from nineteen (3 per cent) to six (0.8 per cent), as many of the passenger boats had been converted to diesel by that point – a process that was completed in 1966. Furthermore, some of the maintenance duties had been devolved to the pursers, with twelve of the sixty being listed also as engineers. Again, a number of specialist employees were the only ones assigned to their particular role. These included a cabinet-maker, blacksmith, cook, lorry driver, marine engineer, plater, rigger, representative, sign-writer, store woman and upholsterer, as well as those in charge of the wharf, camping store and sail shop respectively.

Of the 508 surnames listed in the 1950s, 111 recur in the 1960s (21.9 per cent), suggesting that some families continued their association with the firm. Indeed, there were twenty-one addresses providing more than one employee.[24] The proportion of women employees had dropped slightly (10.1 per cent, down from 12.8 per cent in the 1950s), but as the 1960s data set was larger, this still represented an increase in real terms from fifty-eight employees to seventy-six. Again, the majority were in administrative roles (thirty-five), although the most common single occupation was the courier (twenty-seven), used by the Windsor office to escort excursion parties. For the first time, there were a number of female employees doing roles that had previously been the exclusive preserve of male staff members – three pursers, two employees in charge of stores and a single deck hand.

Recruitment

Over the course of the twentieth century there was also a considerable change in where Salters' recruited its staff from. Many of the firm's skilled workers came through the apprenticeship system, which was operating from at least 1859.[25] Although the expansion of the motor industry caused many smaller employers in the city to stop this form of training by the 1930s,[26] Salters' continued to offer it until the late twentieth century. Nevertheless, the competition in the job market may explain why the length of the apprenticeship was progressively reduced from seven years in the 1880s to four by the late 1950s. Furthermore, the training at the firm by the second half of the twentieth century was handled in an informal manner. Only some of those learning the trade were put on official apprenticeships and the onus was on the individual to develop their skills beyond the basic training.[27] By the 1970s it had become very difficult to find craftsmen and the firm was relying upon trainees from local schools.[28] The apprenticeship system eventually fell out of favour, because of the problems in dealing with disciplinary issues and the difficulty in retaining staff once they had completed their training (see p. 181).

As noted above, Salters' also gained a number of employees from several families that enjoyed long associations with the firm. This suggests that jobs at the business were considered a good career option. Families with the Thames 'in the blood', included the Knights (boat-builders)[29] and the Palmers (carters),[30] who had both contributed more than one generation of employees to Salters' by the end of the nineteenth century. From the Sick Club records between 1906 and 1940 we can see a number of instances of the same surname belonging to at least two individuals: Archer (1919–30), Beechey (1920), Beesley (1909–40), Butterfield (1909–27), Gillams (1906–40), Jackman (1906–22), Morgan (1933–40), Nutt (1922–34), Paintin (1906–13), Palmer (1910–17) and Taylor (1917–40).[31] Those who were shown as training their own children during the First World War period included the 'sawmill foreman' E.J. Shaw, who was in charge of (amongst others) his son Cyril, a 'woodworking machinist', and the 'oar and scull maker' B. Collar, who had his son Frank (who in 1932 went on to start his own successful business)[32] as the 'assistant paddle maker'.[33] By the end of the twentieth century there were still a few families connected with the business, like the Dunckleys and the Andrews, but the younger generations were no longer remaining at the firm.

Salters' also sourced many workers who had skills that were transferable. The previous jobs of 213 workers who joined the firm between 1916 and 1919 are recorded (Table 6.1) and the largest occupational group were joiners (sixty-six employees), although the firm also attracted some boat-builders, engineers, skippers, painters and carpenters. Salters' also received two employees (the brothers Fred and G.W. Tull) who had previously been tug skippers from Kingston. It did not appear to have gained many staff directly from Oxford's other boating community at Fisher Row, partly because many of those working on the waterways there had already left the area by the start of the twentieth century.[34] Nevertheless, members of some of the well-known families, like the Bossoms and Beesleys, tried to remain on the river in alternative occupations,[35] and as Salters' outlasted many other Thames businesses, a few inevitably ended up at the firm, like F.J. and T. Beesley in the inter-war period.[36] There were also a large number who came from the armed forces or from trades wholly unrelated to boating. Arthur North, for example, went from driving the Corporation refuse cart to crewing on the Oxford to Kingston steamers.

Table 6.1 The most common previous occupations of Salters' employees during the First World War[37]

Occupation	Number
Joiner	66
Army/Navy/RAF	20
Errand boy (different trades)	14
Assistant (different trades)	9
Painter	8
Boat-builder	7
Grocer (including grocer's assistants)	6
Carpenter (or related trade)	6
Engineer	6
University employee (inc. porters/assistants)	5
Builder	3
Great Western Railway employee	3
Publican (or in the brewery trade)	3
Driver	3
Scholar	3

Salters' appears to have been a source of summer employment for those who did not have jobs outside the university term – a perennial problem in Oxford until the 1920s. This may account for the large number of errand boys and assistants coming to the firm, as many trades would have been much quieter in the summer (although that age-group was also more transient). Only five employees came directly from jobs associated with the university, such as J. Bourton, a college porter, and P.H. Brown, a stoker from Keble College. None had been university students before joining Salters' and even in the 1950s and 1960s very few made the transition (less than 0.1 per cent of the staff listed as leaving). The comparatively small number is partly because the full boating season tended to start a little earlier (in late May) than the end of the academic term (normally in June). Nevertheless, there were some university occupations that complemented each other well. Former employee Albert Andrews was appointed Oxford University Boatman in 1950, but he was able to work for Salters' during his sixteen-week vacations, when the crews were not rowing.[38]

Finding people willing to work the summers only was an on-going challenge for Salters', but at the end of the nineteenth century the business started an initiative that helped to provide year-round employment for many of its staff members. A flexible system of labour was adopted in which workers in the boat-letting side of the business were retained during the autumn, in order to build houses for the staff, and they would then be lent to a gas or a coal and coke company, for their busiest period, before returning to the firm in the late spring.[39] It is likely that the system, in this precise form at least, did not last very long, as the majority of the firm's house-building was confined to the late 1880s and early 1890s, and after this period its seasonal needs grew much greater, as the passenger boat fleet expanded (see chapter 4). Nevertheless, Salters' always retained a few of its steamer and boat-letting staff over the winter, because there were many preparatory tasks that needed to be done to get the craft ready for the summer.

Over the course of the twentieth century there was a significant change in where (geographically) the employees were sourced from. Between 1916 and 1919 the addresses of 302 employees were given and 282 of these (nearly 95 per cent) lived in Oxford.[40] Twelve of the remaining twenty came from either London or the Caversham area, whilst the rest hailed either from nearby towns and villages or from other Thames locations. The addresses do not guarantee that they were all brought up in the place shown, but they suggest that, as in Oxford's nascent car industry at this time,[41] the firm was relying largely upon local labour.

The addresses of those living in the city show that the firm was also drawing much of its workforce from the area very close to Folly Bridge. Many lived in South Oxford (seventy-five), with more employees (sixteen) coming from Marlborough Road, where the firm owned a number of houses, than from any other street. A heavy concentration of workers (thirty-five) lived in St Ebbe's, which was just north of Folly Bridge and was historically a slum area, and there were many (fifty-four) spread across East Oxford near the Iffley Road slipway. Fewer lived in affluent North Oxford (twenty-two), although five of these were in Islip Road (2 miles from the city centre), possibly because they may once have been involved with the boathouse there on the river Cherwell. Smaller numbers resided in the working-class suburb of Jericho (nine), the village of Headington (thirteen), and the Botley Road area to the west (twelve).[42]

By the 1950s, however, the majority of the workforce was being drawn from outside the city, which was partly because the data included a greater number of the seasonal staff and partly because the expansion of the motor industry had caused a shortage of local labour and housing.[43] The city was still the most common place for the workforce to come from, but only just over a third (36.7 per cent) now came from it. Instead, the majority of the staff members came from either nearby towns and villages, like Kennington, or other Thames locations, like Windsor. Of the latter, the largest proportion (7.6 per cent) came from Caversham or Reading, which was partly owing to the yard Salters' had there. Perhaps the most surprising statistic is that 10.3 per cent of the workforce (sixty-eight employees) came from Southampton, an altogether different kind of boating area. Another change was the number of workers from Wales, with 2.5 per cent coming from either Barry or Cardiff (seventeen people in total). Recruitment for the motor industry ensured that by 1938 around 10 per cent of the city's insured workforce was Welsh,[44] and it is possible that some of these ended up at Salters'. The firm was, however, independently advertising in both Southampton and Wales for its seasonal staff.[45] The fact that many of the summer employees did not change their addresses suggests that many had permanent bases to return to after the season was finished. Many of the deck hands, for example, were teenage boys who presumably returned to their parents' houses over the winter.

As well as being more geographically spread out across the UK, the staff members living in the Oxford area (243 in total) were also more dispersed around the city than they had been forty years earlier, although this was partly a reflection of the suburban development that had occurred. This suggests that the firm was no longer as closely connected with the local community as it once had been. Nevertheless, again, the largest concentration of staff lived in the close vicinity of Folly Bridge, with many living in South Oxford (forty-four employees) and Marlborough Road once more being the most common address (eight). Several lived in St Ebbe's (fifteen) and the Jericho area (eight), although fewer were now living in south Oxford than east Oxford (forty-seven). The latter was where the majority of the new housing had been built for the car industry, and it was the area with the highest concentration of skilled labourers.[46] It was also closer to the firm's slipway, where four employees were listed as living, which included two on board *Wanderlust* (the ex-St John's College barge) and another on *The Santiago*. This was probably another form of subsidised accommodation, as the firm had sold most of its residential property in the 1950s (see chapter 5).

By the 1960s the proportion of staff members living in Oxford had declined further to 29 per cent. Although many still came from nearby towns and villages, the number coming from further afield had risen significantly. Windsor now accounted for 7.4 per cent of the workforce (up from 4.2 per cent in the 1950s) and there was also a small rise in those coming from the Southampton area (11.2 per cent, up from 10.3 per cent). Perhaps the most noticeable change, however, was a massive rise in Welsh employment. In the 1950s a mere 2.8 per cent of the employees came from across the border (mainly Barry and Cardiff), but by the 1960s those coming from Wales accounted for just under 15 per cent of the entire workforce.[47]

The trend of recruiting from outside of Oxford continued beyond this and in the 1970s, for example, the firm drew some of its staff from the boating communities of Norfolk.[48] The need for skilled workers was receding by this stage, however, owing to the introduction of fibreglass construction in the boat-building department (see chapter 2).

The Employment Market in Oxford, 1918–70

In order to understand why the firm began sourcing more of its staff from outside Oxford, it is necessary to look at the level of wages offered at Salters' and the socio-economic development of the city in the early twentieth century. Carpenters and joiners were being paid 8d an hour in 1913,[49] which was what skilled builders in Oxford were being paid at the time,[50] and we know that some of the workers were members of a trade union, because in July 1918 the Amalgamated Society of Carpenters and Joiners successfully took the firm to an arbitration panel in order to secure an award of 2½d extra per hour.[51] This was a period when 'new unionism'[52] was spreading rapidly across the country and it is likely that the presence of members amongst the employees was the result of the significant enlargement of the workforce during the war.

It is possible that the 1918 pay award protected Salters' from a widespread strike amongst Thames boat-builders during the summer of 1920, although the firm's geographical location almost certainly made a difference. The union demands show that the wages at Salters' were much lower than many equivalent businesses, although one would expect regional differences, firstly because the levels of pay in the Oxford area were especially low,[53] and secondly because many of the firms involved with the industrial action were closer to London (the heaviest concentration of boat-builders on the river being on the section above Chiswick).[54] Nevertheless, it is notable that the average boat-builder's wage (1s 11d per hour for a forty-seven-hour week, with overtime paid at time-and-a-half)[55] was considered low enough to warrant strike action and yet it was still 6d per hour (or 35 per cent) more than Salters' was paying its equivalent staff seventeen years later (see p. 170).[56]

This issue, however, is complicated by the fact that Salters' was paying some employees by piecework, rather than an hourly wage. In 1918, William Brocklesby was offered work building 24ft tub pairs at a rate of 9s per foot, which was apparently a rise of 3s per foot from the war rate (although the firm claimed there were no definite prices fixed in the trade). It is not clear how widespread this method of payment was, however, because George Salter said that they had considered offering a salary.[57]

Paying staff by piecework was a way in which the firm reduced its financial risk from the market uncertainties, whilst also incentivising faster work. By the 1930s this system was already dying out in some Oxford industries, such as the printing trade, but it remained common in others, such as the motor industry where around 80 per cent of workers were paid in this manner.[58] Salters' was paying its permanent staff an hourly wage by the late 1940s, although Bill Dunckley recalls that a few temporary employees were paid solely by piecework until the 1950s (per boat rather than per foot). He recalls that those employed on this arrangement tended to 'go like stink' for three or four weeks before disappearing until they needed money again. This system worked well for those who wanted to build boats around other jobs or activities, although it attracted some less reliable staff and the high-end craft were left to the salaried workforce. It also operated as a form of overtime for the permanent employees, as in the late 1940s Bill and colleagues would sometimes build steel canoes in the evening for the additional cash.[59] It is likely that the piecework system fell out of favour in the 1950s and 1960s when the firm's output of boats declined (see chapter 2).

By the mid-1930s the majority of the firm's boat-builders were on between 1s 4½d and 1s 5½d an hour depending on their seniority, although the range extended from around 1s, for the less experienced craftsmen, to 1s 8d, for the leading racing boat-builder (William Brocklesby, who was on a regular wage by that point).[60] Although the levels of pay were significantly lower than those in the boatyards nearer to London, they were competitive compared with other businesses in the city. In 1937, bus conductors in Oxford were on a wage of 1s to 1s 1⅞d an hour, whilst drivers were earning between 1s 2d and 1s 3⅞d an hour. Levels of pay were higher in the building industry, where labourers earned around 1s 2d an hour and craftsmen could expect to earn around 1s 6½d an hour, although work dropped off during the winter. These figures did not come close to the hourly rate earned by those on the Morris assembly line, where employees were typically being paid 2s 6d an hour for a forty-four-hour week, but the industry suffered from regular periods of unemployment during the summer.

Until 1936 it was customary in the assembly plant to turn works off for several weeks at a time, especially in the three months from June to September; that is, before work began on the new annual models for the Motor Show:

> In 1936, in an attempt to regularise production and employment, Morris Motors Ltd. decided to abandon the wholesale introduction of new models once a year and instead to produce new models at irregular intervals. The result has been that long periods of unemployment have been abolished. Latterly, however, there has been a considerable extension in the number of short 'stand-offs', varying from a few days to one or two weeks ... [61]

Morris' had an unemployment insurance scheme, however, which acted as a sort of subsidy, allowing it to send employees home, knowing that they were unlikely to seek alternative jobs because they were virtually assured of re-employment after a short period. Yet the quieter periods ensured that there was relative parity between the different trades in the city, because over the course of the year the workers averaged approximately 70 to 80s per week. This figure would have been similar to that in the building trade, where craftsmen would typically earn 71s 8d a week working forty-six and a half hours a week in the summer, but where overtime was common during boom periods.[62] Likewise, boat-builders at Salters' might have been on a lower hourly wage than those at Morris, but there were a number of employees who would work more than fifty hours per week during the busy periods (the spring months), which made their weekly pay packet competitive (Table 6.2). An employee working a forty-seven-hour week at the lower rate of 1s 4½d an hour would earn 64s 7½d, which was similar to a bus driver's wage, whilst those working fifty-two hours on the higher rate of 1s 5½d would take home 75s 10d, which was more than many comparable trades. Although some staff chose to work less, Salters' guaranteed the full-time workers a forty-seven-hour week (the industry norm in 1920),[63] although this reduced to forty-four in 1948[64] and forty by the mid-1960s.[65]

Table 6.2 Wages in Oxford (1937)[66]

Occupation	Hourly wage	Weekly hours	Weekly pay
Morris Motors (on the assembly line)	2s 6d	44 hours	70s–80s (average over the year, taking into consideration periods of unemployment)
Building industry (craftsmen)	1s 6½d	44 hours (winter) to 46½ hours (summer)	67s 10d (winter) to 71s 8d plus overtime (summer)
Building industry (labourer)	1s 2d	44 hours (winter) to 46½ hours (summer)	51s 4d (winter) to 54s 3d (summer)
Salters' boat-builder	1s 4½d to 1s 5½d	**47 hours to 52 hours (spring)**	64s 7½d (47 hours at the lower rate) to 75s 10d (52 hours at the higher rate)
Bus company (driver)	1s 2d to 1s 3⅞d	48 hours guaranteed, but average 52 hours	60s 8d to 68s 9½d (52 hours)
Bus company (conductor)	1s to 1s 1⅞d	48 hours guaranteed, but average 52 hours	52s to 60s ½d (52 hours)

Yet the higher wages in the motor industry were starting to cause problems for local businesses by that point:

> The demand of the motor industry for labour has seriously affected the supply of workers in the Oxford district available for some other employments … the comparatively high wages, which youths may earn 'on the line' seriously rival the lengthy training and lower wages of an apprentice … The skilled men enjoy more regular employment, but for many youths and their parents this advantage does not counter-balance the lower rate of pay received.[67]

The earliest indication of the motor works posing a problem for the firm was in 1940, when Frank wrote an exasperated letter to his brother, Sir Arthur Salter (who worked for the Transport Executive), to complain about the Admiralty's poor communication and its quibbling over prices (see chapter 2). The reason for his concern was that the delays had cost the business employees:

> In the meantime we are losing our men. They think we are getting slack and they may have to stand off. They therefore go to Morris on aeroplane work, where they are paid 2/- an hour and all sorts of bonuses. The Admiralty won't pay us enough to enable us to pay the men more than about 1/5½.[68]

Yet the higher pay in the motor industry became an even greater problem for the firm after the war. In 1951, the wages at Salters' ranged from £2 8s ⅝d per week for the brush hands, to £8 per week for the skippers and (steam) engineers (Table 6.3).

Table 6.3 Weekly wages of Salters' staff in 1951[69]

Skippers/engineers	£8 0s 0d
Pursers	£7 10s 0d
Clerks	£5 5s 0d
Typists	£4 0s 0d
Deck hands/mates	£2 19s 0d to £3 9s 0d
Boat-builders★	£3 2s ¾d
Carpenters	£3 0s 0d
Brush hands	£2 8s ⅝d
Third-year apprentices/trainees	£2 0s 0d
Guides	15s per day

★1952

The boat-builders and carpenters were amongst the worst-paid employees, although the wages of the apprentices were inevitably lower still, albeit rising in yearly increments. The indenture of Bernard Grossman, dated 5 May 1949, for example, shows that his apprenticeship as a ship's plater and general marine engineer received a starting salary of just £1 4s 1d per week, although 'board, drink, lodging, clothing and proper clothes' were also provided. This rose by 6s 1d in his second year and then by around 10s every subsequent year, until reaching £3 2s 3d per week by the fifth and final year of his apprenticeship (correlating with the pay of a boat-builder).[70]

Table 6.4 Annual wages in Oxford (from a 1951 survey)[71]

Semi-skilled machine minders	£485
Skilled workers	£444
Salters' skippers and steam engineers (skilled)	£416
Salters' boat-builders (skilled)	£161.36

In 1951, over £10 per week was considered a very good wage[72] and therefore some of Salters' pay was certainly on the low side, especially for the boat-builders, who, after completing a five-year apprenticeship, were on around a third of what a semi-skilled machine minder in the motor industry received (Table 6.4). Even the highest-earning employees, the skippers and steam engineers, were earning around 16 per cent less than their counterparts in the car factories. This was a relatively small difference, but the equivalent hourly wage at Salters' was much lower, because the steamer employees worked long hours and seven-day weeks, and, importantly, there was no guarantee of work over the winter. Nevertheless, the firm was still paying its staff more than was earned by some of the other professions on the river, such as lockkeepers.

Many trades lost staff to the motor industry, as John Greenford, a former employee who left Salters' in 1967 to work in the pattern shop at Morris (thereby securing a 44 per cent increase in wage), explained: 'That was the big thing about the car factory in the sixties: it did rob a lot of people. It was full of tradesmen in there, even on the line. That was pretty bad really, but that's what it was – right through Oxford.'[73]

The stretched labour market and the lack of affordable housing in the city after the war, forced many businesses to seek workers from outside Oxford.[74] As Salters' could not guarantee its summer staff employment over the winter, it was susceptible to losing them to other employers. This is the reason why former employee Bryan Dunckley left the firm to join the motor works in the 1960s. Yet he only did so because he was able to secure the comparatively appealing job of driving newly built cars out of the building (thereby avoiding having to work on the assembly line), whilst he was able to do occasional weekend work on the steamers, for additional cash.[75]

Unsurprisingly, the flow of staff members was seldom in the opposite direction, although this was partly because Salters' had a general policy of not taking employees from the motor works, because they were used to higher wages and less work.[76] James Robinson was one exception, as he was taken on, albeit after he had reached retirement age. He responded to an advertisement for a part-time job, only to be told at the interview that given his experience (as a pattern maker at Pressed Steel), he needed a full-time job, resulting in his appointment as the sawmill foreman in 1962.[77] It was unusual for employees to be retained beyond the age of 65, although exceptions were made for those who were particularly good or useful, like Jim Nicholls, an ex-Royal Navy man, who retained his job as a skipper until his late 70s.[78]

The motor industry should not be viewed as completely antagonistic to the interests of Salters', however, because it contributed to the growing size and prosperity of the city as a whole, which meant that there were more potential customers to participate in leisure on the river. Furthermore, Morris produced a small number of engines for the boat firm and its factory was included within the range of circular tours that Salters' offered from the 1930s onwards (see chapter 4).

Although the motor industry was a particular attraction, there were other professions to which Salters' was liable to lose its staff, because its craftsmen had skills that were transferable to them. There was an acute demand for housing in the city – partly because of the needs of those working in the motor industry – and the loss of employees to the building trade became a constant 'bone of contention' for Salters'. Carpentry work was a 'doddle' for skilled boat-builders, but once they left the firm, they rarely returned.[79] A particular draw for those in the racing boat department were watermen jobs offered by Oxford colleges or schools specialising in rowing, because they tended to offer higher wages, less intensive work and other perks, like accommodation. There were fewer options for unskilled workers who wanted to remain on the river, however, although some ex-staff members became lockkeepers. Salters' was well aware of the competition it faced in the employment market and therefore it not only offered employees good job security (provided they could do the work), but also maintained a pragmatic open-door policy for any proficient ex-employee who wanted to return to the firm.

Discipline

The competition in the labour market also meant that Salters' struggled to find reliable workers. This is shown by the declining standards of discipline at the firm in the 1950s and 1960s.

Complaints about the levels of pay were commonplace at the business from at least the 1930s onwards. Len Andrews, for example, recalled that when any Salter family member used to visit them in the workshop, the staff would whistle the tune to the following song:

> We are but little children meek,
> We only earn three bob a week,
> The more we work, the more we may,
> It makes no difference to our pay.[80]

Yet, unlike at the Cowley motor works, where industrial disputes were common, there was never any strike action at Salters'. There were some successful attempts by the staff to improve their rates of pay, however, including a 'round-robin' petition signed by the Oxford and Kingston skippers in 1947, in order to gain a rise of 10s a week (thereby reaching the psychologically significant total of £7 per week or £1 per day).[81]

Although it was strictly forbidden, there were also a number of attempts by staff members to elicit tips from customers. One of the earliest examples of this was recorded by a visitor to the yard in the 1870s, who was obliged to pay a Salters' employee for 'swabbing' his canoe whilst it was stored overnight (to prevent rats eating the bottom, it was claimed), despite having turned down the offer when he arrived.[82] Working on the passenger boats provided even greater opportunity for such ruses and the classic passing round of the skipper's hat was one of a number of ways in which the workforce tried to encourage donations. In the 1950s, those on board the steamers were responsible for over 80 per cent of the disciplinary issues that resulted in employees leaving the firm. Thirty left in acrimonious circumstances (the equivalent of three per year) and half of these were deck hands, which was the occupational group with the reputation for being the most dishonest amongst the canal community too.[83] This is perhaps unsurprising, as those at Salters' were amongst the lowest-paid employees and they were typically teenage boys (the youngest staff members) who worked the summers only.

This is not to say that some of those in higher positions did not cause problems, as of the seven skippers or drivers to leave the firm because of disciplinary issues, four were sacked (three of whom were 'no use' or 'incompetent'), two were 'sent to prison' and another was dismissed for failing to refuel the *Mapledurham*. No further information accompanies the latter, but as this was the largest-capacity boat on the Upper Thames, one can see why letting it run out of fuel might have been grounds for dismissal. The conversion of the craft from steam to diesel, however, did catch out some employees, as they previously relied on the steam engineer to tend the engine and there was also a visual indication of the level of fuel. Moreover, wood could previously be collected from the riverside as an emergency back-up. This was, however, the twilight of the steam era and finding trained engineers was becoming more problematic. In 1958, three were employed on a trial basis and all were dismissed, one for being 'undesirable', another for having 'no knowledge of the work' and the last for being a 'thorough nuisance'.[84]

By the 1960s the standard of discipline had declined further, as there were forty-five disciplinary comments written on the records of employees who had left. Indeed, the fact that there were almost 15 per cent more employees listed in the card index (755) than in the previous decade (662) suggests that retaining staff was becoming more of an issue, especially when one considers that both the firm's rental and passenger boat fleets were smaller than in the 1950s and the boat-building department was also receiving fewer orders.

Again the deck hands accounted for the largest proportion of issues (57.8 per cent), with the majority being listed as either 'unsatisfactory' or 'no use'. The latter included five who were dismissed for some kind of collective misdemeanour. Others included a deck hand sacked for an issue relating to *Goring*'s diesel oil, another for a knife-related incident, a steam engineer for being 'under the influence' and a sawmill trainee for bad timekeeping. Five employees were arrested, imprisoned or had absconded (with the police enquiring after them), which included one who was detained for an incident involving the Reading safe. A further ten were listed as having left without notice, including one who was recorded as having 'left with Alsatian dog' (presumably referring to the last-known sighting of him), and another who worked for two hours before walking out, thereby earning the comment 'Useless' on his record.[85]

Yet, as with the previous decade, no skipper was shown as being dismissed for navigating his boat badly or dangerously. This is surprising given that David Blagrove, the Goring lockkeeper, alleged that the standards deteriorated at this time. He claimed that the firm's policy of recruiting 'redundant merchant navy men' and staff from labour exchanges resulted in the older staff who had a 'deeper understanding of the river and its ways' slowly being replaced by a new generation of reckless younger staff who were, in his words, of the 'cow-boy' persuasion.[86] This suggests that the firm became less selective about whom it hired, which was also the case for other Oxford employers: at the start of the twentieth century one had to be of a certain social standing to be considered for a job as a college servant, but by the 1950s they were taking almost anybody.[87] Although disciplinary standards were slipping at the firm at this time, any navigation incidents that occurred were obviously not deemed serious enough to warrant anyone's dismissal.

The greater number and range of employees causing problems also shows that disciplinary issues were becoming more widespread at Salters'. It was no coincidence, therefore, that a number of measures were introduced in the 1960s to try and gain greater control over the workforce. Keeping track of the highly mobile steamer crews remained a constant challenge, although the close-knit nature of the firm (see p. 177) ensured that the management usually found out if something was amiss. After a purser was discovered to be 'skimming' from the takings, by issuing tickets in pencil which could subsequently be altered, Salters' issued ticket machines and started to employ inspectors. The most significant decision, however, which changed the working environment considerably, was to abolish sleeping on the steamers, in order to try to reduce the time that the crews spent together on board unsupervised.

The disciplinary issues should not be over-stated, as they still only accounted for 4.5 per cent and 5.8 per cent of the staff departures in the 1950s and 1960s respectively, which shows that the vast majority of employees left the firm amicably. Indeed, perhaps what is most remarkable is that there were many low-paid workers willing to return to Salters' year-upon-year, which suggests that the job offered certain non-pecuniary attractions.

Work Environment: Steamer Crews

The distinctive nature of those working on Oxford's waterways has long been acknowledged. Robert Burton (1577–1640), the author of *The Anatomy of Melancholy*, was said to have visited Folly Bridge whenever he felt in need of some light relief. According to Bishop Kennet, 'nothing at last could make him laugh, but going down to the Bridge-foot in Oxford, and hearing the Barge-men scold and storm and swear at one another, at which he would set his Hands to his Sides, and laugh most profusely'.[88]

Over two centuries later, another distinctive waterway community developed, which became known as the 'Salters' navy'. Like those employed on the canal, they formed a cohesive social group that was based on occupation rather than class. Indeed, the working environment was highly unusual and immensely enjoyable, which was crucial in helping the firm to recruit and retain many of its employees, despite the low wages.

The majority of those assigned to the passenger boats were employed from the end of May to the end of September only, although there were always a few who were retained over the winter for preparatory tasks, like maintaining or repairing the boats and engines for the forthcoming season. The latter greatly looked forward to the summer, as this was when they would take to the water to work (and live) on board the steamers.

Once the passenger boat season started, the employees were split into crews consisting of a skipper, steam engineer, waitress, one or two deck hands (depending on the size of the boat) and a purser (on the scheduled cruises only).[89] The skippers took great pride in their craft and, as they were ultimately in charge of the whole boat, the crew were expected to obey their orders. The steam engineer was the next most senior staff member and he was in charge of keeping the engine stoked, as well as operating the throttle according to the commands of the skipper (as relayed via the telegraph). The deck hands were responsible for operational duties like taking the funnel down when approaching low bridges and manning the ropes at the locks and the landing stages.

The waitresses and the pursers boarded the boats each morning and were responsible for serving tea and snacks in the saloon, and selling tickets on board respectively. The others slept on board in the forward cabin (known as the 'crew's quarters'), which, on the larger craft, was divided into two with the engineer and skipper in the roomier and lighter section by the wheelhouse, and the mates in the narrower, darker part by the bow. This arrangement was unusual because, unlike other Thames firms, Salters' had to be able to operate its steamers over a long distance and from many locations. Furthermore, sleeping on the boat was the most practical way of ensuring that the boiler was lit early enough to gain steam for the morning and that the firm's property was protected from vandalism. There were a number of instances from the 1980s onwards (when the crews no longer slept on board) of steamers being damaged, including boats being broken into because they carried alcohol on board. In 1987, someone in Reading set *Goring* adrift; its rescuers unsuccessfully went to court to claim the steamer as salvage.[90]

Many of the crews worked the whole (summer) season without a day off, which meant that they spent more consecutive days on the water than even the majority of those in the canal community, who tended to sleep on board only when they were delivering their cargo – after which they returned to their homes on land.[91] The hours were very long, with the steam engineer often surfacing at five or six in the morning in order to light the boiler. The services normally finished at about 7.00 p.m., but it could take until 10.00 p.m. to finish all the chores, including scrubbing the decks, polishing the brass and cleaning the boiler. The engines were 'spotlessly kept',[92] although keeping the rest of the boat dirt-free was no easy task, as every four days coal had to be shovelled on, requiring everything to be washed down again. Ex-employee Steve Long, who began working for the firm in the 1970s, recalled that there was a friendly rivalry between the crews about the appearance of their boats and this was especially the case when a boat needed to be moved from one part of the river to another, where its condition would be scrutinised by other staff members.[93] 'Boat-moves' like this were sometimes done overnight, if the craft was needed elsewhere the following morning, although, with the exception of last-minute bookings, staff generally knew what they would be doing at least seven days in advance, as they were given their itineraries at the start of the week.

For many of the staff, the major attraction of crewing on the boats was that it allowed them to be outdoors during the summer in a job that was active, but without being too taxing. The working environment was much more pleasant than being employed on the canal, as the boats only operated during the warmest months. This also protected the workforce from some of the health problems associated with living on boats all year round.[94] Furthermore, the steamers had large awnings and a saloon, which shielded the employees from any extremes of the weather.

The job also appealed because the crews were able to enjoy 'messing about in boats'. Like those in the Navy, many of the employees developed a strong sentimental attachment to the craft they worked on and this was particularly the case for the skippers, who often became inextricably linked with 'their' boat. The workforce was also proud to be part of a long-standing Thames tradition.

There was also an element of escapism connected to the job, as being on the steamers provided an opportunity to 'get away from it all'. H. W. Wack's description of the waterway as 'Thamesland' is quite fitting, as it was like being in a different world.[95] The crews were able to enjoy the idyllic scenery of the river and, as they were on board for seven days a week,[96] it was easy to become divorced from the rest of society. As Bryan Dunckley explains:

Living on a boat down at Windsor … you'd been cut off from society and all of a sudden you'd come out in the traffic [on land]. It was like being in another world … So we never used to come ashore really. Didn't read papers, so you didn't know what the other side of the world was doing! It was a life of its own![97]

This separate existence was summed up in a Thames poem:

Time goes by, they say it alters;
not at all if you work for Salters.
Ring out the bell from every steeple;
it makes no difference to boating people.[98]

The sense of 'otherness' that the crews felt was shared by other waterway occupations, but they did not develop the kind of elitism that the watermen of London were famous for, for example, probably because their working community was easier to enter and not as heavily regulated.

Yet there was little chance of the crews becoming an insular community, like those working on the canals, because it was an extremely sociable existence, which was another attraction of the job. Working on the boats was a bit like being in a family, which was partly the result of the firm trying to care for its staff through a system of paternalism (see chapter 7). The crews were close-knit, and although the relationships inevitably varied from boat to boat, on the whole there was good camaraderie. Crews sometimes raced one another in friendly competition and they would often socialise together in the evenings when the steamers moored up alongside each other.

The staff also had interaction with passengers on a daily basis – and often large numbers of them. The different groups that came on board meant that the job was very varied and a number of staff agreed with the journalist S.P.B. Mais who claimed there was 'never a dull moment' on board.[99] The lively private parties were particularly popular as the crews were able to enjoy the on-board entertainment, which was often provided by the piano that was standard issue on some of the craft in the middle of the twentieth century. John Springer's most vivid memory was a party of 500 Welshman performing *Cwm Rhondda* ('Guide Me, O Thou Great Jehovah') whilst on board two

Party on a steamer in the 1940s with on-board piano visible.

separate steamers.[100] Furthermore, the crews were able to enjoy the carnival atmosphere that surrounded special events, like the Henley Royal Regatta, when a number of steamers would often be hired out for corporate parties.

They also felt part of the wider river community, which included lockkeepers and those whose businesses were connected with the Thames in the towns and villages that the boats passed through. In fact, like sailors, the crews were renowned for having relationships with women at their different ports of call, as the steamer employees (as well as many of the office managers)[101] were mainly bachelors. Bryan Dunckley described the job as a 'young man's paradise', where staff enjoyed 'the life of Riley'. Starting a relationship could have further ramifications, however, as he recalled being asked to swap with the skipper of *Hampton Court* who wanted to end his shift in Kingston, where there was a nurse with whom he had begun a relationship.[102] Once a staff member married, there was often pressure from their partner to come ashore, which could result in them leaving the firm. Indeed, many of the seasonal staff saw the job as being something one did whilst young and single, before settling down into a steady profession. As former employee Christopher Raworth explained, 'if it had paid more I would have done it all my life'.[103]

Yet although it was simply an interim job for some, the wage was not an issue for others, because the job offered free board and lodging, which made it relatively easy to save money. As Bryan Dunckley explains, this was another appeal of the job:

> In those days, you had a hot dinner, both the ways, you had people in the kitchens up at Oxford here making a hot dinner and down at Windsor. So you had a good cooked dinner, you had enough tea on board so … even if you had no wages, you were made up really.[104]

John Springer recalled that even in the days of rationing, the crews were 'fed marvellously'. A gang of waitresses would come on board for the larger parties and they would work hard to ensure all of the passengers were fed, often in a number of sittings. Any food that was left over was then distributed amongst the crew: 'After party trips we would find leftover lobster, chicken, loaves, seven pound tins of creamed Russian salad, a pound or so of butter, tea and sugar. We thrived on it.'[105]

Furthermore, the passengers not only provided the staff with food, but could also be a source of tips for the crew. The potential for this additional source of income was greatest on the larger craft, because they carried the most people, and this, combined with the greater skill needed to navigate larger vessels, ensured that working on them was considered to be more prestigious. The additional money was enough for Bryan Dunckley to be able to store his pay packets unopened,[106] whilst there is even an example of one employee, Alan Smith, who remarkably managed to work for the firm for five summers (from 1946 to 1950) without ever officially receiving a wage. The latter had been, in his own words, 'smuggled on board' as an 'illicit crew member',[107] which further underlines how enjoyable the job was and how the level of pay was not important for some. Moreover, it is also demonstrates that the steamer crews were far from being too poor to live ashore, which was the stereotype associated with those working on the canals.[108]

The crew's uniform (*c.* 1890–1910).

The existence of an illicit crew member also highlights another appealing part of being on the steamers, which was that it offered staff a lot of independence, as they could not be closely supervised. Furthermore, the level of scrutiny appears to have reduced once the third generation of the Salter family took over. Len Andrews recalled that 'when John and George [Salter] was alive, you wasn't allowed to go on the boat with your coat off, however hot it was! They'd pull you up over it.'[109] As this suggests, the steamer crews had been expected to remain smartly dressed at all times, in a shirt, tie, suit and hat. Although the requirements were relaxed in the second half of the twentieth century, the uniform also helped prevent the crews from becoming a marginalised community like those working on the canal, who had many negative stereotypes circulating about them and who stood out because of their distinctive dress.[110]

Yet it was the freedom the staff enjoyed that became a problem for the management once standards of discipline started to fall after the Second World War. After sleeping on board was abolished in the 1960s, in order to reduce the amount of time the crews spent on the boats unsupervised, the work experience was never quite the same. Nevertheless, for many the appeal of the job remained, as it was seen as more of a way of life than an occupation. The nostalgia felt by ex-staff, even today, is perhaps best summed up by Sam Jefferson's article, 'Salter's of the Earth', in which he describes the 'remarkable experience' of skippering the steamers.[111] The final word, however, should perhaps go to the firm's longest-serving employee, Bill Dunckley, who started working for Salters' in 1944 and remains the firm's senior engineer: 'When I was on the boats it was the best thing since sliced bread, you know, it was brilliant … couldn't get enough of it. Still can't.'[112]

Bill Dunckley at the slipway with punts, a skiff, a steamer and a motor boat in the background. (Photo by author in 2012)

Work Environment: Boat-Builders

The working environment may have been extraordinarily appealing for those working on the steamers, but the same could not be said for the 'onshore' roles at Salters'. This was another reason why the number of skilled craftsmen at the firm declined over the course of the twentieth century, once the local employment market was transformed by the industrialisation of Oxford.

The boat-builders worked in the different workshops dotted around Folly Bridge (see chapter 5). Although each room was slightly different, the overall conditions remained largely unchanged throughout the twentieth century, apart from the introduction of innovations such as electric lighting, electric tools and rudimentary heating. One of the best records of the conditions inside the workshops was a series of photographs taken by former employee, John Greenford, in the 1950s. These show that some of the workshops could become quite cluttered, although a clear space was always needed for the construction of craft.

The boat-builders had to be highly skilled and many of them took great pride in their work. Some even refused to do menial *ad hoc* jobs, because they deemed it below their station. They also had to be very flexible, because boat-building was a very 'irregular business',[113] where both the number and types of craft ordered could change considerably from month to month, as well as from year to year (see chapter 2).

Bill Gillams, the firm's foreman at Folly Bridge in the 1930s, was known for being a particularly versatile and talented craftsman, as he not only designed many of the boats (by building them first, as the saying went),[114] but also constructed parts for the steamers. These included a set of seats for the *River Queen*, having taken a template from those on the buses.

The majority of the other craftsmen specialised in a certain type of vessel, although changing market forces inevitably dictated how busy each would be. The senior boat-builders were assigned to the larger and more technical craft, like the racing vessels, whilst the junior employees were responsible for the smaller and simpler models, like the dinghies. This was another reason why Salters' struggled to retain its trainee craftsmen, because after the Second World War the firm built a smaller range of craft, of which a much higher proportion were the basic corporation boats (see chapter 2). This resulted in some junior staff members becoming disillusioned with the job, because they wanted to construct the more elaborate boats.[115]

Indeed, it was the younger employees who were particularly prone to leaving Salters', whilst the older craftsmen slowly declined in number, as individuals reached retirement age. This was partly because there was a perception amongst the staff members that boat-building was a dying industry – as confirmed by the declining number of orders at the firm in the 1950s and 1960s (see chapter 2). This meant that some of those thinking about their long-term futures started to look elsewhere, especially as they could command higher wages in other industries. Their perception of the industry proved to be correct, as the introduction of fibreglass construction in the 1970s and the closure

A first-floor workshop at Grandpont Yard in the 1950s. (Reproduced by permission of John Greenford)

of the racing boat department in the 1980s brought an end to the skilled craftsmanship
that had been a hallmark of the firm for over a century (see chapters 1 and 2).

• • •

This chapter has shown that at the start of the twentieth century Salters' was a significant
employer in Oxford, driven by a highly skilled and competitively paid local workforce,
in a city that had no large industry. This changed in the inter-war period, when the
rapid enlargement of the motor industry caused a fundamental shift in the job market.
Salters', like many other 'traditional' businesses, was unable to compete with the wages
offered by the new dominant employers. Nevertheless, it was flexible enough to adapt
and it started to source more of its staff from outside Oxford. Ultimately, it was the
appealing and alternative lifestyle that was offered on the steamers that was crucial in
helping it attract employees. Free board and lodging meant that the low wages were not
so much of an issue for the workers and over the course of many decades thousands of
employees, from across England and Wales, came to work for a few months of the year,
as part of the 'Salters' navy' – although many eventually went on to other careers. The
firm struggled to retain its lower-paid skilled craftsmen, in particular, which was another
reason why the focus of the business shifted from boat-building towards the provision
of leisure facilities. Yet this was also inevitably the result of managerial decisions, and one
cannot understand why the business evolved as it did without examining the role that
the Salter family played in running the firm.

Notes

1   *Oxford Mail*, 1 July 1955.
2   S. Pollard, 'The Decline of Shipbuilding on the Thames', *Economic History Review*, vol. 3,
     no. 1 (1950), pp. 72–89.
3   Black, *Our Canoe Voyage*, p. 298.
4   R.A. Church, *The Dynamics of Victorian Business* (London, 1980), p. 124.
5   SA Sick Club Book.
6   *Lock to Lock Times*, 5 August 1893, p. 1.
7   Whiting, *View from Cowley*, pp. 5–6.
8   Day, 'Modern Oxford', p. 216.
9   *Allen's Activities*, vol. 4, no. 13 (autumn, 1952), pp. 4–16.
10   T. Sharp, *Oxford Re-planned* (London, 1948), p. 57.
11   Ibid.
12   SA War Munition Volunteers Form for George Ashley. The document is undated, but the
     Employment List (1916 to 1919) shows he worked for the firm from 9 July to 13 November 1918.
13   SA Account Book 1915–29.
14   Email from David Nutt (describing the experience of his father at the firm),
     30 December 2004.
15   *Jackson's Oxford Journal*, 30 July 1859.
16   313 employees were listed between 1916 and 1919.
17   D.I. Scargill, 'Responses to Growth', in Whiting, *Oxford*, p. 113.
18   SA First World War Employee List. She is also shown as being the first female
     contributing to the Sick Club in 1917.

19   1901 census.
20   A plumber is not mentioned.
21   Conversation with Derek Bromhall, 21 June 2010.
22   SA 1950s Card Index.
23   SA 1960s Card Index. The occupations of only fifty-eight were listed. Thames Catering Company's employment records do not survive.
24   This does not mean that they necessarily worked at the same time, as the data set is for the whole decade.
25   *Jackson's Oxford Journal*, 10 December 1859.
26   E. Ackroyd and A. Plummer, 'Industry', in A. Bourdillon (ed.), *A Survey of Social Services in the Oxford District*, vol. 1 (Oxford, 1938), pp. 81–84.
27   Interview with John Greenford, 15 November 2012.
28   COS Radio interview with Arthur Salter, OXOHA: MT 536 (1971).
29   *Oxford Times*, 22 February 1952, p. 4.
30   SA Carmans Boat Works and *Oxford Times*, 6 March 1931, p. 24.
31   The dates show only the periods in which two or more were listed, so single staff members may have been working before or after these dates.
32   The brand name is now owned by Freeland Yacht Spar Ltd in Dorchester: www.collars.co.uk (accessed 10 November 2011). Another ex-staff member to set up his own firm was John Tims, one of the original employees, who established his own yard in Staines in the 1870s, which is still run by his descendants.
33   SA First World War Employee List.
34   Prior, *Fisher Row*, pp. 259–324.
35   *Jackson's Oxford Journal*, 3 November 1855, 10 August 1867, 23 February 1889, 29 July 1893 and 6 May 1893.
36   SA Sick Club Book.
37   SA First World War Employee List.
38   Interview with Albert Andrews, 26 March 2005.
39   *London Calling*, no. 289 (29 April–5 May 1945), p. 4 and Salter, *Memoirs of a Public Servant*. There was a large gas works by Folly Bridge and some coal was transported on the river.
40   'Oxford' includes the bordering villages of Marston, Cowley, Headington and Iffley, which are now within the modern ring road.
41   Ward, Stewart and Swyngedouw, 'Cowley and the Oxford Economy', p. 72.
42   SA Employment List 1916–19.
43   Scargill, 'Responses to Growth', pp. 110–30.
44   Mogey, *Family and Neighbourhood*, p. 4.
45   Interview with Bill Dunckley, 21 September 2004 and with Paul Richmond, Bryan Dunckley and Bill Dunckley, 4 December 2010.
46   P. Collison and J. Mogey, 'Residence and Social Class in Oxford', *American Journal of Sociology*, vol. 64, no. 6 (May, 1959), p. 601.
47   SA 1950s and 1960s Card Indexes.
48   *Oxford Times*, 18 August 1978, p. 11.
49   SA Piecework Folder 1913–26.
50   W.C. Walker, *Some Reminiscences of an Oxford Builder 1882 to 1960* (Oxford, 1960), p. 59.
51   *The Labour Gazette*, vol. 26, no. 8 (August 1918), p. 333.
52   E.T.J. Butchart, 'Wages and Unemployment in Britain, 1855–1938' (Oxford University DPhil thesis, 1996), p. 307.
53   *Report: Oxford Diocesan Social Services Committee* (1908), p. 33, in Day, 'Modern Oxford', p. 217.
54   *The Motor Boat*, vol. 2, no. 49 (15 June 1905), p. 387.
55   Ibid., vol. 32, no. 832 (18 June 1920), p. 589 and no. 845 (17 September 1918), p. 269.

56   SA Boat-Builder Documents 1934–37.
57   SA Letter from George Salter to W. Brocklesby, 4 December 1918.
58   Ackroyd and Plummer, 'Industry', pp. 87–89.
59   Interviews with Bill Dunckley, 4 August and 15 September 2011.
60   SA Boat-Builder Documents 1934–37.
61   Ackroyd and Plummer, 'Industry', p. 90.
62   Ibid., pp. 88–102.
63   *The Motor Boat*, vol. 32, no. 832 (18 June 1920), p. 589.
64   SA Labour Book 1945–48, pp. 121–55.
65   SA Wage Rates 1965–72.
66   Ackroyd and Plummer, 'Industry', pp. 88–102 and SA Boat-Builder Documents 1934–37.
67   Ackroyd and Plummer, 'Industry', p. 77.
68   Letter to Lt-Commander R. Fletcher MP, 5 June 1940 (sent to author by Sidney Aster, Sir Arthur Salter's biographer).
69   SA 1950s Card Index.
70   SA Indenture of Bernard Grossman, 5 May 1949.
71   H.W.F. Lydall, 'Personal Incomes in Oxford', *Bulletin of the Oxford University Institute of Statistics*, vol. 13 (1951), p. 388, in R.C. Whiting, 'Association and Separation in the Working Class, 1920–1970', in Whiting, *Oxford*, p. 150.
72   Mogey, *Family and Neighbourhood*, p. 132.
73   Interview with John Greenford, 30 May 2012.
74   Mogey, *Family and Neighbourhood*, p. 157.
75   Interview with Bryan Dunckley, 17 August 2004.
76   Interview with John Salter, 20 December 2011.
77   Conversation with James Robinson's daughter, Olga Nichols, 27 January 2011.
78   Davis, 'Memories of Salter's Steamers', pp. 53–54.
79   Interview with John Salter, 20 December 2011.
80   Response to a letter from the author to Graham Andrews (Len's son), 11 October 2004. This was a modified version of a British war song derived from the hymn 'We are but little children meek'.
81   Interview with Bill Dunckley, 21 August 2004.
82   Black, *Our Canoe Voyage*, pp. 299–355.
83   H. Hanson, *The Canal Boatmen 1760–1914* (Manchester, 1984), p. i.
84   SA 1950s Card Index.
85   SA 1960s Card Index.
86   Blagrove, *Quiet Waters By*, p. 89.
87   Mogey, *Family and Neighbourhood*, p. 6.
88   J. Granger, *Biographical History of England from Egbert the Great to the Revolution* (London, 1804), p. 367.
89   In addition to these, some boats also had drivers in the early years.
90   *Daily Telegraph*, 26 February 1987, p. 3. A boat was also set adrift in Oxford in 1930.
91   Freer, 'Canal Boat People', pp. 132–36.
92   Blagrove, *Quiet Waters By*, p. 87.
93   Interview with Steve Long, 16 May 2011.
94   Ibid., p. 268. The Salters' workforce also had the advantage of being predominantly young men.
95   H.W. Wack, *In Thamesland*.
96   It was not until the 1990s that the working week (in the summer) was reduced to six.
97   Interview with Bryan Dunckley, 17 August 2004.
98   B. Eade, *Along the Thames* (Stroud, 1997), p. 32.

99   *Oxford Mail*, 1 July 1955, p. 8.
100   *Canal and Riverboat*, November 1981, pp. 39–41.
101   There were duty managers based at Oxford, Reading and Windsor.
102   Interview with Bryan Dunckley, 17 August 2004.
103   Conversation with Christopher Raworth, 5 June 2013.
104   Interview with Bryan Dunckley, 17 August 2004.
105   *Canal and Riverboat*, November 1981, pp. 39–41.
106   Interview with Bryan Dunckley, 17 August 2004.
107   Letter from Alan Smith to Brian Hillsdon, 2 November 1992 (sent to the author).
108   Freer, 'Canal Boat People', p. 334.
109   Interview with Len Andrews, 31 August 2004.
110   Freer, 'Canal Boat People', pp. 132–50.
111   *Canal Boat* (February 2011), pp. 60–63.
112   Interview with Bill Dunckley, 21 August 2004.
113   *The Motor Boat*, vol. 33, no. 854 (19 November 1920), p. 476.
114   Interview with John Salter, 20 December 2011.
115   Interview with John Greenford, 30 May 2012.

7

The Family

This then was the stock from which I came; undilutedly English, Thames Valley English, every member of it for a century deriving from within 100 miles from London. It was typical of the stuff of Victorian England. Energetic enterprise carving a new business out of the undeveloped opportunities of the time, unhampered by restrictive regulations or elaborate industrial or labour organisation. In the second generation, some culture, varied public service, a strict non-conformist religion, Gladstone Liberalism, vitality and staying power. Here in miniature was one of the main strata of nineteenth-century England, socially below the professional, rising beyond the manual to considerable, but still limited and individual, business success. Of such families was the main strength and support of Gladstone's age.

Sir Arthur Salter, 1961[1]

John and Stephen Salter came from a family of carpenters and publicans, and it was their success in the sport of rowing (see chapter 1) that enabled them to amass a 'modest fortune'.[2] They accumulated a large amount of property and were amongst the early residents of Boars Hill, an area that became popular with Oxford's rich and famous.[3]

John believed in giving his sons (John Henry, Thomas Alfred, James Edward and George Stephen) the same kind of upbringing as he had had. Instead of sending them to a good school – as he could well afford to do – he started them working for the firm at the age of 14 on an artisan's wage.[4] All six family members were working for Salters' in 1871,[5] but after Stephen left the business in the mid-1870s and John retired to Boars Hill a decade later, the firm passed down to John, James and George, whilst Thomas opted to return to Wandsworth.[6]

The second generation's upbringing meant that they were regarded as 'boat-builders', which almost disqualified James' oldest son from being able to row at university, as it was questioned whether he should be classed as a 'professional'.[7] Yet to describe them solely as such would be to do them a great disservice, as the three brothers, and particularly John and James, achieved considerable fame in the city. Indeed, they had a significant impact on the religious and political life of Oxford, which also inevitably had ramifications for their firm.

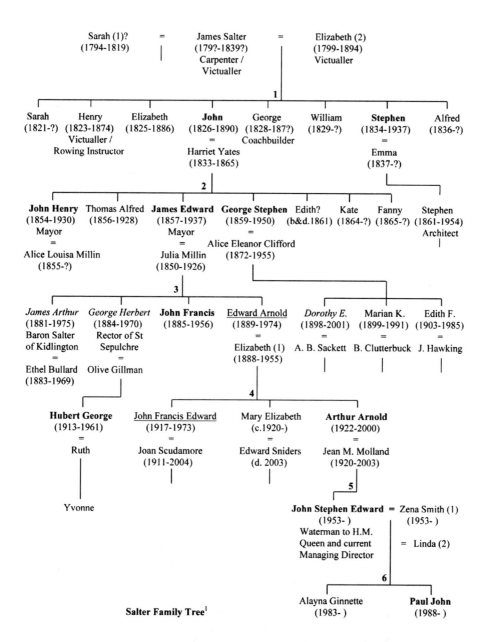

Salter Family Tree[1]

Salter family tree. Information collected from baptism records, censuses, obituaries, family memoirs and gravestones. Those listed are family members within one generation of those managing the firm. **Bold** denotes those with a managerial role, *italic* denotes non-executive directors, underlined denotes those involved primarily with the catering side of the business. The third generation were all known by their middle names, i.e. 'Arthur', 'Bert', 'Frank' and 'Arnold'.

Religion and the Salter Family

A short history of the Wesley Memorial Chapel was produced in 1968 to commemorate its 150th anniversary and this included recollections from past clergy. One of them was from Reverend J. Bodgener, who described what his predecessor, B. Brash, had said about the chapel at the beginning of the century. Significantly, the first individuals he mentioned were the Salter brothers (although he was mistaken as to who was the oldest):

> … the congregation consisted mainly of individuals, and this was true enough – but what individuals! There were three Salter brothers all regularly seated in their pews on Sunday morning. James Edward, the eldest, was of all men the most modest and retiring, quite unassuming and full of old world courtesy … John Henry, the middle brother, was appointed Sheriff in 1889, and for distinguished services honoured with the degree of Master of Arts by the University … Better known to the members of the congregation and in the city was the youngest brother – George. For many years he was Superintendent of the Sunday School and intimately connected with all the activities of Church life.[8]

Indeed, the name of Salter was not only 'known in all boating circles in England', but it was a 'household word also in Methodist circles' in the city.[9] The family were amongst a small number of wealthy businessmen who were the local equivalent of the 'workhorses' running Methodism at the national level.[10]

The religious climate in Oxfordshire in the middle of the nineteenth century has been described as a 'hornets' nest' with the different denominations involved in 'combative proselytising'. Nonconformists were growing in confidence 'both economically, through association with leading industrial and manufacturing interests and politically through links with Liberalism'.[11] Furthermore, religious tests were abolished at Oxford University in 1854 (for most courses) and 1871 (for fellows), and although Anglican

The Salter brothers: George, James and John (inset). (Reproduced by permission of Robert Sackett)

influence remained pervasive, 'the dawn of a new day for Nonconformists in Oxford'[12] was reached in 1886, with the opening of Mansfield College.

The Wesleyan Methodist denomination grew rapidly after the death of John Wesley in 1791. The parent chapel in Oxford (the Wesley Memorial Chapel) moved to a site on New Inn Hall Street in 1818, and by 1851 it was one of the best attended places of worship in the city.[13] After overcoming serious financial difficulties in the 1860s it was able to move to a new larger chapel on the same street in 1878 (its present location), which greatly improved its status in the city. The additional capacity facilitated a period of spectacular growth when its membership almost doubled in two years, from 537 in 1881 to 935 by 1883.[14] The catalyst for this influx was the hugely successful preacher Hugh Price Hughes, who ensured that revival missions became 'a constant feature' in and around the city at this time. He was also known for spurring even the richer members of his congregation into service,[15] which may explain why his arrival in 1881 coincided with the period in which the Salters became more actively involved with the chapel.

The second generation of the family became Wesleyans owing to the influence of their housekeeper, Hannah Long.[16] Given that the youngest of the three brothers, George, worshipped in the old building,[17] it is likely that they were all members of the congregation by the time the new chapel was built in 1878. Yet it was the middle brother, James, who was the first to become actively involved at a committee level. In 1882, at the age of 24, he is listed as being amongst those who attended the quarterly meetings, where the chapel's policy was decided.[18] This date is significant as it shows that his religious activism preceded his standing for (secular) political office by over a decade. This suggests that the former may have been an important training ground for the latter, as the denomination prided itself on being 'one of the most highly organised bodies in existence'.[19]

James' organisational skills were probably honed even earlier still, as he played a crucial role in the expansion of the Oxford branch of the Young Men's Christian Association (YMCA). The organisation, which became 'one of the phenomena of the day', sought to provide the right kind of leisure activities for young people as 'a wholesome alternative to the deleterious diet of drinking, smoking and gambling'.[20] The Oxford branch, founded in the middle of the nineteenth century, had an inauspicious start, as its first incarnation suffered from a lack of funds and was dissolved in 1868, whilst its second, established in 1871, was initially in a 'low estate', as it had to move premises seven times in its first two decades. James Salter, who joined in the mid-1870s (at the age of 17)[21] and became its secretary by the mid-1880s, was involved with the organisation as he believed that young men were the most difficult group to get through to, and therefore it was important that people cared for them.[22]

James was responsible for identifying a piece of land on George Street, which he pressed the Association to buy, despite his colleagues believing it could not be afforded.[23] The whole project ended up costing approximately £5,000 and the four-storey building, opened in 1891, included three shops on the ground floor (to provide rent), a 300-capacity lecture theatre on the first floor, classrooms, a library and a gymnasium on the second floor, and a caretaker's apartment on the top floor.[24] This enabled the movement to grow from 109 full members (and twenty-seven associates) in 1888 to 616 members by 1894, with its regular activities by that point including services on Sunday, a Bible class, a Literary and Debating Society (members of which subsequently took on the Oxford Union), educational instruction (in French, Greek, shorthand and the violin), as well as rowing, cricket, football and athletics clubs.[25]

By 1899 James had become president of the branch and his wife, Julia, would later become a vice president of the city's Young Women's Christian Association.[26] His contribution to the organisation was recognised at an event held in his honour in 1910. During the ceremony he was described as 'the best member the YMCA had ever had', and that 'they could not add anything to the lustre that shone around the name of Salter'.[27] Despite a large fire to the George Street property in 1917, the Association remained an influential presence in the city until after the Second World War, when financial problems eventually forced it to move from its headquarters and to scale down many of its activities.

Given his dedication to the YMCA, it is perhaps unsurprising that at the chapel James was also best known for his work amongst children. He helped with the Sunday School from at least the early 1880s (passing his exams to teach scripture in 1888) and by the turn of the century he had become the education secretary. He presided over a period in which the Circuit was enlarged and its programme increased rapidly, from fourteen Sunday schools with 199 teachers and 1,251 scholars in 1903, to thirty-eight schools, 353 teachers and 2,387 scholars by 1914.[28] When he later became a local politician (see p. 198), he was 'only too pleased' to use his influence to help youth work in the city,[29] and at one event he was applauded for the support he had given 'to every cause which had had for its object the welfare and advancement of young people'.[30]

James was also involved with the Circuit Mission Committee from 1884 and the Temperance Committee from 1900, and his seniority in the chapel was confirmed when he served as one of the two Circuit stewards in 1888 and one of the two representatives to Synod from 1898 to 1900. He also became one of the chapel's longest serving committee members (beyond both of his brothers), as his official duties did not end until 15 March 1934, when he finally resigned from his last post as treasurer of the Circuit Mission Fund, at the age of 77. By this stage, James' son, Frank, was continuing the family's tradition of service (first appearing on a committee in 1907 as secretary of the chapel's bazaar),[31] although he was not as actively involved as those from his father's generation.

John Henry followed his younger brother into service on the chapel's committees in 1887, although, unlike James, he was already a local politician by this stage (see p. 197). His interest in finance at the council may explain why the first committee he appeared on, accompanied by James, was one to raise £2,000 in order to liquidate the chapel's debts and to fund the building of more places of worship. He assumed charge of presenting the accounts at the quarterly meetings and he also acted as treasurer for the foreign missions committee from 1894 onwards.

The minutes of the meetings suggest that he was more dominant than his brother, as he was responsible for making many policy suggestions. He became one of the two senior stewards from 1896 (and again between 1910 and 1918) and his other roles included serving on the Circuit Choral Union, the temperance committee and the magazine committee. He was also one of the two Wesley Memorial Chapel representatives sent to the Nonconformist Council, which was set up in 1895, and in the 1920s he was involved in the early negotiations that would eventually lead to the merger of the Methodist denominations in 1932.[32] He was not, however, just an arch-bureaucrat, as in 1891 he passed his exams to be qualified to teach in the chapel. By 1902, he was amongst the forty-six Oxford-based Wesleyan preachers, from both town and gown, although he was one of the few not to be listed as a cyclist.[33]

As at the firm, the third brother was also actively involved. George joined his first committee in 1891 as secretary of the Foreign Mission Committee, aged 31, and he, too, became a senior steward (in 1902), a representative to the Synod (in 1908 and 1909), and a long-serving Sunday school teacher. By 1906, he was more involved in the quarterly meetings than his brothers,[34] which suggests that John and James were increasingly preoccupied with their political duties by that point.

Furthermore, he and his wife, Alice, often provided an open house on Sunday evenings where members of the chapel could congregate. One of George's sons-in-law described the home (at 57 Banbury Road) as 'a very special social centre that by the beginning of the post-war years linked university with town, opened doors to the magic of the Thames and boats, and enabled intelligent Methodist people to foster a network of human contact'.[35]

Alice organised many activities for the congregation, which inevitably included trips on the river. Furthermore, she also undertook pastoral visitations and was chosen to be the chapel's sole representative at the Oxford Temperance Council of Christian Churches, as well as serving as the vice president of the local branch of the British Women's Temperance Association.[36] Other female family members inevitably helped out at events, and there was also an unidentified 'Miss Salter' shown as having served as the treasurer for the Women's Department from 1934 to 1947.

The family was also involved in many evangelistic initiatives. By the end of the 1880s the chapel was holding regular services on Broad Street, which had become a notable hub for religious and political gatherings. Some of these resulted in disorderly conduct and, in February 1889, the chapel was threatened with a summons by the police if it held another gathering there. After advice from the chairman of the board, it decided to continue the practice, which resulted in James being amongst those whose names were taken by the police.[37] This demonstrates that he was willing to put his religious convictions ahead of his respectability.

The family also focused its attention on supporting the surrounding villages, 'where struggling little Methodist chapels were maintaining a precarious existence'.[38] The brothers (and James' son, Frank) were on the committees overseeing numerous places of worship around Oxford (Table 7.1). John was also responsible for laying the cornerstone at Combe chapel in 1893,[39] and his name adorns one at the Wesley Hall in 1904 (now the Cowley Road Methodist Church), a building designed by his architect cousin (see chapter 5).

Table 7.1 Salters who were committee members of a chapel at any time up to the period of 1913[40]

	John	James	George	Frank
Bladon	X	X		
Combe	X			
Cranham Street Mission	X	X		
Dorchester	X		X	
Eynsham	X	X	X	
Forest Hill	X	X		
Headington Quarry	X			
Horsepath				X
Islip	X	X	X	
New Headington	X			
New Hincksey	X	X	X	X
New Inn Hall Street	X	X	X	
Tackley		X	X	
Wesley Hall	X	X	X	
Wootton		X	X	
Woodstock			X	

As prominent local businessmen, the Salters were also important for providing financial assistance to the chapels. Raising adequate capital was a continual challenge because, as James explained, they belonged to a 'missionary church', which he had never known to be out of debt because 'they had faith that the work, which had been done from the very highest motives, would be paid for'.[41] According to ex-employee Len Andrews, the Salters were well known for being 'charitable' and inevitably Wesley Memorial Church 'did very well out of them'.[42] There are no surviving comprehensive chapel accounts for this period, although one can gain an indication of the level of the family's support from some of the fundraising initiatives they were involved with. In 1895, for example, the chapel's debt extinction fund raised £748 7s 4d and this included £20 from each of the brothers, the joint sixth largest donations made by the twenty-five donors concerned. As there were three of them, theirs was the second largest contribution from a single family (and 8 per cent of the overall total), although it was considerably less than the donations made by the restaurateurs Alfred and James Boffin (of 107 High Street), whose contributions of £265 and £80, respectively, accounted for almost half of the money raised.[43]

Yet arguably one of the Salters' greatest contributions to Methodism stemmed from their political rather than financial clout, as John and James used their public profiles to raise the chapel's prestige. One only has to look at the Liberal Oxford Chronicle at the beginning of the twentieth century to see how active they were in promoting Methodism. As mayor in 1902–03, for example, John started a tradition of taking the entire Corporation to the Wesley Memorial Church, if the superintendent of the Oxford circuit, Rev. Grainger Hargreaves, was preaching.[44] Furthermore, he described the post-holder as being:

> ... a gentleman appointed to preside at missionary meetings, to open bazaars, and attend similar functions at the different churches of the municipality in which he resides and that he was permitted to fill up his spare time by going to the meetings of the City Council and occupy the chief seat on the Bench of the City Magistrates.[45]

As this suggests, a lot of John Salters' time was committed to activities that were not directly related to his business. Furthermore, although the comment was meant in a light-hearted manner, the brothers considered their political activities to be secondary to their religious work. Similarly, when it came to their business, the family were willing to override certain economic considerations because of their Wesleyan Methodist convictions.

Religion and the Business

The Salters were unlike many other prominent Oxford families, such as the Morrells and the Halls, the famous local brewers, or – further afield – the Hobbs, the Henley boat-builders, because they became Methodists. Yet it was not until the second generation that the firm was run by individuals with strong religious convictions and, as one would expect, this inevitably had a number of ramifications for their business.

The association between religious belief and business acumen is one that has received much attention from scholars. In *Capitalists and Christians*, David Jeremy examines some of the common traits possessed by Christian business leaders between 1900 and 1960. He argues that Cadbury's represented the pinnacle of 'sensitive community-based entrepreneurship', which required treading a fine line between employer provision and respect for the freedom of the individual employee. This form of management could have significant financial repercussions, however, if certain fundamental business principles were overridden by religious convictions. Yet there is little evidence to suggest that Christian employers in major businesses used their faith either to proselytise to their workforce or as an instrument of social control. Instead, he argues that the greatest impact of religious convictions on family firms may have been in helping to inculcate an atmosphere of self-criticism (although this is a phenomenon that is difficult to measure), as well as encouraging some industries to adopt old modes of paternalism.[46] Patrick Joyce argues that the impact of the latter should not be underestimated:

> The paternalism of the family firm was vastly more important than is generally recognised. In the changed technological and cultural environment after mid-century this piecemeal, unsung paternalism cut more deeply into operative life than had the paternalism of the early founders of industry.

He suggests that the 'feudal' form of paternalism, where duties and rights bound the big employer to his workers, was less likely to cause resentment than the 'familiar' form, where a common lifestyle was shared by the master of a smaller business and his men.[47]

Although Joyce was describing the types of relationships that existed between employers and employees in northern factories at the end of the Victorian period, the former appears to have been similar to the system that operated at Salters'. Former employee Albert Andrews described the Salters as being 'very understanding' and he noted that they used to walk around the workshops chatting to the staff members (a practice still going on in the 1960s), in much the same way as William Morris had initially done with his staff.[48]

An important part of the benevolent paternalism was the provision of housing for the staff, which was an initiative that also helped to tackle some of the wider labour issues they faced (see chapters 5 and 6). David Nutt recalls that his father, William (an ex-employee), was paying less rent on their Salters'-owned Buckingham Street property than their neighbours, and that when it was eventually sold, it was offered to them at less than the market rate.[49] Although the firm sold most of its residential property in the 1950s, it always retained some housing to offer to key workers as an additional incentive.

Another area the firm helped its staff with was the provision of health care. Before the formation of the National Health Service, the firm would buy 'turns' (like a ticket book) to see a local doctor, and if a staff member was ill, they could arrange to see one of the Salters who would dispense these if the illness was legitimate.[50] By 1906 there was a Sick and Share-out Club operating amongst the employees. This provided income for staff members if they were ill (for three or more days) and it also operated as both a form of Christmas bonus and life insurance (as an additional levy was collected if an employee or his wife died).[51] Between 1925 and 1950 the annual premium was £1 6s per year (or 6d per week – the same rate that the Morris Motor Works paid in the mid-1930s).[52]

Unlike some of the large employers in Oxford, the firm did not have any sporting clubs connected with it, probably because many employees worked on the passenger boats all summer without a day off (see chapter 6). There was, however, both an annual staff outing, from at least 1874,[53] and a Christmas meal at the Marlborough Arms. Furthermore, other aspects of paternalism included providing financial aid, letters of introduction and even sometimes paying bail on an employee's behalf.

Although the paternalism was bound up with the family's religious beliefs, it persisted beyond the second and third generations of the family, who were the most active in Methodist affairs. The Salters were conscious of the problems in the local employment market (see chapter 6) and they tried to provide their employees with good job security. Furthermore, if a seasonal staff member asked, they would also try to give them some work in the winter, even if it was only an occasional task. In the 1960s, for example, Bryan Dunckley was assigned to selling paraffin on the estates around Oxford, having cleaned out one of the firm's tankers. Although this initiative was short-lived, as the firm received complaints that it had taken business from someone else's round in Garden City (Kidlington), the gesture had been appreciated. He summed up the relationship as 'They didn't pay you a lot, but I'll give 'em their due. They did back you up ... Can't fault 'em.'[54]

The Salters did not consider the provision of leisure services to be inconsistent with their faith. By the middle of the nineteenth century, Methodists had established a reputation for being hostile towards popular forms of festivity. This attitude slowly softened from the 1870s onwards and the leisure market was transformed once 'the heirs of Wesley and Baxter had decided "pleasure" was not only no longer sinful, but it was essential to their mission'.[55] Indeed, their passenger boat services represented a wholesome activity that many religious groups took advantage of, which could include a visit to a temperance establishment, if required. Furthermore, the family's involvement with the likes of the YMCA and Sunday schools helped the firm to tap into the important youth market. They were also willing to provide a number of free outings for charitable causes, such as an annual trip to Nuneham for the children of the Cowley Poor Law School.[56]

The Salters were also prepared to accept a considerably reduced level of income – not to mention assisting their competitors – by not operating scheduled services on a Sunday until 1933, even though it was already a popular day of leisure on the river a century earlier. Although referring to the downstream services from the capital, Armstrong and Williams argue that 'the steamboat helped in the process of secularisation of Sunday', which was 'a crucial shift in attitudes needed if popular tourism was to occur'.[57] Fred Millin, who ran the family's operation in Edgbaston, certainly believed it to be the most significant day of leisure: in his negotiations to take over the Reservoir business in 1911, he wrote to John Salter to say that he believed running on a Sunday would generate a 'large increase' in takings of just over 20 per cent. This, he argued, was because:

> ... on Saturday afternoons there is cricket, football, tennis etc and cheap excursions to all parts. On Sunday this is all stopped and consequently there are thousands who would be only too glad to have the privilege of boating. There are also a great number of people in a town like B'ham, whose only day for a little recreation is Sunday.[58]

Although Millin was referring to the Midlands, Sir Arthur Salter suggested that on the Thames 'a host of rival firms got their start through the fact that Salters' resolutely refused for many years to let boats, or run steamers on that day'.[59] Although this is difficult to assess (see chapter 4), it is obvious that other businesses could have benefited from this policy, especially as some went so far as to publicise that they operated on a Sunday in their marketing. In 1912, for example, the Oxford boat proprietor George Harris advertised that his boat *Sovereign* ran to Abingdon on 'whit-Sunday and other Sundays during the season'.[60]

Salters' was operating private hires on Sunday by the mid-1920s (see chapter 4) – probably partly to cater for the likes of church parties – but the decision to start running scheduled services on the Sabbath was made 'very reluctantly' under pressure from the younger generation of the family and it was strongly influenced by economic considerations. The firm was badly affected by the Depression, as its overall turnover dropped by over a quarter from £40,574 12s 6d in 1930 to £28,825 0s 5½d in 1932 – the latter representing its worst yearly figures since the First World War. The Oxford and Kingston service was posting an average turnover of approximately £10,000 per year during the 1920s, and yet in 1931 the revenue it produced was only £6,231 7s 1d. The addition of the Sunday service provided an immediate and much-needed fillip, as the steamer income rose by a quarter from £6,797 18s 5½d (1932) to £8,479 9s 6d (1933),[61] although this was partly because of a particularly nice summer. This suggests that the financial ramifications of not operating on a Sunday were indeed around the 20 per cent figure that Fred Millin had estimated. Furthermore, as the firm had the largest fleet on the river, one can see how starting to operate on a Sunday would have represented a significant challenge to competitors.

A similar self-imposed restriction was that although the steamers did not have to be licensed for alcohol to be served on board – a legal loophole that was only recently closed – the Salters only served non-alcoholic beverages on them. The family was certainly well informed about the drinks trade, as they had been brought up in a tavern, and it may have been partly their father's drinking that contributed to the second generation becoming teetotal. There was also an on-going and vigorous debate in Oxford about the social impact of drinking. At the end of the nineteenth century, the received wisdom was that the city's sole industry was beer,[62] as it boasted seven breweries and over 300 licensed premises in 1883.[63] James believed that temperance was, next to the gospel, 'one of the greatest agencies for the uplifting of mankind', and he and his brothers were active in trying to promote the cause. In this respect they considered themselves as carrying on the work of a number of famous citizens, such as T.H. Green, Henry Fry and George Rolleston.[64] The Salters even kept the licence for the defunct 'Boat House Tavern' in order to prevent it being reallocated.[65]

Although the decision not to serve alcohol on the steamers may have endeared the firm to certain clients, like youth organisations and church groups, it would have lost the business money, as at the beginning of the twentieth century boating excursions and drinking were closely linked with one another. Indeed, in 1904 a number of newspapers whipped up a public outcry about the behaviour of those on board passenger boats, and the problem of 'floating beer-houses' even received parliamentary attention.[66] The Thames Conservancy dealt with the problem of rowdy behaviour by making the captain of the craft responsible for the passengers on board. Despite the Thames Boating Trades Association arguing this was unfair, the measure was said to have had an 'excellent effect', as there had been a 'marked decrease in river rowdies' by 1907, although there were still occasional problems in some areas.[67]

There does not seem to be any evidence, however, of the Salters being selective over whom they hired passenger boats to. Although it is conceivable that they may have occasionally turned down certain groups, they regularly accepted bookings from those connected with the drinks trade, including from the Licensed Victuallers of Oxford, with whom the brothers often clashed in public meetings.[68] It is not clear whether they would have allowed passengers to bring their own drink on board, although customers were able to purchase alcohol in advance from the firm by the late 1920s.[69] This was another pragmatic decision made as a result of pressure from younger family members, although by that stage many temperance organisations were less active, as they had failed to persuade the wider population that drinking was a social evil.[70]

One should also acknowledge the impact that Methodism had on the Salter family themselves. The Buddenbrooks thesis suggests that it was the desire of business owners to pursue a gentrified existence that caused them to become distracted from the primary focus on production and profit (see introduction). Yet strong Nonconformists were supposedly less susceptible to this, as they did not aspire to join the established Church of England.[71] Nor were they likely to focus on pursuing pleasure and the 'good life'. Indeed, the religious convictions of the Salters appear to have inculcated the kinds of quality that the so-called 'ultra-evangelicals' were renowned for: that is, hard work and 'character'.[72]

Yet these religious convictions did not just inform the way in which the family did business; they were also inextricably bound up with their political beliefs.[73] It is perhaps unsurprising, therefore, that when the brothers entered local politics, their activities would closely mirror those they had been involved with in the chapel.

Politics and the Salter Family

The commercial development of Oxford during the late nineteenth century was 'rapid, impressive and varied'.[74] As the region grew in prosperity from the 1870s onwards, the city emerged as a centre for a number of specialised trades, including printing and publishing. This contributed to Oxford's growing economic independence, although a great deal of commerce still revolved around the fluctuating needs of the university. The burgeoning prosperity of the city also led to the emergence of an increasingly wealthy and independent middle class in local politics, led by figures like the Conservative Walter Gray (steward of Keble College) and the Liberal Robert Buckell (auctioneer and estate agent). This elite group contributed to the city's growing civic pride and played a key role in the drive to gain county borough status for Oxford in 1889, following negotiations with the university.[75] Amongst these individuals was John Salter, who was followed into public service by his younger brother James. Between them they both enjoyed long and distinguished careers as local Liberal politicians.

The Salters were amongst a new generation of public servants to emerge in the aftermath of a number of scandals that rocked the political establishment in Oxford. They were not among those who were implicated in the malpractice surrounding the tainted general election of 1880, for example, which resulted in the city being disenfranchised by a Royal Commission,[76] nor were they involved with the Oxford Building and Investment Company, the collapse of which (in 1883) discredited a number of old Liberal leaders, most notably the company secretary, Alderman J. Galpin, who was forced to resign amidst allegations of corruption.[77]

John was involved with the Liberal Party for over a decade before he decided to stand for election, as he was responsible for nominating a number of candidates in the 1870s, as part of the Oxford Reform Club. He was also personally responsible for much of the work that led to a junior branch of the club being formed in 1882, which boasted 500 members by 1883.[78]

After being elected to the South Ward by a margin of only eight votes,[79] he went on to enjoy a political career of over forty years of service, which included being made an alderman in 1898 and mayor in 1902. Described as a 'man of exceptional and varied talents', he was 'for over a quarter of a century, one of the three or four leading figures in

Oxford's municipal life'.[80] When he received the freedom of the city in 1926, the *Oxford Times* recorded that he had 'established a reputation for sound judgment [sic] second to none of his colleagues and in difficult matters the city council often looked to him for guidance – and not in vain'.[81]

Although his political career began after the death of T.H. Green in 1882, John was a keen supporter of the influential reformer, sharing a number of mutual political interests, such as promoting temperance and a desire to raise the standard of education in the city. John served as vice president of the City Education Committee and, following its rearrangement, as chairman in 1927. He was an advocate of efficient secondary schools and he favoured, for example, schemes to build new schools in Cutteslowe and at the White House Ground.[82]

Perhaps his most significant work was in reforming the financial systems of the council, which included modernising the system for collecting the district and poor rates (which had previously been gathered separately), as well as overhauling the outdated commission system. His obituary recalled: 'His was the brain and the influence behind those dramatic changes in municipal financial methods which have lifted Oxford from a system that was antiquated, parochial and amateur to one which is regarded as a model of efficiency.'[83]

With the oldest brother deeply involved in politics, the second generation of the Salter family was very much like the Hobbs family of the other Oxfordshire boat company at Henley. In their case the founder of the firm, Harry (another owner of a waterside tavern), had six sons who assisted in the business, and again it was the oldest of these, William, who became a (Conservative) councillor and eventually mayor (twice in his case).[84]

Yet for the Salter family, it was not merely the oldest who entered political service, as James was elected to the council in 1896, also as a Liberal in the South Ward. He served as sheriff in 1908 and, like his older brother, he became mayor (in 1909) – an appointment that involved attending George V's coronation and welcoming Theodore Roosevelt when he visited Oxford – as well as an alderman (in 1922). He also played a particularly important role at the Board of Guardians, as its vice chairman. He was described by the chairman, Rev. L.R. Phelps (Provost of Oriel College from 1914 to 1930), as his 'right-hand man'[85] who had 'no superior in the city, when it came to the knowledge of the poor of Oxford, the sympathy shown to their sufferings and the earnest desire to help them'.[86] Their unwavering partnership was crucial in maintaining the cohesion of the board, as, like in many of the city's organisations, there were often tensions between town and gown.[87] His other roles included promoting public health as chairman of the city's Bath Committee, which was involved with opening a number of new facilities (including swimming pools), and being a governor of the Radcliffe Infirmary.

With two family members on the council, the Salters had considerable political power, not least because they both served into old age. Their shared principles ensured that they almost always voted along the same lines and between them they were involved with many different aspects of Oxford life. Collective representation on the council was not uncommon in the city at the time, as the families of Buckell, Lewis, Vincent, Salter, Cooper and Kingerlee were all providing more than one councillor in 1909.[88]

Yet, what does seem to be more distinctive was the *way* in which they conducted their affairs. They had certain qualities that made them particularly effective politicians, traits that presumably also served them well in the tourist industry. John had a reputation for being a 'very amiable and courteous gentleman',[89] who showed 'sympathy and a kindness of heart' to those he dealt with, whilst taking criticism magnanimously, rather than personally.[90] He was widely liked, as his obituary recorded that 'it is not often that a man of strong political views enjoys the confidence and affection of all classes of his fellow citizens' and that a 'great deal of his popularity might be traced to the delicate sense of humour which found a cause for smiling even when serious business was afoot'.[91] He also enjoyed 'warm respect' from the university and he was awarded an MA *honoris causa* in recognition of his civic work and part in cementing town and gown friendship.[92]

If anything there was even more affection for James on the council. Indeed, he had such a gentle demeanour that some questioned whether he had what it took to be mayor.[93] Yet he won over his detractors by his quiet, steady and efficient work, and Sir Robert Buckell claimed that his 'simplicity, geniality and courtesy', as well as his 'kindly spirit', was unparalleled by any of the previous post-holders.[94]

Politics and the Business

It is difficult to assess the impact that the public service of John and James had on their business, as they were involved in so many decisions that affected Oxford during their long and distinguished careers. Although it is likely that they considered it inappropriate to use their political influence overtly to benefit their firm, some of the work they were involved with inevitably impacted their livelihood, both positively and negatively. Furthermore, their prominence in civic affairs would certainly have helped to raise the profile of their business, although being on the council inevitably took up a lot of time, which is why the firm was fortunate to have three industrious and dynamic brothers in charge.

In terms of their business interests, arguably the most important political debate that the family was involved with was the dispute that flared up in the 1880s over the future of the Thames. This was an early example of the Salters being active in trying to protect the river on which their livelihood depended, and it may well have been a primary reason for John being drawn into political service in the first place. The issue dated back to at least 1853, when a report into the drainage of the Thames Valley had recommended dredging the river above Iffley, the construction of a new mouth for the river Cherwell and the removal of Iffley lock. These ideas resurfaced in 1869 when the engineers of the Oxford Local Board suggested a number of schemes to reduce flooding and improve the public health of the city. This led in 1871 to the creation of the Thames Valley Drainage Committee, which drew up formal plans for the work. By 1883, sufficient funds had been accumulated, but objections were raised by the Oxford Waterworks Company, which claimed that removing the lock might jeopardise the city's water supply.

The dispute came to a head in 1885, when fierce lobbying broke out on both sides, each receiving support from a cross-section of town and gown. A number of boating men decided to set up their own rival scheme to outbid the vote, as they were concerned that the beauty of the river would be destroyed and its suitability for boats impaired.[95] Unsurprisingly, John Salter, who was elected to the town council in April, was active in the debate, speaking to the mayor 'several times' about it, as well as requesting a special discussion to be held on the matter. He argued that although preventing floods and lowering the water table was desirable, removing the lock would be 'disastrous to the river itself' and 'would seriously injure the property on its banks' (some of which, of course, he owned).[96] His point of view eventually won the debate, as it was resolved to retain Iffley lock and to remove Folly Bridge lock instead.

Another pertinent issue at this time, for both the firm and its employees, was that although Grandpont (where Salters' was based) and part of North Hinksey were under the authority of the Oxford Local Board, they were also in the county of Berkshire, which was outside the municipal boundary. This meant that the residents had the inconvenience and expense of being in two jurisdictions. At a meeting of ratepayers in 1885, John Salter proposed a resolution to extend the municipal boundary to match that of the Oxford Local Board and a few months later he presented the council with a memorial from residents to that effect.[97] He was duly assigned to the parliamentary committee that successfully lobbied for the change, which came into force in 1889.

Being on the council also helped the brothers to accumulate expertise in a wide range of areas, which presumably would have helped their business interests. Their political careers certainly brought them into contact with people from many different sectors of society and John's foray into property development in south Oxford (see chapter 5) appears to have been one commercial opportunity that was a direct result of his involvement with the council. Furthermore, the family's understanding of the machinations of local government must have helped once their boat-building department focused more heavily on producing craft for corporations around the country (see chapter 2).

Yet there were also inevitably some occasions when the brothers voted against proposals that might have had potential benefits to their firm. In 1923, the council discussed a plan to build a road bridge over the Thames, which was intended to link south and east Oxford, whilst also providing some employment for the local population. Although it would have provided Salters' with a convenient road between its two main sites (Folly Bridge and the slipway), John was opposed to the idea, as he argued the costs were prohibitive, the area was prone to flooding and building more houses was a better way of tackling unemployment. By contrast, James was in favour of the idea – a rare occasion when the brothers did not see eye-to-eye – although the proposal was subsequently voted down.[98]

It is clear, however, that the political duties of John and James inevitably reduced the amount of time they could commit to their firm. This is why the partnership of the three brothers was so important, as they were able to draw from their collective talents, whilst devolving some of the operational duties to George. Yet, as has been shown, they were also dynamic individuals who were able to take on a wide range of roles and responsibilities. Nowhere was this more apparent than in the exceptional career of John, who was described as being 'clear headed, very active and energetic'.[99] He was not only a businessman, politician, preacher and author, but also chairman of the Oxford

Chronicle Company (which produced the city's Liberal newspaper),[100] the Oxford Amateur Photography Society, and the Thames Boating Trades Association, as well as being a director of Gillman and Co. (the Oxford photography company), W. Sissons (the Gloucester engine company that produced steam engines for Salters') and the Edgbaston Reservoir Company. Furthermore, he was also in charge of a number of charitable organisations, including the Oxford Medical Dispensary and the Lying in Charity.

As one would expect, his (and his brothers') involvement in so many aspects of Oxford life must have helped to raise the profile of their business in the local area. Indeed, their contribution to the city would never be matched by any subsequent generation of the family. When John died in the 1930, one newspaper declared that not only had the city lost the most eminent survivor of the public servants who had rebuilt the local government following the reconstruction of the municipality in 1889, but there had been 'few abler men, and certainly none who have worked more unselfishly for its benefit'.[101] Similarly, at James' funeral (in 1937), the city's rector claimed that they had lost one of the 'oldest, best known and highly regarded citizens'.[102]

The tradition of public service was continued by some of James' descendants, but the close personal attachment to Oxford was lost as those from the third generation onwards chose to reside in the nearby village of Kidlington instead. Undoubtedly the most famous subsequent family member was James' oldest son, Arthur, whose rise to prominence, initially in the civil service, was closely monitored by local newspapers (as a favourite 'son' of the city). Yet although he became Gladstone Professor of Political Theory and Institutions at All Souls College (1934–44) and an Independent MP representing the university (1937–50), his contribution to Oxford was confined to a relatively short time frame, as most of his working life was spent elsewhere. However, his affection for his family's home was shown by his adoption of the title Baron Salter of Kidlington, when he gained his peerage.[103] His chosen trajectory in life highlights another reason why the descendants of the second generation did not match their forefathers' personal impact in Oxford, which is that a number of them left the firm to pursue alternative careers. To understand why this occurred, we need to examine how the family developed and how succession was handled at the business.

Succession

The survival of Salters' inevitably depended on the managerial abilities of the family and one cannot explain the development of the business without examining how succession was handled. There were many factors that influenced this, but it was in the third generation that there was a split between the town and gown sides of the family, with the former taking over the firm. Their inheritance of the business coincided with one of the most difficult periods in the company's history, but the family subsequently took steps to try to strengthen the position of those in charge.

Succession is one of the 'critical tests' for the long-term survival of a family firm,[104] as the way in which business evolves is inevitably dictated by the abilities of those in charge. The founders of Salters' were rowing enthusiasts and their firm initially revolved around the sport, although this inevitably changed after the departure of Stephen, who had been the driving force behind this side of the business. The second generation had a much broader range of personal interests and they took the business in a number of new directions. They were also willing to override some economic considerations because of their religious convictions, although pressure from younger family members eventually resulted in some of the restrictions being overturned in the inter-war period. We also know that certain family members were especially interested in particular types of craft. George always retaining a fondness for the manual-powered vessels,[105] whereas his nephew, Frank, was an outboard motor boat racing enthusiast who influenced the development of that side of the business.

In the fourth generation, Hubert was focused solely on the rental fleet and his death resulted in the firm no longer sending a representative to the Thames Hire Cruiser Association meetings (although Salters' remained a member), whilst it was Arthur's affection and feelings of nostalgia for the racing boats that led him to invest more heavily in that side of the business. It was then John, in the twenty-first century, who transformed the parent company into a property firm. This was a significant departure from the previous regime, as his father had a much more cautious attitude to debt and would not have countenanced the level of borrowing needed to develop some of the yards into residential accommodation.[106]

Yet like many businesses, Salters' never had any formal plan for how succession would be handled. Instead the firm was passed down in an *ad hoc* and pragmatic manner. As the current managing director, John Salter, explained regarding his position: 'I don't think there's ever been any plan. It's just the way it happened – last man standing, I guess.'[107] Nevertheless, a form of hierarchical management was adopted, by which the oldest staff member had seniority (including amongst those in the same generation), although the junior manager's succession was never assured.

As this suggests, there was element of luck to the way in which the management of the firm developed. The number of male family members was crucial, because the female relatives did not get involved in running the business. This is one of the reasons why the descendants of George (who only had daughters) became divorced from the operational duties. The firm was fortunate to have enough heirs to keep it going, but there also had to be sufficient work available to make it a viable career option for any potential successor. Indeed, it was arguably the success and status of the second generation – not to mention John's strong personality[108] – that discouraged some of the immediate descendants from joining the business. Only one of James' four sons, Frank, opted to have a career at the family firm, although 'family responsibilities' subsequently required his brother Arnold to help out with the catering.[109]

Their education also undoubtedly played a major part in their decision whether or not to join the business, as they were the first to be schooled beyond the age of 14, which was a classic hallmark of the so-called 'Buddenbrooks effect' (see introduction). James, the only brother to have sons, was insistent that his children were not deprived of 'the educational opportunities which he so ardently desired'.[110] Arthur was sent to the Oxford High School for Boys – set up to provide for the needs of Oxford tradesmen, at fees within their means – whilst Frank, Bert and Arnold began their schooling at the same establishment,[111] before being dispatched to the Leys School in Cambridge, a college for the sons of lay Methodists, which produced some of the denomination's wealthiest industrialists of the twentieth century.[112] As a result of this education, Arthur (Brasenose), Bert (St John's) and Arnold (Lincoln) all went on to study at Oxford University, whilst Frank, the first of his generation to become involved with the firm, remained at the business.

The impact of his education was best summed up by James' oldest son, Arthur, who admitted that he left university with 'no conviction of business aptitude', but realised that working for Salters' offered what he considered to be 'inadequate scope'.[113] His decision to pursue a different career was certainly a loss to Salters', especially when one considers his talents and subsequent success, although there were a number of occasions when he intervened to help his family's business (see chapters 5 and 6). The second brother (Bert) also chose an alternative career path, opting to continue his education in order to become a clergyman in the Church of England, thereby severing his previous ties with Methodism (as his older brother had also done, although in his case because he lost his faith).[114]

The educational experience of the youngest brother, Arnold, also shaped his future career, but for a very different reason, as he was unable to complete his degree owing to a breakdown. His subsequent investment in property in both Wheatley and Kidlington (the latter being Hampton Manor estate, on Mill Street) could be seen as another classic trait of the Buddenbrooks effect, although his main interest was in poultry farming, which was a continuation of another family tradition (see chapter 5). He assumed charge of supplying food for the passenger boats, but despite proven 'organizing abilities',[115] as shown by his involvement as Pageant Master for the Oxfordshire Historical Pageant at Shipton Manor in 1931 (a show that lasted a number of days and featured a cast of over 2,000 performers), he was better known in the family for his historical interests than for his business acumen.[116] This is because he sold off swathes of agricultural land in Kidlington (including parts of the Hampden Estate in 1954 and 1955),[117] which was then used by developers to produce houses.

It could certainly be argued, therefore, that there was a 'haemorrhaging' of talent, as a result of some male heirs choosing different career paths and George's daughters (and subsequent descendants) becoming divorced from operational duties. There also appears to have been a more conservative attitude to business amongst those who inherited the company from the three Salter brothers, which is another characteristic of family firms. Whilst the second generation launched a number of new business ventures, most notably the Oxford and Kingston steamers and the reservoir at Edgbaston, there was little innovation in many of the firm's departments once the third and fourth generations took over (from 1950 and 1956 respectively).

Another reason why the firm struggled at this time is that the business became compartmentalised between different family members. After the death of George in 1950, Arthur (junior), who was trained in-house as a boat-builder, assumed overall control of Salters' with help from his cousin Hubert, who ran the motor boat fleet, having previously had his own wireless business. Thames Catering was managed by Arnold with assistance from his oldest son, John Francis ('Jack'). Dividing up responsibilities in this manner was common in family firms, but it could result in a lack of cohesion and the lines of communication becoming blurred. This sometimes occurred at Salters': employee Bill Dunckley recalled an incident in the 1950s when an ex-college barge with a slow leak sank at the slipway, because he had been sent down river by one family member and was therefore unable to fulfil his other duty (as assigned by another) of keeping it pumped out.[118] Furthermore, disputes were commonplace in family firms, especially once they passed down to a 'confederation' of cousins who did not share the same kind of close historical bonds or value systems.[119] At Salters' relations were on the whole good, though the family did occasionally fall out with one another, which caused wider friction amongst the employees.

Yet it was the way in which the management and ownership of the firm developed after this difficult period – which was partly by chance and partly by design – that was important in ensuring the longevity of the business. Firstly, there was a reduction in the number of people managing Salters', after Hubert died in 1961 (aged 48) and Jack, who had been involved with catering, was dismissed. The removal of less productive family members from businesses was one way of avoiding the Buddenbrooks effect, but it could have a damaging effect on relationships.

Secondly, a number of events led to one line of the family gaining a greater control of the business. When Arthur took over the running of the business, one of his first tasks was to rebuild the cohesion at the firm, but ironically it was a dispute between two brothers that led to his becoming the largest shareholder. In the late 1960s, the ownership of the firm was fairly evenly split between six individuals, which may have been another reason for some of the problems the firm experienced, as none of them was involved with running the boat side of the business. Yet after the second largest shareholder, Sir Arthur Salter, had a falling out with his younger brother, Arnold, this led to the former, who did not have any children, giving his stake in the business to his nephew, Arthur (junior), in the early 1970s. He did not think the shares were worth much, anyway, because the business had been struggling in the previous two decades (see chapter 4).[120]

Nevertheless, this gave Arthur (junior) a 20.3 per cent stake in the firm, and his control of Salters' increased again after the death of his father, Arnold (who had previously been the largest shareholder with 18 per cent of the business), in 1974. This was then followed by a further consolidation in 1980 when the firm's ownership structure was changed,[121] which resulted in Arthur's side of the family buying additional shares in order to achieve an overall majority. Although there were inevitably differences of opinion about what the future direction of the business needed to be, this was an amicable decision that was seen as necessary to strengthen the business, given the problems the company had been through. The longest serving non-executive director and 'steadying influence',[122] Dorothy Sackett, believed that those running the business should have a controlling stake.[123] This meant that the ownership of Salters' had come full circle. It had grown from a business run by two brothers into one owned and managed by a complicated network of extended kin, each with varying stakes in the business, and then had returned to the control of a nuclear family.

Despite all of the changes that were made, crucially, the shares always remained in the hands of the family, which ultimately protected the firm from the kind of 'outside' influence that caused those running other famous Oxford businesses, like Morris Motors and Cooper's marmalade, to lose control of their brand. Indeed, the Salters took a 'hands on' approach to running the business, although greater responsibility was given to duty managers in the second half of the twentieth century, when fewer family members worked at the firm. It was not until the death of Arthur in 2000, when there was no direct descendant old enough to replace him, that a non-family member was made a director. Neil Kinch, a manager promoted by Arthur's son, John, served as a director of Salter Bros until 2008 and of Salter's Steamers until 2013 (when he left the firm). His roles were then taken over by Paul Salter, the son of John.

• • •

The founders built up the business, but it was the second generation who rose to become well-known pillars of the establishment in Oxford. Their other commitments and their religious convictions inevitably had both positive and negative financial ramifications for the business, but on the whole the partnership of three exceptional brothers appears to have worked well. Although there were many reasons why certain parts of the firm struggled in the second half of the twentieth century, it was significant that some key family members chose to pursue different career paths. Furthermore, those who remained at the firm were not as involved with public service in Oxford (as residents of Kidlington), they were more conservative in their business affairs and they did not enjoy the same level of cohesion as those in the second generation. Although chance then played a part in Arthur Salter subsequently gaining control of the company, it was partly the problems that had previously occurred that encouraged the family to allow him to strengthen his position in 1980. The different individuals each put their own personal stamp on the business and, ultimately, it was their ability to overcome the challenges they faced, including the way in which they utilised the firm's assets, that was crucial for the survival of their enterprise. Furthermore, the shares always remained in the family, which protected the firm from outside interference.

Notes

1   Salter, *Memoirs of a Public Servant*, p. 22.
2   Ibid., p. 15.
3   J. Burchardt, 'Historicizing Counterurbanization: In-migration and the Reconstruction of Rural Space in Berkshire', *Journal of Historical Geography*, vol. 38, no. 2 (April 2012), pp. 162–64. Stephen also owned Egrove Park.
4   Salter, *Memoirs of a Public Servant*, p. 19. However, they were privately educated up to that point.
5   1871 census.
6   1891 census and SA Will of Thomas Salter (1924).
7   Salter, *Memoirs of a Public Servant*, pp. 29–31.
8   J.E. Oxley, *A History of Wesley Memorial Church* (Oxford, 1967), pp. 57–58.
9   *Oxford Times*, 9 July 1910, p. 10.
10 D. Jeremy, *Capitalists and Christians* (Oxford, 1990), p. 296.
11 K. Tiller, *Church and Chapel in Oxfordshire, 1851* (Oxford, 1987), p. xiii.
12 Ritson, *The World is Our Parish*, p. 28.
13 1851 Religious Census. They recorded that their average attendance was normally around 500 in the morning, 120 in the afternoon and 600 in the evening.

14   Oxford Record Office (ORO) Quarterly meetings of the Methodist Circuit, 29 March 1882 and 21 March 1883.

15   C. Oldstone-Moore, *Hugh Price Hughes: Founder of a New Methodism* (Cardiff, 1999), p. 94.

16   From memoirs in the possession of the Sackett family.

17   Oxley, *Wesley Memorial Church*, p. 47.

18   ORO Quarterly meetings of the Methodist Circuit, 29 March 1882.

19   *The Oxford Methodist*, April 1891, p. 19.

20   Erdozain, *The Problem of Pleasure*, pp. 77 and 119.

21   *Oxford Times*, 9 July 1910, p. 10.

22   *Jackson's Oxford Journal*, 17 March 1888.

23   Ibid., 29 June 1901, p. 6.

24   Ibid., 21 March 1891 and 5 December 1891.

25   *Jackson's Oxford Journal*, 17 March 1888 and 24 February 1894.

26   *Jackson's Oxford Journal*, 4 February 1899 and *Oxford Times*, 27 May 1911, p. 5.

27   *Oxford Times*, 9 July 1910, p. 10.

28   ORO Quarterly Meetings of the Methodist Circuit, 25 March 1903 and 19 March 1914. Abingdon, Wantage, Thames and Watlington were added to the Circuit.

29   *Oxford Times*, 2 April 1910, p. 4.

30   Ibid., 12 March 1910, p. 12.

31   ORO Quarterly Meetings of the Methodist Circuit, 20 June 1907.

32   *Oxford Chronicle*, 21 April 1922, p. 13.

33   Ibid., 22 December 1902.

34   After that point the minute books stopped listing all of those attending.

35   From memoirs in the possession of the Sackett family. John Henry Salter lived next-door at number 55.

36   *Oxford Times*, 20 January 1912, p. 10 and ORO Quarterly Meetings of the Methodist Circuit, 16 March 1916.

37   Oxley, *Wesley Memorial Church*, pp. 33–34.

38   K.P. Hughes, *The Story of My Life* (London, 1945), pp. 59–60.

39   *Jackson's Oxford Journal*, 2 September 1893.

40   ORO Quarterly Meetings of the Methodist Circuit 1882–1913.

41   *Oxford Times*, 7 May, 1910, p. 7.

42   Interview with Len Andrews, 31 August 2004.

43   ORO Quarterly Meetings of the Methodist Circuit, 25 September 1895.

44   *Oxford Times*, 12 February 1910, p. 7.

45   Ibid., 6 December 1902, p. 12.

46   Jeremy, *Capitalists and Christians*, p. 414.

47   P. Joyce, *Work, Society and Politics*, p. xx (London, 1982), p. 125, in Jeremy, *Capitalists and Christians*.

48   M. Adeney, *Nuffield: A Biography* (London, 1993), p. 105.

49   Email from David Nutt, 10 March 2011.

50   Interview with John Salter, 20 December 2011.

51   SA Sick and Share-Out Club Rules 1950.

52   Bourdillon, *Survey of the Social Services*, vol. 1, p. 92.

53   *Jackson's Oxford Journal*, 15 August 1874.

54   Interview with Bryan Dunckley, 17 August 2004.

55   Erdozain, *Problem of Pleasure*, pp. 84–155.

56   *Jackson's Oxford Journal*, 18 August 1900.

57   Armstrong and Williams, 'The Steamboat and Popular Tourism', p. 72.

58   SA Letter from Fred Millin to John Salter, 1 December 1911.

59 Salter, *Memoirs of a Public Servant*, p. 20.

60 *Oxford Times*, 25 May 1912, p. 3.

61 SA Salter Bros Ltd End of Year Accounts 1916–33.

62 *Oxford Magazine*, June 1893, p. 413, in C. Day, 'The University and the City', in Brock and Curthoys, *History of the University of Oxford: Nineteenth Century*, vol. 6, p. 457.

63 Bodleian Library Drink Map of Oxford (1883), reference: C17. 70 Oxford (7).

64 *Oxford Times*, 11 June 1910, p. 12.

65 *Jackson's Oxford Journal*, 1 October 1892.

66 *Hansard H.C. Deb.*, 1 August 1904, vol. 139, c.254 from http://hansard.millbanksystems. com/commons/1904/aug/01/sale-of-liquor-on-river-steamers (accessed 20 October 2012). Reference found through the (unpublished) work of Iain MacLeod.

67 *The Motor Boat*, vol. 7, no. 169 (3 October 1907), p. 216.

68 *Jackson's Oxford Journal*, 1 August 1891.

69 SA Cash Book 1927–28.

70 A.E. Dingle, *The Campaign for Prohibition in England* (London, 1980), p. 227.

71 Crouzet, *The Victorian Economy*, p. 408.

72 H. McLeod, *Class and Religion in the Late Victorian City* (London, 1974), pp. 88–157.

73 *Jackson's Oxford Journal*, 1 March 1884.

74 A. Howe, 'Intellect and Civic Responsibility', in Whiting, *Oxford*, p. 21.

75 *Oxford Times*, 11 May 1912, p. 9.

76 See P.D. John, 'Politics and Corruption: Oxford and the General Election of 1880', in *Oxoniensia*, vol. 55 (1990), pp. 131–46.

77 See C. Fenby, *The Other Oxford* (London, 1970). The firm did, however, benefit from the collapse of the business, as it ended up buying some property from it.

78 *Jackson's Oxford Journal*, 31 October 1874 and 7 April 1883.

79 Ibid., 18 April 1885.

80 Salter, *Memoirs of a Public Servant*, p. 18 and *Oxford Mail*, 29 January 1923, p. 1.

81 *Oxford Times*, 23 April 1926, p. 11.

82 Ibid., 17 October 1930, p. 5.

83 *Oxford Monthly*, November 1930.

84 Telephone conversation with Tony Hobbs, 18 July 2005.

85 *Oxford Times*, 19 April 1913, p. 3.

86 Ibid., 20 April 1912, p. 16.

87 Ibid., 8 February 1924, p. 4 and 25 April 1924, p. 27.

88 Ibid., 31 July 1909, p. 7. The majority of these families were Nonconformists.

89 Ibid., 17 October 1930, p. 5.

90 Ibid., 9 January 1915, p. 5.

91 Ibid., 17 October 1930, p. 5.

92 Ibid., 2 April 1936.

93 *Oxford Times*, 9 July 1910, p. 10.

94 Ibid., 12 November 1910, p. 8.

95 Howe, 'Intellect and Civic Responsibility', pp. 25–26.

96 *Jackson's Oxford Journal*, 4 July 1885.

97 Ibid.

98 *Oxford Times*, 2 January 1923, p. 11.

99 *Jackson's Oxford Journal*, 11 November 1899.

100 The company was discontinued in 1929 and the papers from the liquidation of the firm in 1932 remain in the archive.

101 *Oxford Times*, 17 October 1930, p. 5.

102 Ibid., 9 April 1937, p. 5.

103 For more information about his life, see Sidney Aster's forthcoming book *Power, Policy and Personality: The Life and Times of Lord Salter, 1881–1975*.

104 Rose, 'Beyond Buddenbrooks', p. 3.

105 Interview with Bill Dunckley, 21 August 2004.

106 Interview with John Salter, 20 December 2011.

107 Ibid.

108 Salter, *Memoirs of a Public Servant*, p. 18.

109 Ibid., p. 22.

110 Ibid., p. 19. Similarly, the three daughters of George were sent to the Oxford High School for Girls.

111 W.T. Coxhill and R.A. Abrams (eds), *Register of Oxford High School: Part II, 1890–1900* (Oxford, 1915), pp. 30–42. Arthur later became president of the Oxford High School Old Boys Club and one of the four houses to which every new student was assigned was named in his honour.

112 Jeremy, *Capitalists and Christians*, pp. 89–91.

113 Salter, *Memoirs of a Public Servant*, p. 32.

114 Ibid., pp. 21–22.

115 Ibid.

116 Interview with John Salter, 20 December 2011.

117 J. Cooper, 'Kidlington', in A. Crossley (ed.), *The Victoria History of the County of Oxford*, vol. 12 (Oxford, 1990), p. 191.

118 Interview with Bill Dunckley, 4 August 2004.

119 Institute of Directors, *Family Businesses*, p. 15.

120 Interview with John Salter, 20 December 2011.

121 This involved the doubling of the company's share capital, a distribution of bonus shares and the purchase of a greater stake in the business by Arthur.

122 From memoirs in the possession of the Sackett family.

123 Email from Robert Sackett (Dorothy Sackett's son), 20 December 2010.

In Conclusion

Salter Bros. Ltd ... [is] one of the oldest and certainly the best known of Thames boatyards ... In their time they [the steamers] must have carried millions of passengers, and to many people the name of Salter's is synonymous with Thames. The history of Salter's steamers is truly fascinating and worthy of more attention.

The Thames Book, 1975[1]

In many ways the history of Salters', from its beginnings up to the present decade, represented a microcosm of the wider changes that were occurring on the river and in the city of Oxford, as well as in society at large. The firm rose to prominence at a time when a number of other specialised businesses were prospering in the city. Through the exertions of family members and a skilled workforce, the business quickly grew from a small enterprise to become the leading racing boat-builder in the 1860s. Success in contests like the university Boat Race helped Salters' to gain a worldwide reputation and it was one of only a few local businesses to export globally at this time.

The value of the firm had increased more than eightfold by the mid-1870s, largely through the acquisition of property around Folly Bridge, which was required in order to expand the business. It had begun to focus more heavily on the pleasure boating market by this stage, and this became more important to Salters' as the racing-boat department declined, following the departure of Stephen Salter in 1874. The river was entering a 'golden age' for leisure, and the firm helped to popularise the long-distance 'Thames trip' between Oxford and London in the mid-Victorian period, which was connected to the rise of recreational camping. By the late 1880s Salters' had grown its rental fleet to 900 craft, which made it one of the country's largest inland boat-letters.

In 1888 the second generation of the family introduced a steamer service between Oxford and Kingston, the expansion of which opened up the Upper Thames to much larger numbers of visitors. By forging a close relationship with others in the leisure and transport industries, most notably the Great Western Railway, Salters' was able to tap into the growing excursion market and to establish a monopoly over the long-distance journey. The service benefited from a large amount of publicity and it was very profitable in the early years. By the beginning of the twentieth century the firm was the biggest passenger boat operator on the Upper Thames, with its steamers well known both nationally and internationally. Indeed, its dominance on the river, not to mention the boat-building department's thriving export trade, helped Salters' to become 'for a time [perhaps] the foremost of its kind in the world'.[2] It had also built up a substantial property empire in Oxford, which became crucial for the firm's survival in the twentieth century.

Salters' experienced some seasonal cash-flow problems in the second decade of the twentieth century, but it benefited greatly from both a large amount of contract work in the latter stages of the First World War, which helped to swell the workforce to unprecedented levels, and a notable short-term rise in pleasure boating during and directly after the conflict. The firm was largely profitable during the inter-war period, although the retained earnings were carefully controlled, and some of the overheads, like the directors' fees, tended to be adjusted according to the financial performance of the previous year, which resulted in the company's performance oscillating during this time.

In the 1920s the three most important parts of the business were the Oxford and Kingston steamers, the rental fleet and the boat-building department, which each typically generated between 20 and 30 per cent of the firm's total annual turnover. Over the course of the decade, orders received by the latter grew to unprecedented levels, whilst the overall trend was one of falling income from the scheduled services and rising income from boat-letting. This included the rental of self-drive motorised craft,

Profit After Tax

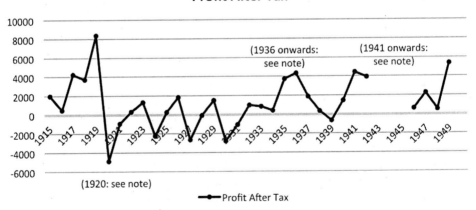

(Figures taken from the End of Year Accounts 1915–49. The figure shows the total profits of the firm after the directors' fees and any taxes had been deducted, though prior to any dividends being paid out. Directors' fees were not collected between 1915 and 1919, and the loss in 1920 was partly because they were larger than normal (to compensate for the missed years) and because of an excess profits duty relating to the previous year. The format of the accounts changed slightly from 1936, when Salters' stopped using a separate income tax account, and from 1941, when money was allocated in advance for tax using an estimated figure.)

which were introduced at this time, and privately hired steamers, especially those used in the increasingly popular circular tours.

The Depression of the 1930s temporarily affected all areas of the business, although it was the boat-building department that suffered the most, as orders failed to recover after falling by approximately a third. The company was also forced to adopt several emergency financial measures, including, most notably, a seasonal loan system, which helped it to maintain cash flow during the winter months. The firm's fortunes improved considerably in the middle of the decade, although profits then slowly declined, partly as a result of falling income from privately hired steamers.

The Second World War was a considerable fillip to business, as the firm benefited from additional contract work and a large increase in pleasure boating, especially travelling on the Oxford and Kingston steamers. The company continued to be profitable in the immediate aftermath of the conflict, but this was followed by two difficult decades. In the 1950s and 1960s Salters' struggled with mounting debts, some managerial problems, the loss of some beneficial relationships (notably with the local rowing scene), conservatism in the boat-building department, losses from the scheduled services and difficulties with the recruitment, retention and disciplinary standards of its staff. The firm was unable to compete with the wages offered in Oxford's developing motor industry and was forced to source employees from outside the city. The jobs on the steamers remained popular, but Salters' struggled in particular to recruit and retain its skilled but low-paid craftsmen, not least because it was forced to sell much of its residential housing in the 1950s, which prevented it from being able to offer many of its staff subsidised accommodation. Furthermore, the firm became increasingly reliant on one side of the business – the passenger boats – which led to a greater dependency on income generated in a narrow time frame each year.

The company's performance improved considerably in the late 1970s, during what was probably the busiest period for pleasure boating in the river's history. The firm's fleet of motorised rental boats grew to its largest size, its racing craft were in the ascendency once again, and both the number of passengers being carried on the steamers and the output of the boat-building department reached new heights. This helped its turnover to grow almost fourfold in a single decade, from £159,681 in 1970 to £633,901 in 1980. Yet despite the profit this helped to generate, the traffic on the river swelled to record levels and the resultant delays forced the company to cut its long-distance service into smaller sections in 1974. This, as well as catering for the growing demand for both short round trips and the private hire market, drew the firm into direct competition with other operators and made it more dependent on Oxford, at a time when its fleet was declining in size.

Salters' experienced a downturn in the 1980s, when the output of the boat-building department declined and it finally bowed out of racing craft construction, but it was the following decade that was a particularly difficult time for the firm. The depression of the early 1990s forced it to dispose of its rental fleet, and sustained losses beyond this culminated in the sale of Grandpont Yard in 1997, which stabilised the company's finances and ensured that Salters' survived into the twenty-first century. The conversion of the property also contributed to the business becoming less visible in the local area

Profit After Tax

(Figures taken from CHC Salter Bros Ltd (and Subsidiary Company) End of Year Accounts 1965–85. The figures were calculated in a slightly different manner from 1983 onwards.)

– a process in which the decreasing size of its rental and passenger boat fleets (and therefore its workforce), the loss of its monopoly over the long-distance steamer service (and some of the advertising that went with it) and the family's declining prominence in Oxford, all played a part.

Ultimately it had been the firm's diversification, as well as its ability to derive income from a wide range of areas relating to its main commercial activities, that had enabled it to dominate many of the markets it focused on. Indeed, adaptability in the fickle and faddish leisure market was of paramount importance: the different departments of Salters' were able to support each other, and the business was able to transform itself from one that revolved around a skilled trade to one that was largely concerned with providing leisure services. The ultimate testament to its flexibility was the restructuring of Salter Bros Ltd in the twenty-first century to become a property company. The divorcing of this from the other parts of the business (run by Salter's Steamers Ltd) was also an acknowledegment of the inherent difficulties of operating in the leisure market, especially in an area of the market that carried a high level of risk and where the vast majority of revenue was generated in a few months of the year.

By tracing the history of the firm, this book has shown, firstly, how the company's development fitted within the socio-economic context of Oxford and the Thames; secondly, the contribution it made to different forms of water-based leisure; and thirdly, how the business managed to survive, given the challenges that family firms face.

By making available and assessing important unpublished material, it has helped to fill a significant gap in the commercial history of Oxford, as it has generally been overlooked that Salters' was once 'a household word in the city of the "dark blues"'.[3] It has shown how the business managed to become a dominant employer in the area, but then had to fight for its survival, when the local employment market was affected by the motor industry. It has also chronicled the demise of skilled boat-building, which was one of many trades around the country that were threatened once industrialisation transformed the economic landscape. Furthermore, it has shed light on the working environment of a distinctive waterway community that has received little attention from scholars: the 'Salters' navy'.

This book has also contributed to the study of how family firms develop and evolve over time. After the initial success of the founders, it was the second generation that became particularly influential, both in Oxford (as leading local politicians and well-known Wesleyan Methodists) and at the firm. Their wider interests and religious convictions had both positive and negative ramifications for the business, but on the whole the firm appears to have done well under their tenure. Salters' experienced some classic weaknesses of such businesses from the third generation onwards, when a number of family members opted for different careers, but the way in which the management and ownership of the company subsequently evolved was important for the firm's longevity. The company shares always remained in the family, which was crucial for the firm's survival, as was the way in which Salters' utilised its property empire.

Perhaps most significantly, this book has made a contribution to the historical study of leisure. The firm was one of the most important businesses connected with the recent history of the Upper Thames, as it was at the forefront of the changes that transformed the river from a working waterway into one of recreation. Indeed, Salters' was amongst the prominent leisure providers of the Victorian age, as it did more to popularise pleasure boating on the waterway above London than any other comparable business. Its dominance, and the extensive marketing it received, also ensured that it became *the* main firm that one associated with the non-tidal river. Yet its major legacy was not so much pioneering new forms of water-based leisure – although it introduced some innovations – but making the Upper Thames more accessible. The delivery and retrieval service for rental craft was an early example of this, but the most notable development came when it combined forces with others in the travel industry to offer customers a range of steamer trips that were part of an integrated transport service. Salters' was, therefore, not only important for the wider river economy, but also an influential force in promoting the Thames (and surrounding area) as somewhere that was beautiful, historic and interesting to visit. Furthermore, by examining the firm's history, this work has traced the development of different forms of pleasure boating on the waterway, including the emergence of camping as a popular pastime – an early form of holidaying on the river – as well as the activities that thrived during the two world wars.

There are several questions that this book has not been able to examine, including the way in which perceptions about the river have changed over time, the role that class identities played in determining types of pleasure boating, and the development of Oxford as a tourist attraction. It has, however, provided the groundwork for further study on the history of leisure on the Thames and in the surrounding area. Indeed, in the 1970s the Oxford Waterways Action Group recommended that there should be a permanent record of the city's waterway heritage in the form of a museum at Folly Bridge.[4] In an era when heritage tourism is increasingly popular, this book has put on display the history of Salters' and has shown the considerable contribution that the family and firm have made to Oxford, the waterway and the surrounding area – a legacy that continues to this day.

Notes

1   H. Salter and D. Dalton (eds), *The Thames Book* (Croydon, 1975), p. 81.
2   Salter, *Memoirs of a Public Servant*, p. 15.
3   *Bow Bells*, 8 June 1894, p. 569.
4   Oxford Waterways Action Group, *Oxford Waterways*, p. 50.

Appendix

Large Passenger Boats in the Fleet (those over 40ft in length)

Dates at Salters'	Name	Built	Dimensions	Hull	Status
1885–1918	*Isis*	1885	45ft x 7ft	Wood	D
1887–1943	*Alaska*	1883	60ft x 9ft 3in	Wood	P
1889–1922	*Oxford* (I) (renamed *Gaiety*)	1889	72ft x 12ft	Steel	P
1890–1915	*Kingston* (renamed *Mamounie*)	1890	72ft x 12ft	Steel	D
1891–1939	*Swan*	1891	49ft 6in x 7ft	Steel	D
1892–1915	*Windsor*	1892	72ft x 12ft	Steel	D
1892–1912	*Cliveden* (I) (renamed *Kamar Ez-Zaman*)	1892	72ft x 12ft	Steel	D
1896–1977	*Henley*	1896	85ft x 13ft 6in	Steel	P
1898–1971	*Nuneham*	1898	85ft x 13ft 6in	Steel	P
1901–present	**Reading**	**1901**	**85ft x 13ft 6in**	**Steel**	**S**
1902–*c.*1990	*Sonning*	1902	85ft x 13ft 6in	Steel	P
1902–1977	*Marlow*	1902	85ft x 13ft 6in	Steel	D
1905–1993	*Streatley*	1905	85ft x 13ft 6in	Steel	P
1907–1920	*The Sikh* (formerly *Kingester*)		45ft x 8ft	Steel	D
1912–present	**Goring**	**1912**	**90ft x 14ft 6in**	**Steel**	**S**
1913–present	**Wargrave**	**1913**	**90ft x 14ft 6in**	**Steel**	**S**
1915–1925	*Sovereign*	1903	59ft x 8ft	Wood	D
1918–1926	*Queen of England*	1902	70ft x 10ft	Wood	D
1921–1931	*Hurley* (formerly *Phoenix* and originally *Caucase*)	1914	66ft x 11ft 6in	Steel	P

1922–present	Oxford (II)	1922	90ft x 14ft 6in	Steel	S
1923–present	Hampton Court	1923	90ft x 14ft 6in	Steel	S
1927–2008	Mapledurham	1927	105ft x 16ft 6in	Steel	D
1931–198?	Cliveden (II)	1931	105ft x 16ft 6in	Steel	L
1937–1962	Grand Duchess	1924	95ft x 16ft 5in	Wood	D
1945–1969	The Majestic	1908	88ft 9in x 15ft	Wood	D
1945–1972	The Original River Queen (formerly River Queen)	1930	60ft 4in x 12ft 6in	Wood	D
1945–195?	Mystery (never operational)				D
1948–1965	Queen of the Thames	1925	94ft 8in x 16ft 3in	Wood	D
1956–present	Mary Stuart (formerly Kagerplas)	1923	68ft 10in x 13ft 10in	Steel	S
1988–present	Lady Ethel	1988	57ft 4in x 14ft 3in	Steel	S
1998–present	Jean Marguerite	1998	44ft 6in x 12ft	Fibreglass	S
2004–present	Maratana	1980	44ft 6in x 12ft	Fibreglass	S
2010–present	Mapledurham Lady (formerly Caversham Lady)	1978	57ft 4in x 14ft 3in	Steel	S

Status: D = defunct; **S** = in Salters' current fleet; P = privately owned/operated by another company; L = laid up

Launches in the Fleet (those between 20ft and 40ft in length)

Dates at Salters'	Name	Built	Dimensions
1893–1923	White Wings	1893	25ft x 5ft 6in
1902–1919	Galatea	1902	36ft x 7ft
1902–1904	Zulu	1902	25ft x 5ft 6in
1904–1921	Sprightly	1904	21ft x 5ft
1905–1906	Leander	1905	24ft x 5ft 6in
1908–1919	Dreadnaught	1908	24ft x 5ft 6in
1909–1918	Iffley (I)	1909	35ft x 7ft 6in
1912–1919	Sea Gull	1912	20ft x 5ft 3in
1913–1918	Coquette (I)	1913	35ft x 6ft
1920–1926	Linda Lee	1913	25ft x 6ft 3in
1919–1926	Swiftsure	1919	40ft x 6ft 3in

1920–1922	Vioella	1920	30ft x 6ft 6in
1921–19??	Iffley (II)	1921	40ft x 9ft 6in
1922–193?	Vioelle	1922	30ft x 5ft 6in
1927–19??	Coquette (II)	1927	40ft x 8ft
1927–196?	Robin	1927	25ft x 5ft 6in
1930–present	**Iffley (III) (originally Leander (II])**	**1930**	**40ft x 9ft 6in**
1931–195?	Redskin	1931	20ft x 5ft 6in

Cabin Cruisers in the Fleet

Dates at Salters'	Name	Built	Dimensions
1922–1932	Ravensbourne	1922	28ft 6in x 6ft 9in
1923–192?	Pilgrim	1923	30ft x 8ft
1925–193?	Rover	1925	30ft x 7ft
1928–1953	Wayfarer	1928	30ft x 8ft
1929–1954	Pilgrim (II)	1929	–
1930–1954	Voyager	1930	30ft x 6ft 9in
1931–1966	Traveller	1931	30ft x 8ft
1932–1964	Gipsy	1932	20ft x 7ft
1936–195?	Rover (II)	1936	30ft x 9ft
1938–196?	Venturer	1938	30ft x 9ft 6in
1939–196?	Pathfinder	1939	20ft x 7ft 6in
1953–196?	Meanderer	1953	30ft
1953–196?	Wayfarer (II)	1953	24ft
1964–196?	Rover (III)	1964	24ft 8in x 9ft 2in
1965–196?	Voyager (II)	1965	24ft 8in x 9ft 2in
1967–199?	Traveller (III)	1967	27ft
1967–199?	Gypsy Moth III (formerly Pilgrim III)	1967	27ft
1968–199?	Gypsy Moth range (I–IV)	From 1968	26ft 8in
1972–199?	Lively Lady range (I–II)	From 1972	–
1973–199?	Serena range (I–III and IX–X)	From 1973	–
1978–199?	Dulcina I–II	From 1978	30ft
1978–199?	Paxina	1978	30ft

Narrowboats in the Fleet

Dates at Salters'	Name	Built	Length
1974–199?	*Romany Queen* range (1–6)	From 1974	50ft
1977–199?	*Romany Princess* range (1–3)	From 1977	38ft

Barges in the Fleet

Dates at Salters'	Name
1858–1920	Green Barge
1858–1???	*Nelson*
1870–1918	*British Queen*
18??–1925	*Cardinal*
18??–1887	Trinity
18??–1882	Brasenose
1862–18??	Balliol
18??–1???	University
18??–1954	Oriel
18??–1???	St Edmund Hall
(Others in 1875)	New (College), *Britannia*, *Lily*, The Large Barge, 'Small'
1903–192?	*The Geisha*
1903–192?	*Psyche*
19??–1934	The Barge
1898–1966	*Wanderlust* (formerly St Edmund Hall and originally St John's)
1920–195?	Green Barge
1926–1966	Ex–Brasenose (formerly St Catherine's)
190?–1963	*Argosy* (formerly Merton's)

Note: Some of the barges may be duplicated in the list, because a number were renamed. The firm also acquired eight modern 'Manor class' houseboats between 1964 and 1968, of which only *Clifotn Manor* survives.

Military Craft Built During the Two World Wars

Date	Craft built	Price per boat (destination, if known)
1915	4 x Julia dinghies	£46 10s (Glasgow)
	60 x Pontoons	
	10 x 20ft Collapsible boats	£60 (Chatham)
	44 x Bipartite pontoons	
	30 x Pontoons	
	30 x 20ft Collapsible boats (Berthon pattern)	£74 (A number of yards, including Sunderland)
	1 x 30ft Admiralty (old pattern) cutter	£150 (Devonport)
	2 x 32ft Admiralty (old pattern) cutters	£195 (Belfast)
1916	2 x 32ft Admiralty cutters	£200 10s (Chatham and Devonport)
	2 x 20ft Admiralty motor boats	£245
	4 x 32ft Admiralty sloop rig cutters	£240 (Portsmouth), £240 10s (Chatham)
	6 x 20ft Collapsible boats (Berthon type)	£80
	2 x 32ft Admiralty sloop rig cutters	£264 (Birkenhead), £271 (Portsmouth)
	2 x 40ft Teak motor launches	(War Office)
1917	2 x 40ft Teak motor launches	(War Office)
	2 x 50ft Teak motor launches	(War Office)
	2 x 27ft Elm whalers	£142
	6 x 20ft Collapsible boats	£80 (Different locations)
	1 x 30ft Sloop rig cutter	£265
	2 x 35ft Seaplane tenders/hydroplanes	£525 (Thornycroft for RAF)
	4 x 55ft Coastal motor boats	(Thornycroft)
	1 x 30ft Carvel gig	£230
	1 x 50ft Steel pinnace (hull)	£1,450
1918	4 x 40ft Coastal motor boats	(Thornycroft)
	1 x 70ft Coastal motor boat	(Thornycroft)
	1 x 30ft Carvel gig for HMS *Dauntless*	£230 (Palmer's shipbuilding yard, Jarrow)
	8 x 12ft Collapsible boats	£45 (A number of yards, including Pembroke)
	6 x 20ft Collapsible boats	£87 (HM dockyard, Sheerness)
	1 x 30ft Carvel gig	£230 (HM dockyard, Chatham)
	1 x 54ft Towing and fuel carrying motor launch	£1,850 (Royal Navy Air Service)
	4 x 12ft Collapsible boats	£50 (HM dockyard, Portsmouth)
	2 x 30ft Motor launches (hull)	£610
	4 x 50ft Wood steam pinnaces (hull)	£2,625 (HM dockyard, Devonport)
	4 x 55ft Coastal motor boats	(Thornycroft)
	20 x Pontoons	£125
	1 x 32ft Cutter for HMS *Despatch/ Euphrates*	£305/£314 (Fairfield shipyard, Govan)
1919	1 x 32ft Cutter for HMS *Despatch/ Euphrates*	£305/£314 (Fairfield shipyard, Govan)
	2 x 27ft Whalers	£160 (HM dockyard, Portsmouth)

Date	Craft built
1940	8 x 32ft Sailing cutters
1941	6 x 25ft Fast motor boats 3 x 41ft 6in Assault landing craft 3 x 41ft Support landing craft 4 x 45ft Launches
1942	6 x 41ft 6in Assault landing craft 4 x 45ft Motor launches 2 x 41ft 6in Landing craft; assault
1943	4 x 41ft 6in Landing craft; assault 2 x 52ft 6in Harbour service launches (steam) 3 x 45ft Motor launches
1944	6 x 32ft Motor cutters 1 x 45ft Motor launch 2 x 52ft 6in Harbour service launches
1945	3 x 45ft Motor launches 4 x 32ft Motor cutters

Index

Lightning Source UK Ltd.
Milton Keynes UK
UKOW04f2235110414

229838UK00004B/6/P